04/19/18S

*'You're promising me a peaceful one, eh? This Year of Our Lord
Nineteen Hundred and Ten? Let's hope you're right.'*

Unfortunately his men can't fulfil Superintendent Lestrade's
wish. Nor can his daughter Emma, who moments later brings
him the news of a tragic boating accident involving members of
her family.

In fact Lestrade's lot is definitely not a happy one: he has a
number of vicious murders to solve, including that of a man
hanged in a church bell tower, of a potential cross-Channel
swimmer and of his old sparring partner Dr Watson. Anarchists
threaten the peace of Europe and the whole of the Yard is
looking for 'Peter the Painter'.

On top of all this Lestrade is roped in to help with the plans
for the Coronation of George V; his daughter is in love; and
Inspector Walter Dew needs help with the disappearance of a
certain Belle Crippen.

And while Lestrade has his hands full a violent London cabbie
lies in wait for the Assistant Commissioner; a Mr Frederick
Seddon is letting out the top flat of his house to elderly spinsters;
and new bride Sarah Rose wanders forlornly round the National
Gallery waiting for George Joseph Smith.

M J Trow's bubbling style and wit with which he has already
enchanted readers in *The Adventures of Inspector Lestrade*, *Brigade*,
and, most recently, *Lestrade and the Hallowed House*, are again in
appearance in this delightful kaleidoscope of fact and fantasy.

by the same author

THE ADVENTURES OF INSPECTOR LESTRADE
BRIGADE
LESTRADE AND THE HALLOWED HOUSE

Lestrade and the Leviathan

Volume IV in the Sholto Lestrade Mystery Series

M.J. Trow

A Gateway Mystery

 REGNERY
PUBLISHING, INC.
Since 1947 • An Eagle Publishing Company

Published in the United States by
Regnery Publishing, Inc.
An Eagle Publishing Company
One Massachusetts Avenue, NW
Washington, DC 20001

Distributed to the trade by
National Book Network
4720-A Boston Way
Lanham, MD 20706

Printed on acid-free paper.
Manufactured in the United States of America

10 9 8 7 6 5 4 3 2 1

Books are available in quantity for promotional or premium use. Write to Director of Special Sales, Regnery Publishing, Inc., One Massachusetts Avenue, NW, Washington, DC 20001, for information on discounts and terms or call (202) 216-0600.

International Standard Book Number:
0-89526-340-8

'. . . To Murder done by night,
To Treason taught by day . . .'

Rudyard Kipling

Contents

Beginnings

The little man on the park bench turned up his collar against the cold. He checked again the half-hunter cradled in his gloved hand. Half-past two. Where was she? He got up, paced up and down past the knot of children feeding the ducks, clicking his tongue at their squeals and chatter. He threw his feet out in his odd little walking style and tilted the bowler further forward on his head.

Again he flicked open the case. Two minutes had passed. Already he was framing the story in his mind, the story to tell Munyon's. There had been a collision. Nothing serious. A horse brought down, delaying the tram. Was that plausible enough? He stamped his feet and walked purposefully back to the bench. Mercifully the children had moved on.

Then there she was, approaching with that merry step of hers, light, jaunty, her hair strained back from the boyish face under the crown of her ribboned hat. He stood up, tipped his bowler and they linked arms. He reached up and kissed her. She smiled and told him to behave himself. They walked past the lake under the bordering elms. Her breath wreathed back as she chattered on absent-mindedly about this and that.

'Ethel.' He stopped her. 'She's threatening to go.'

The girl stopped, looking hard at him. 'She has before.'

'I know, I know. But this time I think she means it. She's going to take out our money. Our savings. It's all we've got in the world.'

'But that's yours,' Ethel said.

'Some of it, yes. Ethel, look, we'll have to . . . stop seeing each other for a while. I can't afford—'

'Peter, I'm your secretary,' she interrupted him. 'How can we stop seeing each other?'

'You know what I mean,' he said. 'I only get commission on my sales . . . the hotel bills—'

'Peter!' She whirled away from him sharply, the pitch of her voice startling the elderly couple on their afternoon stroll through the park. She came in closer, lowering herself so that their eyes were on a level. 'I'm tired of hotels. Of meeting like this. Of being treated as though I were some sort of leper. You've got to do something, Peter. It's got to be me or her.'

He faltered, the huge eyes blinking in the cold behind the gold-rimmed glasses. 'It's difficult . . .'

'You're a doctor, for God's sake,' she hissed.

'Well, I've never actually practised—'

'You haven't the leisure to practise, Peter. You've got to get it right first time.'

'Ethel . . .' He reached out for her small breasts under the folds of her pelisse.

'Oh, no, not until you've done something. I don't know what. I don't want to know what. But until it's done, Peter, you and I are merely colleagues. I'll type your letters and that's all.'

She swirled up the hill, away into the January mists.

He caught a bus, blindly, unthinkingly circling the streets until he realised where he was. Then he got off and walked past his office in Albion House, on to the premises of Messrs Lewis and Burrows, the chemists.

'I'm afraid we have none in stock, sir,' the chemist informed him. 'But we can get some in a couple of days. Not much call for hyoscine, you see. Will that be all right?'

The customer was miles away. 'What?'

'I said it'll be a couple of days. Would you mind signing the register now?'

'Register?' he repeated blankly.

'Yes, sir. The poisons register. Just a formality, you know.'

'Er . . . yes . . . yes, of course.'

And he steadied his hand as best he could to form the words –
'Dr H. H. Crippen'.

The nattily dressed gentleman sipped his umpteenth glass of tea
in the warmest corner of the Warsaw Restaurant. Outside in
Osborn Street the clutter of the Whitechapel day passed him by.
Occasionally he would wave at a passing gonoph or smile and
chuckle to himself at some inward joke or remembrance of
happier times. He checked his waxed moustache in the little
looking-glass he carried and hastily pocketed it in case any of his
chavim noticed his vanity.

'Afternoon, Leon.' A voice brought him back to the present
and a huge dark hulk blocked his view of the window.

'Steinie.' Leon extended a hand. 'It's been . . . weeks. Tea?'

'Why not?' Steinie sat down, an enormous, handsome young
man, immaculate in grey suit and matching titfer.

'Nice.' Leon ran his hands over the cloth. 'Yours?'

'It is now,' beamed Steinie. 'So's this.'

He placed an object wrapped in paper on the table. The older
man looked at him with his deep, dark eyes and easy smile. There
was nothing there to trust, something there perhaps to avoid.

'What is it?'

'Leon, about the rent. . . .' The two men broke apart in their
huddled corner as a third joined them.

'Sol, my dear,' Leon greeted him, with all the false bonhomie
of a viper. 'It has been a while, you know.'

Sol crouched beside his landlord, submissive, like a feudal
vassal paying homage. It was a posture the Jews had always
managed without difficulty. 'I know, believe me, I know,'
agreed Sol. 'But it's the business. Nobody's buying latkes these
days.'

'Not at your prices they're not,' commented Steinie.

Sol's grin turned sour. 'Hello, Steinie. I didn't notice you
there.'

'And I'm a rabbi's uncle,' said Steinie. 'Where's my three bob?'

'Three bob, he says,' Sol raised his hands to heaven. 'I'm on my knees and he wants three bob.'

'All right, Solly, you've got till Thursday.'

Sol groaned in relief.

'Only Thursday, mind you . . . or I'll send Steinie round to bend your neck.'

'You're a saint, Leon Beron, a saint.' Sol all but kissed his landlord's hand.

'What's this, a Gentile I'm turning into? Get out!' and Sol scampered for the door.

'Of course, he's got a pretty daughter,' said Leon, rubbing his well-waxed goatee.

Steinie shook his head and clicked his tongue. 'And you're old enough to be her grandfather.'

'Ah, you're never that old.' Leon poured them both more tea. 'What's in the parcel?'

Steinie's hand slammed down on the landlord's, jamming his fingers onto the brown paper. Leon's eyes widened in realisation. He pulled his hand away suddenly. 'It's a gun,' he whispered as though the words were choking him.

Steinie nodded. 'A Webley. With a box of forty-four cartridges. Want to count them?'

Leon leaned back from the table. 'What for should I want to count them? Why have you got that?'

Steinie leaned forward. 'The burglary business ain't what it was, Leon, old friend. The Bill's getting difficult. I'm not getting any younger. You mentioned a job in Lavender Hill . . .'

Leon snorted. 'That's out of your league, Steinie . . .'

The younger man raised a finger to his lips and dropped it to the package. He shook his head. 'Not with this, Leon.'

Leon shook his head sadly. 'You'll be the death of me, Steinie Morrison,' he whispered.

★ ★ ★

The removals men had been coming and going all day at the large, comfortable house at No. 63 Tollington Park, London N4. The new owner supervised their every move and expected his family to keep out of the way. It was nearly dark when they finished and the senior of the four men approached him on the pavement, cap in hand.

'That's it then, sir. All done,' and he coughed loudly.

His client looked at him. 'Are you waiting for a tip?' he asked in his clipped Lancashire accent.

'Well, sir, I . . .'

'Young man,' he began with clarity if not precision, for the removal boss was easily fifteen years his senior. 'I am district superintendent of the London and Manchester Industrial Assurance Company. I have worked for said company for over twenty years. And I haven't got where I am today by giving money to the likes of you. Do I make myself clear?'

'Perfectly . . . sir,' growled the Londoner and proceeded to tip the contents of an ash bucket on his client's doorstep.

'Come back 'ere,' screamed the new owner, his Lancashire broadening in his annoyance. But the removals men were on their cart and away, hurling abuse at the Northerner.

'Whatever is it, Fred?' His wife appeared in the doorway.

'Nothing!' Fred kicked the bucket as he passed it. A sign perhaps of things to come. 'Mind your business, Margaret. And where's that maniac of a maid got to?'

'Ssshhh, Fred, she'll hear you!' Margaret winced at her husband's lack of discretion.

'I don't care if t' whole bloody street hears me. Her brother and cousin are both you-know-where, chained to t' wall. And she'll be joining 'em before too long!'

'What's that?' A large, dishevelled-looking woman hurtled around the side of the house.

'Ah, there you are.' Fred relented a little, suddenly mindful of the need for dignity in his new abode. 'Clean this mess up.' He scowled at her.

She bobbed a curtsey and proceeded to start on the ashes with her fingers.

'Look at her,' he muttered to his wife. 'Mad as a hatter,' and he took her indoors.

'Well, my love' – the phrase hung in the air like ice – 'this is it. Fourteen rooms.' He strolled the hall surveying his new domain. 'The front basement I shall turn into an office. You may grow some plants in the conservatory. That big room upstairs at the back we'll partition off. Grandfather William can have one half with the boys – by the way, I must up their rent to six shillings. The little buggers eat like horses. The other half the girls can have together with that lunatic of yours.' He gestured to where the maid was still struggling on the doorstep.

'Which leaves the top floor. Four rooms. We would be able to get a few bob for that. And we needn't waste time getting them, neither. I'll place an advertisement in the *Standard* tomorrow.'

And he was as good as his word. It read 'Top floor tenancy now vacant. Four good rooms. All mod. cons. Would suit single lady. Must be well-to-do.'

His wife was surprised he had not complained to the newspaper of the cost of the advertising. He signed it 'Apply Mr & Mrs Frederick Seddon'.

Mr and Mrs Rose walked that afternoon in the hushed halls of the National Gallery. She knew little of paintings, but her husband did. She spent most of the time gazing rapturously at him. He was tall, gaunt almost, with high cheekbones and the heavy moustache of a respectable gent. It was his eyes that really held her. Cold, piercing, grey as a dreadnought and almost hypnotic. He smiled down at her, pointing now and again at the work before them, saying, 'Ah, now that I do like. Oh yes. Oh yes. Rubens.'

'Titian,' the strolling attendant corrected him.

'Bless you,' said Mr Rose through clenched teeth. And whisked his wife away.

'George?' she said.

'Yes, my dear?'

'You know I withdrew all my savings from the Post Office?'

'Yes, my dear.' He smiled benignly.

'And sold the little bit of Government Stock I had put away? You know, for a rainy day?'

'Yes, my dear.'

'Well, when are you going to buy that antique shop you talked about? I don't like the thought of that money lying about. Is it safe?'

'Safe as houses, dearest,' Mr Rose said. 'Do you like this one?' He tried to steer the conversation back to canvas.

'Oh, yes, I do. Who is it by?'

'Er . . . Rubens,' said Mr Rose.

'They've got a lot of Rubens here, haven't they?'

'Well, I expect someone got them as a job lot. Shall we get some for our antique shop, dearest?'

'Ooh, that sounds nice, George. "Our antique shop". That does sound nice.'

'Well, it won't be yet awhile, Sarah,' he said patiently, patting her hand. 'These things take time. And, as I told you, when my Aunt Lucy, the Dowager Duchess, settles on me, we'll have a chain of antique shops.'

'I don't want a chain, George,' Sarah Rose sighed, looking up at him. 'I just want you.'

He stooped to kiss her cheek. 'First we must get a few things for the house. A new bath perhaps?'

'What about one of those new shower contraptions? I hear they're all the rage.'

'Newfangled,' commented George. 'I'm an old-fashioned sort, dearest. I prefer baths.'

'Of course, dear,' she smiled. 'A bath it is.'

'Talking of which,' George hopped from foot to foot, 'I must pay a call, my love. Hold my hat, will you? I shan't be long,' and he pecked her on the forehead.

Sarah Rose, newly wed, so, so deeply in love for the first time in her life, wandered the echoing halls, cradling the shiny topper lovingly. George Rose, newly wed for the third time, took a bus to Clapham and sold all his wife's furniture and belongings.

Mrs Rose was still holding the hat when they asked her to leave at closing time. No, there was no one in the building other than Gallery personnel. No, they had checked the conveniences. Empty. The gentleman must have been called away. Sarah Rose wandered the streets, tears streaming down her cheeks. Through the blur, she happened to notice the name in the hatband. George must have picked up the wrong hat by mistake. The name read George Joseph Smith.

It had not been a good day for Alfred Bowes. He waited in the outer room of the Public Carriage Office for nearly two hours. His feet hurt and he was cold, despite the attempt of the coal fire to lend a glow to the cheerless room.

The tap of a pen on a counter top made him stand up.

'Mr Bowes?' the clerk enquired.

'That's me,' Bowes tried to sound as cheerful as he could, coming from Acton and all.

'I understand you have applied for a licence as a taxi driver.'

'Yes, I have, yes.' Bowes straightened his tie.

'I'm afraid it has been refused,' said the clerk.

Bowes blinked. 'Refused?' he said.

'Refused.' The clerk closed his ledger purposefully.

'Why?' Bowes became indignant.

'Why?' the clerk repeated. 'Why is it not possible for you to become a taxi driver? Because you cannot drive, Mr Bowes. You have not passed the test.'

'Nobody else has to pass a test,' snapped Bowes.

'Private individuals, no. Though, if I may say so, the day must come when they do. But if you wish to operate under licence in London you must satisfy the examiners . . .'

'What if I drive without a licence?' Bowes saw a way through the entanglement of red tape hedging him round.

'You will be arrested.' The clerk was patience itself, and only a few yards from the Monument, too.

'By whom?'

The clerk looked at him. 'By the police,' he said, concluding that the failed applicant was at best feeble-minded; at worst he might even be a Socialist. 'By Mr Edward Henry himself, I shouldn't wonder. These buildings were the premises of Scotland Yard. Take care you don't find yourself in the New ones.'

'Edward Henry? Who's he when he's at home?' The Acton man became cocky.

'When he's at home he is probably Edward Henry. But at his place of work he is Assistant Commissioner of the Metropolitan Police.'

'Is he now?' Bowes appeared far away. It came as no surprise to the clerk. 'Well,' he slapped his fist down on the counter, 'Mr Edward bloody Henry isn't going to stop me getting a licence. I'm going to stop him. You'll see!' he screamed as he reached the door. 'I'll stop him!'

Mr Edward bloody Henry clattered over the cobbles at Scotland Yard the following morning at his usual time. Ever-punctual, the dark-skinned little man belied his years, dismounting and running up the steps into the side entrance. A brace of constables saluted him, a gaggle broke up a cosy chinwag to let him pass and a positive parliament of them rushed to open the lift door.

'Not this morning, gentlemen. Mrs Henry says I'm putting on weight. The stairs.'

And, suiting his action to his word, he bounded up them two at a time. It was as well. For the lift that morning was jammed with the moribund hulk that was Superintendent Frank Froest, sweating in his attempt to beat his chief to his office.

'Late again, Frank?' was all he heard as a little brown whirlwind hurtled past him on the landing.

Froest slammed the ornate gates shut and met a wry smile floating along the corridor towards him, somewhere between a bowler and the upturned collar of a Donegal.

'Not a word, Lestrade,' Froest grunted. 'Not a bloody word.'

Lestrade raised his hands in submission. 'Frank,' he said, 'I wouldn't be so beastly. Anyway, it's your shout at the Horse's Collar at lunchtime. I wouldn't want to jeopardise that.'

'Meaning?' Both men continued to walk past and away from each other.

'Nothing. It's just that Sergeant Horner has been waiting since he was a rookie for a drink from you. He retires tomorrow.' Lestrade had vanished round a corner by the time Froest's bowler hissed through the air to hit the aforementioned sergeant squarely in the teeth.

Lestrade threw his bowler instead at a constable and followed it with his Donegal. 'Tea!' he roared.

A steaming mug of the said brew appeared at his elbow as he lowered himself over an in-tray that would have buried a weaker man. He looked at the constable.

'Are they here?' he asked.

'In your outer office, sir.'

Lestrade stared at the lad. If he'd listened to the old adage about policemen looking younger than you, he'd have retired years ago. Looking at the forms in triplicate, he wondered again why he hadn't.

'Right.' He snatched the mug, with its cracks and chips. Superintendent he might be, but only commissioners and their assistants got porcelain. Still, a saucer only cramped your style. It left no room to be expansive, to interrogate suspects and to lean on villains.

Lestrade had gone up in the world. His superintendent's office was on the third floor, as far away from Fingerprints and the sergeants' stews in the basement as it was possible to be, unless of course you counted the manic manifestations of Special Branch in the attic. He was convinced they hung chirruping from the rafters until twilight like a demented colony of bats, defecating on the buggers below.

'Gentlemen!' Lestrade liked to make sudden entrances. 'No, don't get up. It spoils concentration. My, my. How I enjoy these monthly chats of ours. Walter, you first, I think.'

Chief Inspector Walter Dew shuffled uneasily in his chair.

'Not a lot, sir,' he said. 'We're still watching those lads on the waterfront, but it's over to the bluebottles any day now.'

'Lady Whitridge?' Lestrade asked.

'Oh, she coughed,' Dew said. 'Asked for thirty-three other cases of armed robbery to be taken into account.'

Lestrade shook his head and clicked his tongue. 'And her only sixty-four,' he said.

'Well, it's the surprise,' said Dew. 'Nobody expects it.'

'Like the Inquisition,' the second man at Dew's elbow commented.

'I think we can leave your Roman Catholic analogies out of this, Eli. What's new?'

Inspector Elias Bower flipped open his file. 'Very little, sir. It looks as though we've lost Ambrose, but the Pinkertons will pick him up on the other side.'

'The Other Side? So you're a spiritualist as well as a Catholic?'

'Imagine,' chortled the next. 'Picked up by the Pinkertons. Tut. Tut.'

'We *are* jovial this morning, Alfred. What have you done about the Belmont diamonds?'

'Ah . . . .' Alfred Ward reddened as only sandy-haired men with a guilt complex can. 'I'm afraid we've drawn something of a blank there, sir.'

'We?' Lestrade's barbed banter had been learned at the assorted knees of Meiklejohn, McNaghten and Frost. Even 'Dolly' Williamson had acknowledged his debt to Lestrade in the early years. Only the fatuous scribblings of the good doctors Watson and Conan Doyle implied he was less than thorough.

'Very well, sir, me.'

'Ah,' echoed Lestrade. 'So the padre . . .'

'Was Benito Garcia, as you surmised.'

Lestrade placed his empty mug down complacently.

'And last, John,' he said. 'But by no means least.'

John Kane said two words before he was howled down by his fellow inspectors. 'Theocratic Unity.'

'Now, now.' Lestrade held up his hand. 'Don't ridicule conspiracies, gentlemen. Especially religious ones. One of them nearly did for me a few years back. Do you have anything new on them, John?'

Kane sighed. 'No, sir. Nothing.'

'Could be one for . . .' Lestrade pointed ominously to the ceiling ' . . .upstairs.'

There were universal rumblings of 'God forbid!', 'Never!' and 'Resign!'.

'Well, gentlemen.' Lestrade stroked his nose, searching vaguely as he always did for the missing tip. 'All quiet, then? You're promising me a peaceful one, eh? This Year of our Lord Nineteen Hundred and Ten? Let's hope you're right.'

It was a little before noon and Lestrade was less than a third of the way through his paperwork when the peace of the new year was shattered. The constable in the outer office opened his door.

'A Miss Bandicoot to see you, sir.'

Lestrade rose in surprise as a demure girl in claret velvet hurried into his office. She looked alarmed, her grey eyes wide with worry, but she checked herself as the superintendent dismissed the constable.

When he'd gone she ran into his arms, burying her face in his shoulder and sobbing convulsively.

'Sshh,' Lestrade comforted her, stroking her golden hair and her wet cheeks. 'Here. . . .' He rummaged for a handkerchief. 'Big blow now. Come on, that's the way. Constable!' he roared, 'a cup of tea for Miss Bandicoot. And one for me.'

'Very good, sir.'

Lestrade sat Miss Bandicoot down on the chair facing his. He lifted her chin and smiled at the huge grey eyes, the nose, reddened by the chill January air and the crying.

'You look more like your mother every time I see you,' he said. 'Now,' and he was professional once more, 'what's the matter?'

'Oh, Daddy.' Miss Bandicoot's lips quivered as she struggled with the words. 'Something terrible has happened.'

'I see,' said Lestrade. 'Then you'd better tell me all about it.'

The Lost Boys

So it was that Superintendent Lestrade missed Frank Froest's shout at the Horse's Collar. But, then, if truth were told, it was rather more of a whisper. There were those, hard-bitten policemen all, gathered in the snug of the aforementioned hostelry, who said it was Lestrade and not Froest who should have been placed in charge of the Serious Crimes Department a few years back. But the older of them knew that Lestrade had never been Edward Henry's blue-eyed boy, and even in this year of our Lord 1910 such things counted. Mind you, there was that curious business of the King's coronation which, it was whispered, had given Lestrade his promotion. And Walter Dew his. But neither of these doyens of respectability, these pillars of society whose arms were so long they dragged the ground, could be drawn on that subject.

Inspector Alfred Ward drew heavily on his meerschaum and blew circles to the ceiling.

'Miss Bandicoot?' he said.

'That's the name she gave.' Bower surfaced from the froth on his beer. 'Quite a cracker, the desk man said.'

'Hello, hello, hello.' Kane bent his knees in the time-honoured manner.

'That'll do,' Dew scolded them. He was the senior man, longer in the tooth than the inspectors. He and Lestrade went back a long way. He might be a chief inspector in his own right now, but Lestrade was still his guv'nor.

'Come on, Walter,' Ward nudged the man. 'Who is she? And where's the boss gone?'

'If you must know, she's his daughter.'

'Daughter?'

'Blimey!'

'Get away.' Bower's comment was the last. 'I didn't know old Lestrade was married.'

'Widower,' said Dew. 'And that's more than enough prying for one day, gentlemen. Here's to Superintendent Froest.' He raised his pint. 'May this new-found generosity continue,' and he downed the glass.

'What's it in aid of?' Kane asked.

'What?'

'Frank buying the round.'

'Ah, well, there *is* a story.'

'So you're not going to tell us about Lestrade, but you don't mind spilling the beans on Froest?' Kane ragged him.

'That's different. This is a special anniversary for Frank. You see, there was this chorus girl . . .' and the collective inspectorate of the old H Division bent their heads into the fug of the Horse's Collar to hear Dew's tale of murder, mayhem, greed and lust . . . prior to sucking long and hard on Ward's packet of Dobson's Extra Strong Lozenges lest the whiff of alcohol ascend to Mr Henry's office during the afternoon.

The superintendent and his daughter caught the westbound train to Taunton and took a pony and trap to Huish Episcopi, country seat of the Bandicoots since the Conquest. The conquest, that is, by one Alaric Bandicoot of the then Lady of the Manor, Eleanor Fitzmaurice, *circa* 1791. Not that Harry Bandicoot, the present Lord of the Manor, was a snob about his ancestry. His wife's family *were* bluebloods and Harry's pedigree bore some research in the pages of Debrett, though Burke's might be more apt.

It was a clear, crisp evening as the policeman and his lady were brought to a lurching halt under the Somerset stars. Dogs barked from everywhere and the house flooded with light. A tall, square-looking man, his curly hair still blond, his eyes still a sparkling blue, hurtled down the steps as though to suffocate her.

'Emma, you bad girl. Where have you been? Letitia and I . . . Sholto?'

The big man peered into the night to be sure. He saw a sallow, ferret-faced man, with dark, sad eyes and old scars, the tip of his nose gone above the walrus moustache, streaked now with grey.

'Sholto! It is you?' The two men shook hands and slapped each other's backs until the dust rising from Lestrade's Donegal became too much for them both. 'What you need is a good woman, Sholto!' laughed the bigger man. 'Nettles.' He turned to a waiting flunkey. 'Pay this good fellow,' indicating the trap driver, 'and bid him be on his way.' He flung an arm round Lestrade and, remembering the girl, caught her too. 'Well, Emma, when we found you'd gone this morning, Aunt Letitia and I were beside ourselves . . .'

'Don't be hard on her, Harry,' said Lestrade. 'She did right to come to me.'

'My dear fellow,' and Harry hugged them both.

Lestrade was nearly bowled over at the top of the stairs by an ancient St Bernard he remembered from earlier visits, a massive beast, fond in a slobbery sort of way, but quite unaware of his own strength. Lestrade had never been the kind of man to be able to extricate himself quickly from mishaps, and hit simultaneously by a wet rasping tongue threatening to demolish his bowler and the lascivious thrusting of the beast's hind quarters into his knees there was only one thing he could do and he did. He buckled like a pack of cards and had to be helped out from under.

'You wouldn't think he still had it in him, would you?' Lestrade did his best to be pleasant.

'I'm sorry, Sholto.' Harry brushed the superintendent down. 'Nettles, pour a bucket of water over that dog. Emma, fetch

Aunt Letitia. What can be keeping her?'

Lestrade was helped into the Great Hall. He had always felt overwhelmed by the immensity of the gentry's living quarters and the advent of the Conservative Party's death duties had dimmed the bright opulence of Bandicoot Hall not a jot. A radiant lady in a velvet gown cascaded down the stairs to meet him. They spoke no words, but held each other tight.

'Sholto,' she said at last. 'Thank God you've come,' and she sobbed quietly on his shoulder.

A vast glass of brandy floated under Lestrade's moustache, courtesy of his host. The velvet-gowned Letitia led the protesting Emma away, leaving the men to the crackling log fire in the Tudor grate.

'She told you, of course?' Harry stared into the flames.

Lestrade nodded. 'Now I'd like your version.'

'Well, it's difficult to know where to start.' Harry sat in one leather chair and offered the other to Lestrade.

'At the beginning, Harry?' Lestrade rubbed the rim of his glass.

'Oh, do you still do it that way at the Yard?' Bandicoot asked.

'We may have a fingerprint department now and our own photographic darkroom, but some things never change.'

'Quite. It was Binky Hobsbaum, I suppose.'

'Hobsbaum?'

'An old school chum. He lives quite near here, at Charlton Mackrell. Comes of an old naval family.'

'Really? I would have said Hobsbaum comes of the Mile End Road.'

'Now, now, Sholto, no inverted snobbery. Some of Eton's most famous families are of chosen stock. Rothschilds, Buckhalters, Gulbenkians . . .'

'And Hobsbaums.'

'Exactly.' Harry poured them both another drink.

'Binky has a yacht, well, three, actually. One of them is moored off Minehead. I'd met him recently and we had a bit of a reunion at Christmas – not that that's a festival Binky recognises, of course. One thing led to another and Binky invited us to do a bit of sailing. Well, I don't mind the odd Hellenic cruise, but something came up and Letitia and I couldn't go. Emma as you know was in Switzerland at Monsieur Le Petomaine's Academy for Young ladies, so the boys went alone.'

'Rupert and Ivo? No one else?'

'No. They're seventeen now, Lestrade. Old enough ...' Harry broke off to stare at the fire again '...or so I thought ... to look after themselves.'

'What happened?'

'There was some sort of accident. The day before yesterday. A group of young bloods on deck. One or two older chaps in the party. Some rigging gave way in a heavy swell and ... Rupert and Ivo were swept overboard. So was Holliday. And Ballard Hook.'

'Who are they?'

'Hook was at Eton, a few years before Rupert and Ivo, of course. He was the first to jump in to try to save them. If it hadn't been for him ... well, there'd be nobody upstairs now.'

'He got out?'

'Yes. Swims like a fish. Royal Navy, you see.'

Lestrade didn't. The only sailors he knew couldn't swim at all. 'And Holliday?'

'They couldn't find his body. He was George Septimus Holliday, Provost of Eton College. An old tartar in his day but nearing retirement and very distinguished. Had a European reputation as a scholar. Highly thought of in the Corridors of Power.'

One day, Lestrade knew, he must find out where they were. 'Go on.'

'No, I'm serious.'

'No, I mean, go on with the story.'

'Ah, I see.' Bandicoot topped up Lestrade's glass. 'It seems the tide was running high. Binky was at the helm and he had the Devil's own job bringing her up. It was feared all were lost. Not a body in sight. Then, as they rounded the point near the Parrett Estuary, they saw two figures in the surf, clinging desperately to each other. Ivo and Hook.'

'Ivo?'

Bandicoot looked at his old guv'nor. 'We think so. Letitia says she's certain.'

'And you?'

'Oh, Sholto.' Bandicoot paced the floor. 'My boys were born identical, Rupert half an hour before Ivo. A father's never as close to his sons as a mother to hers. They had different ways, different mannerisms, but Ivo . . .'

'I know, Emma told me – the blow on the head.'

'The doctor says he was smashed against the rocks repeatedly. He's lucky to be alive. We must be thankful,' and he swigged his glass quickly, careful not to let Lestrade see his face.

'Holliday?'

'You must have seen it in the papers,' Bandicoot sniffed. 'His body was washed up on the estuary yesterday.'

A silence.

'And Rupert?'

Bandicoot shook his head. 'It was good of you to come, Sholto. I was angry with Emma when she went off like that . . .'

'She doesn't think it was an accident, Harry,' Lestrade said.

'What?' Bandicoot looked up.

'She thinks someone wanted Rupert dead.'

Bandicoot summoned up every tiny reserve of intellect he had. 'But that's preposterous,' he finally managed. 'He was only seventeen years old.'

'The Black Prince had won his spurs three years when he was seventeen.' Lestrade was summoning up the gems of his Blackheath crammer all those years before. 'There must have been a few thousand Frenchmen who hated *him*.'

'You think the French are behind all this?' Bandicoot was utterly lost.

'No, Harry, I don't.' Lestrade patted his arm. 'I only know that when my Sarah died, two of the dearest friends I have in the world took in all that was left of her – little Emma. You've raised her to be a fine lady, Harry. You and Letitia. The least I can do is repay some of that kindness now. May I see Ivo?'

Bandicoot nodded and the two made for the stairs.

Ivo Bandicoot sat near the fire in the room. His mother sat next to him.

'Ivo,' she whispered. 'It's . . .'

Lestrade held up his hand to silence her. He took the oil-lamp from the bedside table and held it and his face near the boy.

'Hello, Ivo,' he said. 'How are you?'

'Well, sir,' said the boy. 'Apart from the headaches.'

Lestrade noticed the bandages and the faraway look in the large eyes. He had known this boy since he was a baby. It seemed strange to see him so quiet, so lifeless. He signalled Letitia and Harry to go and ushered them from the room. Then he turned to face the boy.

'Do you know me, Ivo?' he asked.

Young Bandicoot strained forward, as though somewhere in the distance a memory stirred. Then he lost it and he slumped back in the chair.

'No, sir,' he said.

Lestrade fumbled in his pockets and produced a pair of handcuffs. He habitually carried these now he was constrained, by force of age and seniority, to spend more time behind a desk than he would have liked. They reminded him of the streets where his heart really lay. They were similar to a pair he had given to the Bandicoot boys years ago and many was the happy hour he had spent bent double round an apple tree in the orchard, shouting to be released when the boys and Emma had forgotten him and gone fishing.

Another glimmer of recognition. 'You're a policeman!' Ivo shouted.

Lestrade smiled. 'Nothing wrong with your deductive powers then, lad. That's good. The late Mr Sherlock Holmes would have been proud of you.'

'Sherlock Holmes? The Great Detective?' Ivo surprised himself.

'Yes, the Great Detective.' Lestrade grimaced. 'I am of course cut to the quick that you should remember him – a man dead before you were born – and that your old Uncle Sholto should mean nothing to you.'

'Sholto? Uncle Sholto?' Ivo brightened. 'I'm sorry. It will take a while. Father has spoken so often of Sherlock Holmes. It seems I can remember the distant things. It's just the near ones I can't quite . . .'

'I know,' and Lestrade patted his shoulder. 'About the accident . . .'

'I've tried, Uncle Sholto. I really have. I remember feeling cold. It was dark and I was tired . . . terribly, terribly tired . . . then nothing. I've been over it all so many times since it happened with Mother, Father, Emma, in my own mind. They've told me Rupert's dead. Is that true, Uncle Sholto?'

Lestrade looked steadily into the boy's eyes. He had played this role so many times. Why was it that death was not real until sanctioned by a policeman?

'Yes, Ivo,' Lestrade said. 'I'm afraid it must be.'

Ivo stared blankly at the fire.

'Now,' said Lestrade, wrenching himself away, 'it's getting late. You need your sleep. We'll talk again in the morning.'

Lestrade did not see Ivo the next morning. Instead, more at the insistence of Emma than the insistence of his own logic, the superintendent bundled himself into the passenger seat of Harry's Silver Ghost, wrapped in Harry's outsize driving furs and gauntlets and gritted his teeth to face his daughter's driving. It was a white-knuckle ride all the way and, by the time they had reached Bridgwater, Lestrade had lost the will to live. They rattled and roared through the winter countryside, hurtling past frozen duckponds and under gaunt, bare trees until at last they screeched to a halt in the twisting lanes of the little village of Lilstock.

Emma wrenched at the brake and jumped onto the roadway, Lestrade floundering in her wake, attempting to keep his fur duster coat out of the ice puddles.

'From what Ballard told us,' Emma said, 'it must have been about there, off Blue Ben, that Binky's boat hit trouble.'

Lestrade stared out under his goggles at the great, grey restless sea.

'The tide was running high, he said, and it carried them along the coast, towards those mud flats. Ballard was afraid they'd run aground on Gore Sand – that's the spit out there.'

Lestrade smiled at his daughter. For all she was his flesh and blood, he didn't really know her. She had been brought up since her mother died by the Bandicoots and until she was seven she had assumed they were her real parents. He still doubted whether he should have told her. But a copper's life made it hard to bring up a child alone. Emma had stayed with the Bandicoots and Monsieur Le Petomaine. Until now, until the near wreck of Binky's boat was threatening to wreck her life.

'Where does Ballard think the boys were washed overboard?' he asked her.

'Around the headland, at Hinkley Point.' She indicated the low, grassy cliffs to their right.

'How far?'

'About two miles, I should think,' she said.

'All right, my darling, back into the car. But Emma, *gently*, please. Your old father isn't as young as he was. I'd like to enjoy my retirement.'

She clipped him round his frozen ear with her muff and he

almost heard the icicle fall. He tugged his goggles down so that she couldn't see that he had his eyes shut and they screamed off in the direction of the estuary.

'Wait here,' he told her. 'There's no point in both of us going down.'

'Be careful, Daddy. What are you looking for?' she called after him.

'Pieces of eight!' he called back and began to scramble down the crumbling redstone cliffs. The tide was out as he reached their base. He'd never known such winds, ripping through the flaps of Harry's driving cap, and it was some time before he heard the other man shouting.

'What the bloody 'ell are you doin'?' A squat little figure swathed in oilskins was slipping crablike along the sands.

'Just walking,' said Lestrade.

'You'm be drowning in a minute,' said the oilskin man. 'See that?' and he pointed to the ground.

Obviously faced with the village idiot, Lestrade decided it was best to humour him. 'Yes,' he said.

'What is it?'

'Sand?' Lestrade had the benefit of a Blackheath crammer and thirty-four years on the Force at his disposal.

'Mud,' the idiot corrected him. 'And I've seen men drown in it. A 'orrible, 'ideous choking death it is an' all.'

Lestrade suddenly realised that this was no idiot after all, until his next remark clouded the issue again. 'See that?' he asked.

'That headland?' Lestrade prided himself on his adaptability.

'That be Brean Down,' he said.

'Ah,' said Lestrade as though the Secret of the Universe had been revealed to him.

'You'm be from that Society, been't you?'

'Society?' Lestrade smelt conspiracies when he heard that word.

'That Society what wants to protect birds.'

'No, I—'

'Ar. That wants to set up that there sanctuary. 'Ad to be a bird sanctuary, didn't it? This bein' the River Parrett and all,' and he danced a little jig in the mud.

Lestrade decided it was best to change the subject.

'How deep is this mud?' he asked.

'Who knows? Down to 'ell, I shouldn't wonder. What do you bird people want to go out there for?'

'Er . . . to check for nests.' Lestrade was hopelessly at sea.

'Nests?' The oilskinned man was incredulous. 'You'm be more barmy than I thought. It's January. There be no nests in January.'

'Ah, no.' Lestrade tried to bluff it out. 'Not in January. But I'm here to . . . get things ready . . . for February.'

A silence as Lestrade hoped he'd hit the right month and the oilskinned man wondered from where it was Lestrade had escaped.

'You'll need my 'orse, then,' he said.

'Horse?' Lestrade scanned the beach for the animal. 'No, I think I'd feel safer on foot.'

'I told you, you'd drown,' the oilskinned man snarled. ''Ere 'tiz.'

And he produced from an upturned rowing boat some yards away a wooden frame, with ropes and wires.

'It's a mud-'orse. 'Ang on yer,' and he rested his elbows on the side props. 'You let go of that and it'll be the last thing you do. An' don't stay out there too long. The tide be turnin'.'

And the oilskinned man disappeared over the redstone ridges muttering to himself in the wind. Lestrade gingerly tested the mud-horse, bracing himself as his elbows found the wood. A rough basket for shrimping lay before him and the whole gadget smelt like Billingsgate at the height of summer. In a strange way, it made him feel at home. He kicked off from the dry mud and made for the distant bar which Emma had called Gore Sand. He didn't really know what he was looking for. Some clue, perhaps. Something tangible as to the whereabouts of Rupert's body. Each step became more difficult, as the clawing mud sucked at his heels, his ankles, his calves. Harry's heavy furs were threatening to pull him down still further. He was less than halfway to the dry sand when he realised the full horror of his situation. The tide had indeed turned as the oilskinned man had predicted and the icy foam was racing along the Stert Flats to his left and right. He turned his horse for home but the damned thing was stuck in the mud. Half a mile away he saw the tiny speck that was Emma waving frantically. He saw her scurry down the cliffs to his rescue and bawled at her to stay back but he knew his voice was drowned by the wind. In desperation, he left the mud-horse where it was and waded on. One step, two. It was like walking in treacle. His third step sucked him down, up to his hips in the slimy stuff.

His life bobbed before him. The Baker business, the Knutt case, it all came flooding back. bAnd he wished he hadn't used that analogy at all. The foam roared round his waist as he twisted and thrashed. Keep calm, he told himself. Keep calm. What would Frank Froest do in this situation? Drown, because he was overweight. Edward Henry? Take the fingerprints of a passing ship, most likely. No help there. What about Harry Bandicoot? And, while he was running through his list of friends and colleagues, Emma's hands caught his.

'Come on, Daddy, pull.'

'Emma, get back,' he bellowed as the surf lashed his armpits. 'How on earth did you get this far?'

'I'm lighter than you are. Can you get that coat off?' She helped him as he struggled out of it.

'Your Uncle Harry will never forgive me.'

'He'll never forgive me if I let my father drown,' she shouted. 'Take hold.' From nowhere, Emma had produced a stout rope which she proceeded to lash round Lestrade's body.

'Where did this come from?' he gasped as the effects of the cold began to reach him.

'One of the essentials of modern motoring,' she grunted,

tying him off nicely with one of those knots Monsieur Le Petomaine insisted were the hallmark of good breeding in a young lady. 'Wait there.'

'I'm not exactly going anywhere, Emma,' he said through clenched teeth. 'For God's sake get back to the shore.'

'Not without you, Daddy. Now shut up and save your breath.'

Lestrade's mouth fell open and the surf bubbled in. Emma vanished behind him and he realised he couldn't even turn his head. In minutes he'd be gone below the surface, but she was back, forcing her aching legs to move the mud-horse. As she pushed, the thing slid forward through the swirling sea and the rope tautened.

'A little bit of help would be nice,' she hissed, fighting for breath. With a sucking, smothering sound, Lestrade's head, cap and goggles disappeared in the mud. The next instant he was up again and the surge of the tide was carrying them all forward, the mud-horse running on the crest of a wave with its boat-keel bottom, Emma somehow hooking her legs up to give it less drag and Lestrade being pulled through the undertow like a hooked turtle, flapping and coughing as the water left his lungs.

When the wave threw them up on the drier mud, the superintendent and his daughter collapsed in a grey-green heap on the mud-horse, laughing between coughs and splutters.

'Emma,' he said, 'you're a remarkable girl. You just saved your old Dad from a fate worse than death.'

'Is there a fate worse than death?' She was suddenly serious.

'Oh, yes,' he said, wiping the mud from his goggles. 'Being up there,' he pointed to the sky, 'listening to Frank Froest and Walter Dew laughing at my demise. Come on. I've got to mortgage my house to buy your Uncle Harry a new coat.'

When Lestrade had bathed and downed the umpteenth tureen of Letitia's nourishing broth, he borrowed more of Bandicoot's clothes, this time a smoking jacket and tasselled cap on the strict understanding he would not go shrimping in them, and roasted his backside nicely over the fire in Harry's library.

'Lieutenant Hook, Mr Bandicoot.' Harry's man introduced the visitor.

'Ballard, dear boy.' Harry shook the man's hand.

'Mr Bandicoot.' Lieutenant Hook was a fine figure of a man, as tall as Bandicoot, though a shade less wide, in the full set permitted by His Majesty's Navy and indeed sported by His Majesty's eldest son.

'May I introduce an old friend, Superintendent Sholto Lestrade?'

'Lestrade of the Yard?' Hook took his hand.

The superintendent bowed.

'An honour, sir. Your exploits go before you, Superintendent.'

'You haven't been bored by Harry's tall stories?' Lestrade asked.

'Bored, no. Tall – I doubt it,' said Hook. 'Though as a boy I used to find the *Strand Magazine*'s version of you a little harsh.'

'Ah,' said Lestrade. 'A man of discernment.'

'Ballard, brandy?' Bandicoot asked.

'Thank you, sir.'

'Are you on leave, Mr Hook?' Lestrade asked.

'My ship is being refitted at Plymouth, sir,' said the Lieutenant, 'but I have other duties and must be away tomorrow. I called to see how Ivo was.'

'Getting better all the time,' said Bandicoot.

'I gather you saved his life?' Lestrade asked him.

'I did what I could,' said Hook. 'You know how treacherous that part of the coast can be.'

'I told Ballard about this afternoon, Daddy.' Emma swept in, gorgeous in the firelight. She linked arms with the lieutenant. Lestrade hadn't realised there was a naval connection. This was a new experience for him. He wondered, fleetingly, of course, whether it should be he or Harry who asked this young man whether his intentions were honourable.

'You are lucky to be alive, sir,' said Hook.

'Luck had nothing to do with it,' Lestrade patted his daughter's arm.

'Another brandy, Ballard? The sun's over the yard arm.'

There was probably a joke there somewhere about the Yard and the law's arm, but everybody missed it.

'What did you hope to find out at Stert Flats, Mr Lestrade?' Hook asked him.

'I don't know,' Lestrade sighed. 'Something . . . I don't know.'

'Gentlemen, Emma.' Hook made an announcement. 'I think we must all face facts. Rupert is dead. Nothing will bring him back.'

Emma buried her face in the lieutenant's shoulder. Harry and Lestrade looked at each other. It was a revelation to no one.

Emma took her father to the station at Taunton the next morning. Ivo looked a little better. Letitia had brightened considerably and spring seemed in the air.

'Daddy.' She held his hand as the train whistled and snorted at Platform Three. 'I am . . . very fond of Ballard Hook.'

'So I saw,' Lestrade said.

'Now, don't growl like an old bear. I *am* seventeen years old, you know.'

'I know,' he said.

'I think the world of him, but he's wrong about one thing. I think Rupert is still alive, Daddy. And I don't think what happened on Binky's yacht was an accident. Do you?'

'Now, Emma . . .' he began.

She held her fingers to his lips. 'I know. I'm a silly little girl who doesn't know what she's talking about. But I am Lestrade's daughter. And something doesn't sit well about all this.'

The stationmaster's flag and whistle ended the conversation. Their fingers broke apart. She blew him a kiss. He promised to write; something at which he was very bad.

He sat in the compartment staring at the poster which said 'Come to Sunny Minehead'. So something didn't sit right for Emma Bandicoot-Lestrade. Well, so be it. He'd keep his eyes open, his tipless nose to the grindstone, his finger on the pulse and other parts of his anatomy where they should be. Well, at fifty-seven, there was arguably nothing else to do with them.

Another beach. Another time. He lay rolled on the shore, bloated, unrecognisable, buzzing with flies. Fishermen with strong stomachs carried what was left of him up the sand. One of them reported to the local constabulary. The local constable reported to his sergeant, who duly mentioned it to his inspector and on up the line. It was days before the chief constable was told. And being a man of proud and fierce disposition he waited a few days more. Only then did he contact the Yard. And so it was that Lestrade came to know.

Winter had moved into spring. Crocuses. Daffodils. Inspector John Kane hurtled along the platform, leaping through the smoke and steam as the whistle blew.

'Here you are, sir.' He passed the flask to Lestrade as the carriage jolted and rattled south-east out of Victoria. 'The stationmaster said that will be threepence.'

'Your round, wasn't it, John?' Lestrade narrowed his eyes inscrutably through the steam.

Kane sighed. That was how men got to be superintendents. He poured himself a cup and sat back.

'And?'

Kane had forgotten something.

'Oh, sorry, sir. No Bath Olivers.'

Lestrade shook his head. 'W. H. Smith,' he said. 'The Railway Library.'

'Ah, yes, sir.' Kane fumbled in his pocket. 'There wasn't much choice, I'm afraid.'

Lestrade looked at the book his inspector had selected and it fell with his face. '*Katie's Secret*, Kane?' The superintendent's eyebrow said it all.

'I thought you'd enjoy a penny dreadful, sir.'

'What is really dreadful,' said Lestrade, 'is that Messrs Mills and Boon should actually expect to get more than a penny for this drivel. It's tantamount to money with menaces. Now,' he poured himself the last of the tea, 'on this bright morning, John, what have we got?'

'Well, there are the sandwiches, sir. I've brought a hip flask. You know how treacherous the Kent weather can be.'

'I was referring to our investigation, Inspector.' Lestrade began to prepare himself for a long day.

'Ah, I see. Well, one body. Male . . . er . . .'

'All right, use the book.' Lestrade couldn't bear the clackety-clack of Kane's silence.

The inspector delved gratefully into the safety of the notepad.

'A body. Washed up on the coast near St Margaret's Bay. Bad decomposition. Probably been in the water two days.'

'Cause of death?' asked Lestrade.

The concentration on Kane's face was a picture. 'Drowning?' he managed at last.

'A shrewd supposition,' said Lestrade, 'but what's the first rule of a detective?'

'Er . . .?'

'That's right, John. Keep an open mind. Let's do that, shall we?'

With their minds wide open, the Yard men rattled, second class, Southern Region, into Deal Station. They were met by a pair of sergeants of the Kent Constabulary, stern-faced and silent, who took them to the Bowling Green public house where the Chief Constable of Kent had taken up residence pending the satisfactory conclusion of the case. Fierce and proud he was indeed and resented the intrusion of the Metropolitan man. After all, he was a Kentishman. His family had driven off Julius Caesar when he had his warships drawn up at Deal a few years back and they had meted out the same treatment to Hengist and Horsa when they had landed at Thanet. And now here were two more invaders. He was fair, without being friendly. Official, without being offensive.

Lestrade wanted to see two things. The body. And the beach where it had been found. The Public Baths, closed now for the winter, revealed the first to him. The Kentishman and the Londoners stood in the makeshift mortuary a little before midday. It was not a pretty sight. Lestrade, whose tipless nose was immune to such things, felt his stomach heave once and then got on with the job. The corpse was naked save a few scarlet rags still clinging to the torso. The fingers and toes had gone, as had the eyes.

'Full fathom five,' murmured Kane, ever the literary one. The others looked at him.

'Know a bit about the sea, do you, John?' Lestrade asked.

'No, sir. Not really.'

'Has the coroner been called in, sir?' Lestrade asked the chief constable.

'No, we were waiting for you chappies.'

'Cause of death then, John?'

Kane circled the blackened, bloated lump a few times.

'Drowning, I suppose.' He was a man who stuck to a story through thick and thin.

'I don't think so,' said Lestrade. He produced a pen from his pocket and began to probe the vacant socket of the deceased's left eye. 'Tweezers, anybody?' he asked.

The chief constable snorted. What a fatuous request, he thought to himself, and how typical!

Lestrade fished in another pocket of his voluminous Donegal and produced the brass knuckles which had been his salvation in many a tight corner. He pressed the catch and the deadly four-inch blade jerked out. The chief constable looked on in alarm. Was this standard issue at the Yard? It made his own swagger cane seem a little paltry. Lestrade inserted the knife alongside the pen, twisted once and produced a smashed lead plug.

'There!' He held it up triumphantly.

'What is it?' the others chorused.

'A bullet. Or what's left of one.'

'You mean he was shot?' The chief constable was lost.

'I'm not an expert' – Lestrade smiled at Kane's wry grin – 'but if you ask the coroner to examine the body now, I think he'll find the bullet entered the head from behind and came to rest . . . here,' and he tapped the exposed bone of the eyebrow ridge.

'So his body was dumped in the water?' Kane had just put his brain back in and busied himself checking wrists and ankles for the marks of ropes.

Lestrade held up his hand. 'Let's not run before we can walk, John. Now, Chief Constable, the place where the body was found, if you please. And I shall need the coroner's report urgently.'

They rattled through the Georgian streets of Deal, the sea crashing and foaming to their left as it hit the sloping shingle of the beach. Lestrade was pleased to see no mud-flats this time and said so to the chief constable, in whose barouche they were bouncing around.

'A dangerous tide, though, Lestrade. See the flags? You've got to be a strong swimmer to cope with the undertow.'

They drove on, past Deal Castle and the Time Ball Tower, clicking in perfect harmony with Greenwich, a little nearer to Lestrade's own manor. The constable reined in the lathered animals at St Margaret's at Cliffe, having hurtled down the zigzag road to the sea, during which Kane's eyes had been shut tight.

They scrambled down the little path that had been cut in the chalk cliffs below the heathland of gorse and heather. The wind whistled and moaned against the heavy iron groynes jutting out into the grey–blue of the English Channel.

'About here.' The chief constable pointed with his cane to the shingly sand.

'What's that?' Lestrade pointed to where a line of surf roared white and deadly out to sea.

'That's the Goodwin Sands,' said the chief constable, 'also called the Ship Swallowers. They're eighty-foot deep, Lestrade.'

Lestrade knew the terror of soft sand now and he instinctively retreated nearer to the cliffs.

'There are four lifeboats in the area and the Walmer Light keeps other vessels away, but we still lose ships – and men.'

'Do you think our body is such a one, sir?' Kane asked. 'Washed up from some ship?'

The chief constable shrugged. 'Who knows?' he said. 'My sergeant here at Deal thinks he's from the *Lady Lovibond*.'

Lestrade and Kane looked at each other. Strain, guessed Lestrade. Age, thought Kane.

'Sir?' they chorused.

'The *Lady Lovibond*, gentlemen, and please don't think me overworked or senile' – he lashed them with his fierce eyes as though he read their every thought – 'was a schooner that ran aground on the Goodwins in the seventeen-forties. It is said that she was steered there deliberately by the first mate who was a rival for the captain's wife. They do say . . .' and the policemen instinctively leaned their heads together '. . . that the *Lady Lovibond* reappears every fifty years. My sergeant swears he saw her in 'ninety-eight, a three–masted schooner in full sail, making knots for the Goodwins.'

There was a silence. 'You can close your mouth now, John,' Lestrade said. 'Whatever that was in the Public Baths, gentlemen, was no ghost. Time for lunch?'

Miss Ethel Le Neve, secretary of Dr Harvey Hawley Crippen, of Munyon's, knocked lightly on the door.

'Come in,' a cackle of female voices responded.

She did so and presented the befeathered lady at the head of the table with an envelope.

'From Mrs Crippen,' she said.

The chairwoman of the Guild of Music Hall Ladies looked at the girl through her lorgnette. Tall, slim, boyish, her eyes dark and shiny.

'It's from Belle,' said the chairwoman after a while. 'She's resigned.'

Intakes of breath and 'Surely not!'s from the others.

'She says she has had to go to America to look after a relative who is ill.' More murmurs. 'She does not know when she will be back.'

'May I see?' one of them asked. The chairwoman passed the member the letter. 'This is not Belle's hand,' she said.

Miss Le Neve smiled warmly. 'Good evening, ladies,' and swept out.

The Cavalry Club stands in Piccadilly, in Lestrade's manor. The superintendent had left John Kane in darkest Kent, where the good inspector had become totally absorbed by the sergeant's salty tales of the sea and the restless ghosts that prowled the Goodwins. Until the coroner's report reached him, Lestrade could do nothing. Kane could cope with the missing persons and he dispatched Alfred Ward to the Ratcliff Highway to enquire in the Port of London if any foreign merchantman had carelessly lost a crew member in the Channel. In the meantime, he had made a promise to Emma and he went about his business.

'Captain Vavasour?' Lestrade entered the room of smoke and brandy fumes.

A tall, elegant young man in the scarlet mess dress of the Life Guards stumbled over a prone comrade and shook his hand.

'My name is Lestrade. Superintendent of Scotland Yard. This' – he indicated the square figure behind him – 'is Chief Inspector Dew.'

'Charmed.' The captain clicked his heels. 'You'll have to

excuse this . . .' he waved extravagantly to the room, spinning though it was in his vision, '. . . but I did leave instructions that we were not to be disturbed.' He looked up and down the corridor for the long-vanished minion who had shown Lestrade and Dew up.

'It is a matter of some importance, sir,' Lestrade explained. 'May we sit down?'

'My dear fellah!' Vavasour threw some cushions onto a settee. 'How can we help?'

'What is it, Algy?' Another scarlet-clad toper emerged from under the table.

'Chappies from the Yard, Gracie. Coppers. Haw, haw!'

'Haw, haw!' Gracie chorused.

'And you are, sir?' Lestrade ventured.

'Oh, yes, I'm sir, all right. Captain, don't y'know.'

'I do know, sir.' Lestrade had the perfect patience of the soberest man in the room. He knew the fumes would have got to Dew by now. 'I would like to know your name.'

'Oh, I see. Oates. Sixth Inniskillings.'

'Indeed? Two birds with one stone, eh, Walter?'

'We'd like to ask you a few questions, gentlemen.' Dew was at his most professional.

'Look,' said Vavasour, kicking the fallen comrade out of the way, 'if it's about that girl in the Haymarket, I'd just got my breeches hooked up, that's all. Those infernal breastplates, you see—'

'It's not the girl in the Haymarket, sir.'

'Not?' Vavasour breathed a sigh of relief that threatened to explode Lestrade's cigar. 'Oh Lord, it's not that . . . Look, I sorted that business out with the vicar. He told me the choirboy didn't hit the right notes any more anyway—'

'No, sir, it's not the choirboy either,' said Lestrade.

Dew was busy scribbling things down.

'I gather that both you and Captain Oates were guests on board the yacht of Mr Binky Hobsbaum last month.'

'We were. And I didn't smash the tantalus in his cabin.' Vavasour was quick to assure the Yard men with the exaggerated gestures of an inebriate man trying very hard to appear sober.

'There was a storm—'

'Storm?' Oates cut in. 'That was a squall, Chief Constable.'

'Superintendent,' Lestrade corrected him.

'Only a squall, Chief Superintendent,' Oates resumed.

'What happened?'

'Er . . .' Oates tried to focus on his brandy balloon. 'Oh' – his memory worked for him – 'we got her under control.'

'And the Bandicoot boys?'

'Not my type,' drawled Vavasour.

'Did you see what happened to them?' Lestrade could feel his knuckles turning white.

'Went over, didn't they, Gracie?'

'Yes,' Oates confirmed. 'That old idiot. What was his name, Algy? Holliday? You know, the old buffer who taught us Latin at school.'

'Yes, that's right. Bit of a blow, what? Drowning and all.'

'Did you see what happened?'

'Well, no,' said Oates. 'We were starboard aft. Holliday and the boys were port side forrard . . .'

'Are you getting all this, Dew?' Lestrade noticed his subordinate struggling with the technical terms.

'Actually, all this talk of squalls and so on . . .' Oates looked decidedly green.

'Hooky did the right thing, of course,' said Vavasour. 'Damned fine to leap in like that. I thought he was a goner, didn't you, Gracie? Ripping swimmer, of course. Gracie, are you all right?'

Oates was on his feet, swaying, lurching for the door.

'I'm just going outside,' he slurred. 'And may be some time.'

'Can't hold it,' sighed Vavasour. 'Well, there it is, he may be an Old Etonian, but he did join a damned line regiment. That's almost like being a ranker, wouldn't you say?'

'So Lieutenant Hook went over the side to save the others?'

'Yes. Look, Superintendent, I've had a few brandies tonight and I'd had a few brandies on old Binky's yacht. As far as I know, old Holliday was spouting some political claptrap – all in Latin, of course – and a bloody great wave must have hit him. I heard somebody shout "My God, what's happening?" and when we reached the stern, Hook was struggling in the water. I couldn't see anybody else at first. We threw out lines of course at once, but we lost them. Gracie – er – Captain Oates and I grabbed the helm and swung her about, but it was ages before we sighted them again.'

'Hook and Bandicoot?'

'That's right. Holliday and the other Bandicoot boy – no sign. Look here,' Vavasour seemed to sober suddenly, 'it was only an accident, you know. We all did what we could.'

'I'm sure you did, Mr Vavasour,' said Lestrade. 'Enjoy your party,' and he left.

Dew closed his notebook with a flourish and leaned heavily over the elegant, sprawling young officer. 'Don't imagine we won't be talking to you again, sir,' he said. 'There are a few matters I'd like to investigate further. The girl in the Haymarket, the choirboy. You won't be leaving town, will you, sir?'

Vavasour staggered to his feet and looked shakily down at Dew. 'I won't,' he said as confidently as he could, 'but I can't speak for old Gracie. That's what this little do is all about tonight. A celebration. He's going with Scott in the summer – you know, to the Antarctic.'

'Where might that be, sir?'

'The South Pole, man. You catch a thirty-six from the Bayswater Road,' Vavasour had the measure of his man now, 'though what he wants to go with a naval chappie for, I can't imagine.'

'I shan't want to see Captain Oates again,' said Dew. 'But

you're a different matter,' and he made for the door.

Vavasour slumped drunkenly in a corner of the settee, crossing his ankles on the back of his unconscious comrade. 'Fancy wanting to go all that bloody way with a naval chappie. Still, there's no accounting for taste. Not when you're as tight as Oates . . .'

And he rang the bell for more brandy.

Alfred Bowes, hansom-cab driver, stood in the front entrance of Scotland Yard on that Thursday afternoon. Before him stood the immobile hulk of Tom Peabody, Sergeant of H Division, Metropolitan Police. Eighteen years' experience. Wife, yes. Kids, four. Known to his mates as Buildings. And he'd seen it all in his day. Growlers with tales as long as your arm. But this man was different. And persistent.

'Look, sir,' Peabody was saying, 'watch my lips. Before I can let you past this desk, I've got to know what it is you want.'

'All right.' Bowes drew himself up to his full five foot two. 'I want to see Mr Edward Henry.'

Peabody flashed a glance to a passing colleague.

'Do you now? And why might that be?'

'It's personal.' Bowes' face darkened. 'Between me and 'im.'

'Well, I'm very sorry, sir. But if you intend to see Mr Henry on these premises, I shall need to know the personal nature of your personal business.'

Bowes slammed the desk with his fist and whirled round in a circle.

'Like I said,' he shouted, 'it's personal,' and he collided with Frank Froest as he reached the door. He bounced off the superintendent's paunch and scuttled outside, snarling and cursing.

'What was that?' Froest asked the desk sergeant.

'Some growler, sir, living up to his reputation.'

'Growler?'

'A hansom-cab driver, sir.'

'Thank you, Sergeant. I am familiar with the term. What did he want?'

'Mr Henry, sir. Said it was personal.'

'Did he now? Well, keep your eyes open, Peabody. Better have somebody watch his lordship's horse in the yard. Perhaps the growler's after some new horseflesh.'

'How *was* lunch, sir?'

But the repartee whistled harmlessly along the corridor. Superintendent Froest had already vanished.

'Read it to me again, John.' Lestrade lolled back in his chair at the Yard.

'Coroner's report on unidentified remains discovered at St Margaret's Bay, Kent, on Tuesday, eighteenth February, nineteen ten—'

'Just the essentials, John,' Lestrade broke in.

'Right, sir. Body was male, any age between twenty-five and fifty. Cause of death, a bullet fired from above—'

'Above?'

'That's what it says, sir.'

'And what do you make of it, Kane?'

'Well,' the inspector's brow took on a furrowed aspect, 'if the bullet entered from above, that means the deceased was lying on his face.'

'In bed? On the deck of a ship? On a pavement? Where?' Lestrade was talking to himself. 'What does the coroner make of the clothes?'

'It says here "Probably part of a Union Jack", sir.'

Lestrade looked at his subordinate. 'Yes, I thought you said that the first time.' He sucked his teeth and reached for the fourth cup of tea that morning. Still no saucer, still cracked. Still, he preferred it that way. 'How many people do you know wear Union Jacks, John?'

'Could it have been a nightshirt, sir?'

'What does he make of the white grease we found under his fingernails?'

'He doesn't mention that, sir.'

'Surprise, surprise. Who did this post-mortem?'

'I believe it was . . .'

Lestrade held up his hand. 'What we call in the business a rhetorical question, John,' he said.

There was a knock at the door and Inspector Alfred Ward dripped in.

'God, it's raining cats and dogs out there.'

'Don't drip on my carpet, Inspector,' said Lestrade. 'It's got to last until next Christmas. What have you got?'

Ward sneezed.

'Apart from a cold,' Lestrade and Kane chorused.

'The Port of London wasn't very helpful, sir.' Ward wrung himself out in Lestrade's lobby, where the young constable wrestled manfully with the upright Remington. 'No crew members missing. No missing persons from any foreign freighter.'

'Customs?' Lestrade asked.

'Well,' Ward was summoning up his every resource, 'in Bolivia the peasants have this strange dance, I believe—'

'I was referring to His Majesty's Customs House, Inspector. Did you try there in your quest for a missing person?'

'Oh, I see. Well, they were as tight-lipped as ever. You know how they are. Wanted to know if I had anything to declare.'

'What did you say?'

'I told them declaring was something they did in Australian cricket, sir.' Ward smirked, his large shoulders quivering with apparent mirth.

'That must have had them rolling in the aisles, Inspector.' Lestrade knew how to hurt a man. 'Have you got a sergeant handy, John?'

'Blenkinsop's off sick, sir. Martin's on leave until Wednesday.'

'Who does that leave?'

'A new man, sir – Blevvins.'

'Any good?'

'Er . . . thorough, sir.'

Lestrade looked at him. 'Wheel him in, then.'

John Kane vanished into the cream and green of the Yard corridor.

'All right, Alfred. Put your feet up. When does your shift end?'

'Half an hour, sir,' Ward bubbled, his nose running the gamut of shades of red.

'Get home, then. I may need you later.'

'Blevvins, sir.' The squat young man nearly knocked over the exiting inspector. 'At your service, sir.'

'Are you, now?' Lestrade looked him up and down. He wasn't an Etonian, like Harry Bandicoot when he had stood before him an eternity ago. And he wasn't a walking encyclopaedia, like Dickens or Jones. But he had the words 'over-zealous' written all over him.

'Know the West End, Sergeant?' Lestrade asked.

'Like the back of my fist, sir.'

'Good. Get down to Messrs Lillywhites in the Strand. Or Oxford Street, whichever you prefer. I want samples of their production lines over the past – say – five years.'

'What are we looking for, sir?'

Lestrade looked up. 'Lillywhites, Sergeant. Watch my lips. Take a couple of constables with you – for instance, the one out there who's driving typewriter keys into my head.'

'Very good, sir.' The sergeant spun on his heels.

'And Blevvins.'

'Sir?'

'Don't knock anybody over.'

'Very good, sir.'

It was the next day that Miss Hinchcliffe, spinster of a number of parishes, was admitted into Lestrade's office. She was a flutter of veils and handkerchiefs, and sobbed quietly throughout most of the interview.

'How may I help you, ma'am?' Lestrade asked.

'Do you have any brandy?' she sobbed.

'Er . . . I'm afraid not,' said Lestrade. 'Tea, perhaps?'

She nodded. 'It's about my brother.'

'This is Inspector Kane.' Lestrade indicated his assistant, whose hairline was barely visible over a pile of papers on his desk. 'He will make a few notes if he may. Now, about your brother.'

'He's missing, Superintendent. Vanished. Gone.'

'Name?'

'William Percy Hinchcliffe. You know . . .'

'Er . . .' Lestrade did not.

'The famous author.'

'Ah.' Lestrade saw Kane's eyebrows appear briefly near his hairline and sensed the smirk beneath it.

'Several novels. Four plays. A number of essays of international importance.'

'Of course. When did you last see your brother, Miss Hinchcliffe?'

'Nearly five weeks ago. He lives in a neighbouring village – Fingalsham in Kent.'

'Kent, Miss Hinchcliffe?' Bells were ringing in Lestrade's head.

'Yes.'

Tea arrived and to the astonishment of the company Miss Hinchcliffe proceeded to pour the contents of a silver hip flask into her cup. 'For my condition,' she said by way of explanation as she saw their faces and patted her ample chest as though that said it all.

'How old is your brother?' Lestrade asked.

'He is forty-five, Superintendent. Some years older than I.' She lashed the policemen with her eyes, defying them to say a word. Lestrade noticed Kane's eyebrows rising again.

'And why do you assume he is missing, madam?'

'Because he joins me for luncheon each Sunday, Superintendent. And he did not come four weeks ago.' She snorted into a lace handkerchief.

'Did you try to contact him?'

'I did. I have no faith in these newfangled speaking devices.' She looked disparagingly at the one on Lestrade's wall. 'I sent my man. He found no sign of anyone at my brother's house.'

'Your brother lives alone, Miss Hinchcliffe?'

'He does. Mildly eccentric, you know, like all authors. Won't have a servant in the house.'

'Is he a Socialist?' John Kane spoke for the first time.

'Please,' Miss Hinchcliffe was indignant, 'that is a disgusting thing to imply.'

'And was the house locked?' Lestrade moved on, ignoring John Kane's bid for transfer to the Special Branch.

'No, it was not.' Miss Hinchcliffe recovered herself. 'Percy did not have locks. It was always open house at Fingalsham.'

'Were there any signs of a struggle, Miss Hinchcliffe?'

'None. Superintendent, what are you suggesting?'

'Nothing, Miss Hinchcliffe. I am sure there is no cause for alarm, but I must explore every avenue. Tell me, did you contact the local constabulary?'

'Good heavens no, Superintendent. I always have the best—'

'That's very kind, ma'am,' Lestrade gushed.

'—but Superintendent Froest was not available, I understand.'

Lestrade's face fell. 'Rest assured, Miss Hinchcliffe, we will do all we can.'

She rose to go.

'I have a sergeant who will take a statement in my outer office,' he said; but suddenly Miss Hinchcliffe reeled sideways as the door caught her in the hip flask.

Blevvins had arrived. Kane and Lestrade lifted the spinster up.

'*This* is the sergeant I had in mind.' Lestrade's look would have frozen a more human man.

Miss Hinchcliffe let out a scream that brought coppers rushing from every door on every landing.

'What have you done, Blevvins?' was the most oft-heard cry in the seconds that followed. When they had engineered the hysterical Miss Hinchcliffe into a chair and Blevvins had disappeared momentarily in search of the straitjacket the Yard kept for serious cases, Lestrade attempted to unravel the woman's mind.

'What is the matter, Miss Hinchcliffe?' Ever the subtle approach.

'That . . . that terrible man!' she sobbed dramatically.

'Yes,' said Lestrade. 'I know Sergeant Blevvins isn't everybody's cup of tea—'

'It's what he had in his hand!' she howled.

Lestrade looked at Kane, who looked at the constable in the outer office, who shrugged.

'It's Percy's!' She collapsed in a distraught heap.

Lestrade was a little nonplussed. 'Do you mean the sergeant had forgotten to adjust his dress?'

Miss Hinchcliffe fetched Lestrade one around his head with the handbag that held the hip flask. 'Don't be disgusting. You are a Servant of the Public.' She seemed to recover a little while he dabbed away the blood with his cravat. 'I mean, he was carrying Percy's bathing costume.'

'His bathing costume?' Lestrade stood up sharply.

'Here it is, sir.' Blevvins arrived with the straitjacket. 'Can I put it on her, sir?'

'Never mind that. That pile of clothes you dropped . . .'

'Well, I'm sorry, sir. That stupid old party made me—'

'Thank you, Sergeant,' Lestrade cut in. 'Are they from Lillywhites?'

'Yes, sir. They were closed yesterday and the manager was

none too keen to lend them, until I . . . persuaded him.'

Lestrade picked out one of the fallen garments and held it up. 'Percy's?' he asked.

'Indeed it is.' Miss Hinchcliffe was indignant.

Lestrade looked at the bathing costume in his hands. It was made in the red, white and blue configuration of the Union Jack.

'You're bleeding, sir,' observed Blevvins. 'Did this old lady—'

'It's all right, Sergeant. It will heal. Which is more than can be said, I fear . . . Miss Hinchcliffe, was . . . is your brother a swimmer?'

'Of course. Why else would he wear a bathing costume?'

'You'd be amazed, dearie—'

'Thank you, Sergeant. How good a swimmer was he?'

'Excellent, Superintendent. Why . . . why are you using the past tense? What has this oaf' – she stabbed the air at Blevvins – 'done to my Percy?'

'Lady, I wouldn't touch anything of yours with—'

'That will be all, Blevvins.' Lestrade dismissed him. He turned to the quivering spinster. 'Miss Hinchcliffe.' He held her hands. 'I have reason to believe that your brother is dead. His body was washed up on the beach at St Margaret's Bay on . . .' But he was talking to the wall. Miss Hinchcliffe had slipped sedately through his fingers to join Messrs Lillywhites' samples on the floor.

'Constable,' Lestrade called. The young man helped carry the spinster out.

'We could do with a few female constables at times like these, sir, eh?' Kane proffered. Lestrade's look withered him.

'You didn't know Matthew Webb?' Lestrade asked. 'No, before your time.'

'I don't follow you, sir.'

'No, I don't suppose you will. Matthew Webb was a Master Mariner. One of the best swimmers this country has produced. He swam the Channel in 'seventy-five.'

'You mean . . . the body on the beach . . .'

'. . .was the result of an attempt to do the same, yes.'

'How do you know it wasn't an ordinary swimmer, sir? Just getting the air.'

'The grease under the fingernails, John. The grease the coroner missed. That worried me.'

'What was it?'

'Porpoise oil. Webb covered himself in it for his swim. It helps keep out the cold. For a dip in the briny you don't need it, but for a twenty-mile swim across the Channel . . .'

'But surely, sir, Hinchcliffe wouldn't have just dived in? Don't you need boats and things in case of trouble?'

'Webb did,' Lestrade remembered. 'But this man was an author, Kane. Mildly eccentric, didn't his sister call him? How eccentric did he have to be to try the Channel, I wonder? And anyway,' Lestrade grabbed his bowler and Donegal, 'Percy Hinchcliffe wasn't alone. His murderer was with him.'

Leon Beron knocked confidently on the door at No. 28 Settles Street. The muffled talking stopped abruptly. There were whispers, the scraping of furniture.

'Come on, Sol, I know you're in there,' Beron shouted, and was about to redouble his knock when the door sprang open to reveal a smart young man with swept back short hair and a foreign-looking beard and moustache.

'Who are you?' Beron asked him.

'I was about to ask you the same question,' said the young man in a clipped European accent.

'Leon Beron,' came the answer. 'I own this building.'

The young man's shifty face broke into a broad grin and he extended a hand. 'I am Peter Schtern,' he said. 'Come in.'

In the room, lit only by an oil lamp, was a circular table with a dark red cloth. Around this sat a group of people Beron had never seen before. One of them stood up at his entrance.

'This is my good friend George Gardstein,' said Schtern. The young man clicked his heels; 'Joe Levi . . .' another one stood up; 'Fritz Svaars . . .' a third. 'And this,' he patted the shoulder of the only woman present, 'is Luba Milstein. You already know Sol of course.'

The nervous tenant emerged from the shadows. 'Leon, it's good to see you, my dear.'

Beron nodded, not taking his eyes off the others. Something didn't smell right. 'It's . . . about the rent, Sol.'

'Oh, of course.' Sol vanished into the shadows momentarily. No one else moved. No one else spoke. 'Here,' he said, pressing a large wad of notes into Beron's hand. 'A little more, yes. The next six months already.'

Beron blinked at the amount in his hand. 'The latke business picking up, Sol?' he asked.

'Yes,' Sol laughed brittly. 'Yes, that's right,' and he ushered Beron to the door. When they got there, the landlord turned to his tenant. 'Who *are* these people, Sol?'

'Friends, Leon. Well, friends of friends, you know.'

Beron nodded slowly, unconvinced. And Sol closed and locked the door.

'Do you think he heard anything?' Gardstein asked.

'Better watch that one,' said Schtern. 'Just in case.'

'He's suspicious already,' said Svaars. 'That'll only make it worse.'

'Not if it's done by somebody he knows, eh, Sol?'

The tenant swallowed hard. 'No, Peter, not me. Leon wouldn't go for that. But . . . there is somebody who would keep an eye on him . . . It'll cost.'

Peter nodded. 'It always does,' he said.

The Dead Ringer

Superintendent Sholto Lestrade received a letter on 8th May. It bore the crest of His late Majesty, Edward, the Peace Maker, whose great heart had ceased to beat two days earlier. The equerry who brought it said it was the last thing he had written in his own hand. No one else had seen it and there were no copies.

'So the King is dead,' mused Lestrade, savouring the moments of their relationship – the then Prince of Wales gasping for a cigar that night of rainless lightning at the Commissioner's Ball; the rotund lover sauntering with Daisy Warwick under the elms at Ladybower and the huddled bundle awaiting apparent murder in the darkened corner of the Diogenes. 'Long live the King,' he said and thanked the equerry for the note. It said little: *Lestrade. Last year in Marienbad. Take care of them for me as you always have. Bertie.*

Marienbad? Lestrade crossed to the curling map on the far wall. Germany, wasn't it? Playground of the rich? A second home for Edward VII. What happened there last year? And who must Lestrade take care of? And why? He was fifty-seven himself. He suddenly felt old and cold in the May sunshine.

There was one case pinned to Lestrade's wall below the map. The murder by person or persons unknown of Percy Hinch-cliffe. The remains had been placed in the modest family vault at Fingalsham. There were few mourners. Lestrade had gone himself in the hope of spotting something – anything –

untoward. Nothing. For all his sister had described him as a famous novelist, his readers weren't exactly flocking to pay their respects. Neither did the writing business pay too well. Lestrade applied for and got a warrant and he and Blevvins combed the late author's cottage. It yielded little. The man was a keen fitness fanatic, running or swimming along the Kent coast most days when the weather permitted. He was also an advocate of peace.

'Bloody coward!' had been Blevvins' sensitive and informed comment.

Hinchcliffe's latest creation lay spread in the untidy heap of the room which served as his study. It bore the title *The Terrors of Tamara* and seemed to be, to Lestrade's casual glance, about the rigours of life at Cheltenham Ladies' College. The bills outnumbered the outpourings of fiction. Evidently, Percy Hinchcliffe was a sharp dresser – the Homburgs alone would have cost Lestrade a year's salary. And, evidently, he travelled much abroad.

It was a Saturday not long after the King died that Lieutenant Ballard Hook, RN, came to Bandicoot Hall. He rode into the courtyard leading a pretty grey pony by the snaffle rein. It was Emma who saw him first, leaping down the stairs two at a time in her pale blue riding habit. Her Aunt Letitia met her at the bottom and raised a disapproving eyebrow.

'What's this?' She held Emma's hands in hers, looking at the girl's fingernails.

'It's all the rage in Germany, Aunt Lettie,' she said. 'Girls paint portraits of . . . gentlemen they admire . . . on their nails. Rather good, don't you think?'

'No, dear,' Letitia chided gently. 'Rather vulgar, I'm afraid.' She beamed at the downcast girl. 'Now, don't be long on your ride. Uncle Harry and Ivo will be back from Taunton in time for lunch. Don't be late. And Emma . . .' she called after the girl's retreating figure, gazing at the horseman through the door, '. . . don't get too fond of Mr Hook.'

'Why ever not, Aunt?' Emma asked.

Letitia smirked, wishing silently she were twenty years younger. 'I believe he's a dangerous man – where women are concerned.'

The girl lowered her voice and stared under her eyebrows in a gesture that was pure Lestrade. 'I hope so!' she said.

He dismounted briskly, kissed her hand and laughed at the ten portraits of himself staring up at him. He lifted her easily into the saddle, bowed to the watchful shadow of Aunt Letitia and swung up beside Lestrade's daughter.

'Race you to the river!' she shouted and lashed the pony with her whip. She was a better horseman than her father – not in itself difficult – and had been taught to ride by Harry Bandicoot. Not that Harry had ever mastered the art of side-saddle – that had been Letitia's province.

They raced through the blossom-laden orchards, the horses black and grey, Emma turning every now and again to check her pace and look for Ballard. He was laughing, slapping his mount's neck with the reins and standing in the stirrups. Suddenly Emma heard a cry as they reached the lush green meadows slanting down to the river. She saw Ballard's horse rush past her, riderless, and tugged hard to bring her animal round. He was lying near the hedge behind her, sprawled in the grass. Her brain whirled. She couldn't hear herself shouting, stumbling from the saddle and racing up the meadow. She fell to her knees beside him, cradling the pale face. His black hair was blown across his eyes, which were closed. Think, girl, think! she told herself. Pulse. Find a pulse. She had difficulty gripping the sailor's arm, trembling as she was. Nothing. She looked up and down in desperation. There was no one in sight. Only the horses, cropping the grass nearby, flicking their tails against the first flies of summer.

She unwrapped the veils that held her hat in place and laid her head on his chest. She hadn't time to focus her ears before strong arms had spun her over onto her back. She cried out, staring up into the strange, dark eyes of the lieutenant.

'Ballard Hook!' she shouted. 'You were shamming all the time. There's nothing wrong with you.'

'I wouldn't say that,' he grinned. 'I landed very hard on an unmentionable place.'

'Serves you right,' she said. 'Why on earth did you do it? You might have killed yourself.'

'The risk was worth it,' he answered her, 'for this.'

He leaned down and kissed her. She twisted under him, but his hands held her wrists fast. The same strong hands that had saved her brother's life. Slowly she relented, her breasts heaving less with effort and more with anticipation. He pushed himself upright again, looking down at her. She was a beautiful girl, the clear eyes sparkling under the crown of hair. He reached down and undid her tresses so that the hair cascaded over her shoulders.

'Ballard,' she whispered.

He closed her lips with another kiss, hotter, more hungry than the last. Slowly, with infinite gentleness, he unbuttoned her bodice and she let his fingers explore the strings of her corset.

'You've done this before,' she said.

'Never,' he lied with a straight face, and they both collapsed in laughter. She rolled over so that he lay on the grass again and this time she undid his buttons and slipped open the waistcoat and shirt. 'But *you* have.'

They laughed again.

'Is it a leap year?' she asked him.

He looked bemused. 'Next year, I think,' he said. 'Why do you ask?'

'There is an old custom,' she said, 'that in leap years, ladies can ask gentlemen to marry them.'

'Marry?' Hook's eyes widened.

'Tut, tut,' Emma scolded him. 'A man who doesn't fear the dreadnought's guns is afraid of a word?'

He laughed again, freeing her small young breasts from the chemise. 'Not afraid,' he said and pulled her to him. She hesitated briefly, her breath tight in her throat. He sensed it. 'Trust me,' he said, 'trust me.'

She did.

'Let's have it, then,' said Lestrade to Sergeant Dickens as they alighted from the hansom at the Aldwych.

'Sir?'

'The church, man.' Lestrade gestured to the Edifice in Question. 'Your words of wisdom.'

'Right, sir. St Clement Danes. Built in sixteen eighty-one to the specifications of Sir Christopher Wren. Possibly on the same site as earlier churches to mark what was a burial ground of Harold Harefoot and other Danish gentlemen. The tower, created in seventeen nineteen, is one hundred and fifteen feet high and was designed by Gibbs, whose pew was in the north gallery. It was also the church of Dr Johnson—'

'Ah, now that's one I do know something about: "O rare Ben Johnson".' An unusually lyric Lestrade was standing before Clement Danes that morning.

'I think you'll find that's Samuel Johnson, sir.' Dickens knew his super well enough to know he'd respond well. He didn't.

'As I said' – Lestrade covered his tracks – '"O rare Sam Johnson". Take your hat off,' and the Yard men went inside. It was cool there after the stifling heat of the late morning. The constable on the door was to blame really for what happened next. He had neglected to tell Lestrade and Dickens about the loose mat on the newly polished floors. It was Lestrade who, for all sorts of reasons, paid the inevitable penalty of this ignorance. He dropped inexorably to the ground prior to sliding half the length of the aisle in his eagerness to locate their quarry.

'No, sir, surely it's back here.' Dickens pointed to the tower.

Lestrade got up with all the dignity he could muster. Well, with greying hair and a face like old parchment, a limp could only add to the mystique, surely? This, at any rate, was what he told himself.

'Lead on, Dickens,' he said.

The sergeant found the door easily enough and negotiated the twisting stair.

'Be careful here, sir,' he called back to Lestrade. 'Mind how you go.'

'It's how *he* went I'm interested in,' Lestrade's voice echoed in the silent church.

Dickens looked up at the ropes swaying and creaking from the belltower. It was a while before his eyes acclimatised to the dark. Then he saw the soles of the feet and the dangling figure above.

'Come on, lad.' Lestrade tapped his sergeant's ankle. 'Keep climbing.'

The Yard men reached the first level where ladders replaced the steps. It was painful for Lestrade, but he made it. Now they were level with the corpse, twirling in the half-light that cut in diagonal shafts from Gibbs' latticed windows. Dickens turned away, sickened by the sight. Lestrade, the older man, was made of sterner stuff. He took it in with the weary eyes of a man who has seen it all before and yet has seen too much.

'Got your notebook, Dickens?'

No answer.

'Come on, man. Get down to the next level. And don't throw up. There's enough mess in here as it is. Write this down.'

Numbly, the pallid Dickens licked his pencil stub and waited, some feet below the feet and he didn't look up again.

'Male. Age, fortyish. Respectable man by his appearance. Good suit. Polished shoes. Half-hunter.' He put his glove on and stretched out against the ladder to check the noose. 'Mustn't upset Inspector Collins,' he muttered, more to himself than to Dickens, 'though I don't think he'll find much of a fingerprint on this lot.'

He looked at the blue lips, the grotesque, bulging tongue and the hideously crossed eyes. The rope bit deeply into the neck, pulpy and angry. The same type of rope (Bell. Anglican. For the use of) tied the wrists. There was a stain on the immaculate pinstripe of the trousers, spreading from crotch to waist.

'Cause of death. Strangulation.' He came down the ladder. 'It probably took him half an hour to die,' he said. 'Well, Sergeant. Oranges and lemons, eh?'

'Sir?'

'Oranges and lemons? You know, the nursery rhyme?'

'Er . . . no, sir.' Dickens was lost.

'Were you never a child, Sergeant? No, don't answer that. You were a pamphlet when you were younger, weren't you, before you grew into a bloody encyclopaedia.'

He noted the sergeant's crestfallen look.

'Never mind,' he slapped his shoulder, 'we'll let the uniformed boys cut him down. You can buy me a saveloy in the Coal Hole and tell me your theories on the case.'

Sergeant Dickens didn't have any theories on the case. The blue-lipped corpse hanging among the bell ropes of St Clement Danes had unnerved him and Lestrade stood him a Scotch. Dickens bought another to help him get over the shock of the superintendent buying the first.

'What do you make of it, sir?' Dickens tried to focus.

Lestrade lit a cigar and tilted his hat back on his head. 'Our man is clever. No obvious footprints and probably no fingerprints, either. And he's very powerful.'

'Powerful?'

'The stairs, man,' said Lestrade. 'No sign of the dust being disturbed. The killer must have been at work late last night, judging by the appearance of the body. No time for dust to re-form as completely as that.'

'But . . . if he didn't climb the stairs with the body, how did he get him up there?'

'That's where his strength comes in. He must have tied the noose around his neck on the floor and hauled him up.'

Dickens blew through the superintendent's smoke cloud. 'So we're looking for a circus strongman?'

'No, Sergeant,' said Lestrade. 'As usual, we're looking for a needle in a haystack.'

* * *

Edward Henry was the man entrusted with the arrangements for the forthcoming coronation. And as he began to draw up the blueprints, as though to spur him on, he received a knighthood from the new man at the Palace. He also received a great deal of scorn from the men at the Yard. Somebody wrote a placard with the legend 'Lord Love Us' and pinned it above his office door. He accused everybody, in the model of the archetypal police-man, and each time he spoke to one of his men, his eyes followed them suspiciously. Arguably, he was never the same again.

So it was that Sir Edward Henry received a visitation, if not from the Lord, then from the next thing to Him, in the form of the Very Reverend Cuthbert Auldwinkle, Vicar of St Clement Danes. Lestrade was about to reach for his second tripe sandwich, lovingly prepared by the good Mrs Dew, when he too had the call.

'Progress?' a voice trilled.

Lestrade looked up. 'You have the advantage of me.'

'Probably. I am the Very Reverend Auldwinkle, of St Clement Danes. It was in my room of God's House that this foul deed was perpetrated. Your bishop – er – I beg your pardon – commissioner told me you were handling the case. What progress?'

'I am afraid I am not at liberty to discuss that with you, sir, but I am glad to meet you at last. We have been trying to contact you.'

'I've been upcountry.'

'Upcountry?' Lestrade caught the bemused look on Sergeant Jones' face as he glided angelically across the corridor beyond the superintendent's open door.

'Windsor. I am Chaplain Extraordinary to His Majesty. I spent many years in Africa, Superintendent . . . er . . .'

'Lestrade.'

'Quite. Ever been among the fuzzy-wuzzies, Lestrade?'

'No, I . . .'

'Dervishes?'

'They whirl, don't they?'

'Not when I've finished with them. Muscular Christianity, Lestrade. God is Love. And the heathen must be taught that.'

The veins in the Very Reverend's temples throbbed crimson beside the wild white hair.

'Quite. So you attend St Clement Danes—'

'When I can. Between the Lord's work and the King's work, it's a full life.'

'Can you shed any light on this unfortunate matter?' Lestrade asked.

'The Light of the World!' Auldwinkle pointed skywards with all the fury of the Evangelist. 'Thomas Portnoy was one of my ringers.'

'Ringers?'

'Campanologist, man.'

'Er . . .'

'That's bellringer, sir.' Jones glided past again.

'Thank you, Sergeant,' Lestrade's teeth were clenched, 'your verger had no idea who he was.'

'New man. Short-sighted. What can you expect?'

'Address?'

'I shall be giving one on Sunday, yes.'

Lestrade looked at him.

'Ah, I see. He lived in the Albany. He was a writer.'

'A writer, sir? Do you mean a novelist?'

'Good heavens, no. He wrote spiritual tracts. You know of course *The Lord's Way*?'

'Would that be the pub in Threadneedle Street, sir?' Jones had passed the outer-office door again.

Auldwinkle rounded on him with the force of a whirlwind. 'It's a quarterly magazine, dolt.' Auldwinkle scrutinised the young sergeant. 'Are you a Son of the Church?' he bellowed.

'Well, I . . . er . . .' Jones cowered with the guilt of the ungodly.

'Did Mr Portnoy have any enemies, sir?' Lestrade endeavoured to save his man from the Wrath of the Lord.

'One or two Papists, perhaps.' Auldwinkle descended from the height of his missionary zeal. He was wasting his time on Jones, Lestrade knew. Sired by the man who years ago ran the River Police, he must be a Baptist.

'Anyone in particular?' Lestrade asked.

'Who'd want to see Portnoy dead? No.' Auldwinkle's crimson brow furrowed. 'No,' he shook his head emphatically, 'but I cannot accept it as God's will,' he said.

'Neither can I, sir,' said Lestrade. 'Whoever strung up your bellringer doesn't have a godly bone in his body.'

Lestrade, Blevvins and Jones interviewed Portnoy's fellow-ringers. There was much talk of Great Peter and Great Tom, hum and quint, and at least nine of them appeared to be tailors, but of the late Thomas Portnoy they all knew little. He was a reserved recluse, living they believed modestly on an annuity and writing religious works. No one could imagine why he had been in the church on that day and at that hour, nor why the act of stringing him up had not caused the bells to strike. The coroner had by now informed the Yard that Portnoy had died between midnight and three, a time of silence on the edge of the City when passing coppers on the beat would have seen a light or heard the muffled discordant peal of a man slowly strangling to death. Blevvins remained convinced that the oft-mentioned Bob Minor or the old man known as Grandsire Triples must be involved somewhere, possibly with the aid of an accomplice called Stedman. He consigned all this to his notebook and Lestrade made a mental note to have Blevvins checked at the earliest opportunity.

It was the other of the encyclopaedic sergeants at the Yard who shed the light that the Reverend Auldwinkle could not. Lestrade was in his office one morning as June broke, twirling in his fingers the noose that had despatched Thomas Portnoy, when the sergeant commented, 'Ashanti.'

'Bless you,' Walter Dew said, on his way to the lift, off duty.

'What did you say?' Lestrade looked up.

'The knot, sir,' said Dickens. 'It's called an Ashanti knot.'

'You know about knots?' Lestrade shouldn't really have been surprised.

'Yes, sir. A knot is defined as a loop, or combination of loops, used for fastening two ropes together, fastening a rope to some object, or for making a knob or swelling in or at one end to—'

'Yes, yes.' Lestrade reached for his cigar case and began puffing furiously. 'Why Ashanti?'

'The Ashanti knot is so called because it was traditionally used by Arabs and others to bind African slaves together when they were brought to the coast prior to being sold—'

'Africa?' shouted Lestrade. 'Dickens, get your hat. We're going to Windsor,' and all that remained of the superintendent was a whiff of smoke.

They missed their quarry at Windsor. The Very Reverend Auldwinkle of Clement Danes was not being strictly faithful to the itinerary he had given to Lestrade. On this Tuesday he ought to have been attending the King, but His New Majesty was abroad and Lestrade and Dickens had travelled forty-five miles to talk to a man whom they could have found a few hundred yards from their front door. At least Lestrade had an opportunity to rub shoulders with the aristocracy. In fact, he did rather more than that. He collided with a stand of banners in Henry VII's chapel and spent the best part of the day being bandaged in Windsor Infirmary.

So it was that Sergeant Dickens did his best to outface the redoubtable missionary of Clement Danes. Auldwinkle knew nothing of the Ashanti. His African work had taken him to the Belgian Congo and east into the Sudan. In fact, he had got to Khartoum all those years ago, ahead of Wolseley's relief column, and Dickens found himself subjected to a lecture on the role of

Christianity among heathens who may or may not have been descended from the lost tribe of Israel. By the time he had finished, Dickens was in serious need of a relief column himself and he staggered back to report to his super, whose head was swathed in bandages and gave him the appearance of an ice-cream cornet.

Now it had never been known for Lestrade to show the kind of exuberance he did when Dickens collapsed in his office. It was probably the blow to his head, but he actually slapped the sergeant's back and gave him a cigar.

'Tell me again,' he said. 'What was it Auldwinkle said as his parting shot?'

'He said that Mr Portnoy had never seemed the same since the death of his friend Hinchcliffe.'

'Rapture,' murmured Lestrade, his mind racing ahead.

'No, sir. Concussion, surely.' Dickens admired the expert safety-pinning of the nurse.

Lestrade's nicely purpling eyes lashed him. He crossed to the pinboard on the far wall.

'So, Dickens. We're on to him. It's not two murderers, it's one.'

'Sir?'

'How many people do you know, Sergeant? Two hundred, three hundred?'

Dickens opened his mouth.

'How many friends have you? Twenty, thirty?' Lestrade reconsidered. '*Any?*'

Dickens continued his goldfish impression.

'And how many of those friends have died mysteriously?'

Dickens closed his mouth. 'None,' he said.

'Exactly. It defies the laws of coincidence that two friends should meet their ends in ways other than the ordinary. Why then should two friends die?'

'A common motive?'

Lestrade toyed with giving the man another cigar, but he had been generous enough for one day. 'Odd, though, that there was no mention of Portnoy in Hinchcliffe's papers. Who looked over Portnoy's rooms?'

'Sergeant Blevvins, sir.'

Lestrade's euphoria plummeted. 'Oh,' he said.

'He did catch some villains conducting a lottery on the pavement outside the Albany, sir.'

'A lottery?'

'Well they said it was a raffle . . . I ask you!'

'Raffles at the Albany? Mmmm, not very likely,' agreed Lestrade. 'Did Portnoy's papers tell us anything?'

'Sergeant Blevvins couldn't make much sense of most of it, sir. Very deep, he said it was. Some of it in a foreign language he took to be Greek.'

'Yes,' sighed Lestrade. 'I'm afraid many things are Greek to Sergeant Blevvins.'

'Got a minute, Sholto?' Frank Froest's paunch appeared in Lestrade's doorway, followed by the rest of him. Yard men, not given to flights of fancy or idle speculation, had commented on the man's similarity to the late and not very lamented Nimrod Frost – 'His Nims' – whose demise a few years ago had allowed in the nut-brown nizam who now occupied the third floor. In name and form, Frank Froest was an uncanny shadow. Some men in darkness muttered. Was this Nimrod Frost come back from the grave to watch over his boys at the Yard?

'Come in, Frank.' He pushed the nearest pile of paper aside.

'How's the head?' Froest observed the absence of bandages. It was this astuteness that had got him where he was today – grovelling.

'You're grovelling, Frank.' Lestrade had not missed it. He waved Froest to a chair.

The big man chuckled. 'You ferret, you never lose a chance, do you?'

Lestrade laughed.

'I've got a problem.' Froest was serious.

'Tried sulphur?' Lestrade was equally grim.

Froest ignored him and opened another button on his waistcoat, a garment that could have carpeted some entire houses Lestrade knew.

'Got anybody free at the moment?'

'What's this for?' Lestrade was suspicious.

'All right, guv,' Froest lolled back, 'I'll come clean. Some friends of mine came to see me this morning. Mr and Mrs Nash. They've just got back from America.'

'Go on, Frank, I'm all ears.'

Froest would have agreed, but he needed Lestrade's help.

'Mrs Nash is a music hall artiste. Works under the name of Lil Hawthorne.'

'The one with the boa constrictor?' asked Lestrade.

'No, no. You're thinking of Sarah Bernhardt. Anyway' – Froest reached for his pipe – 'they paid a call on another friend, a Dr Crippen. Seems Crippen's wife was another hall girl – under the name of Belle Elmore.'

'And?'

'She's supposed to have gone to America and died there.'

'And?'

'And the Nashes found no one there who remembered seeing her. Odd?'

'Perhaps. But the bad news is I can only spare Walter Dew.'

Froest groaned. 'So be it,' he said. 'Lord Love Us has got me running round in circles on this damned coronation. I ask you – Head of the Serious Crimes Squad.'

'It's the way of the world, Frank,' said Lestrade.

'Sholto, keep an eye on Dew, will you? I don't want to let the Nashes down.'

Lestrade nodded.

Journeys into the Unknown

The Lanchester lay at a crazy angle on the sharp bend below Box Hill. Around it swarmed innumerable uniformed constables, a vicious-looking sergeant in plain clothes and a sallow, ferret-faced man in an obsolete Donegal and shabby bowler. They didn't pay superintendents enough.

'Mr Lestrade, sir,' the sergeant called.

'What is it, Blevvins?'

'I found this on the back seat, sir.'

Lestrade looked the sergeant in the eye. 'Do you know what a fingerprint is, Sergeant?'

'Yes, sir, it's a—'

Lestrade snatched the outstretched piece of paper from him. 'Never mind, Blevvins. When they ask me my views on this case, I shall tell them you did it,' Lestrade shook the paper, 'and here's my evidence.'

He read the torn fragment: ...*time spent in inevitable repairs might be killed pleasantly.*

'What do you make of it?'

'It's part of a newspaper, sir.'

'Splendid, Blevvins. And what significance do you attach to it?'

'Sir?'

'Never mind. Take the wagon, will you, and get back to the Yard. I'll be staying over. By the time I get back, I want to know where that came from. Get Dickens and Jones to help you. Start in Fleet Street. That's where they keep all the news-papers. All right?'

'Very good, sir.'

'Who found the body?' Lestrade asked.

'Crabbe, sir, Surrey Constabulary.' A young officer saluted him briskly.

'Good man, Constable. Tell me about it.'

'I was cycling in an easterly direction, sir, last evening, prior to partaking of an evening meal—'

'We are not in court, Constable,' Lestrade reminded him and lit a cigar. 'In your own words.'

The constable relaxed a little. 'Well, sir, like I say, I was on my bike, just about to knock off duty, when I came across this 'ere motor.'

'A road accident, surely?' Lestrade tested him.

'That's what I thought at first, sir,' said Crabbe, 'but there was no tyre marks on the road. And no damage to the vehicle itself.'

Lestrade nodded. 'And the deceased?'

'In the position she is now, sir.'

'Injuries?'

'Not consistent with those pertaining to a horseless carriage accident, sir.'

Lestrade looked quizzically at him.

'Sorry, sir. Lots of blood, but from the ears and nose. No outward bash, except for the forehead.'

'Very good, Constable. What then?'

'I pedalled like hell for the nick, sir. Made me report and the sergeant run round to the chief constable's house.'

Lestrade nodded. He walked around the constable. Then patted his shoulder. 'That's good policework, Constable,' he said. 'If you ever get tired of Surrey, pay me a visit. The Yard can use men like you and I think we can make you a sergeant, Crabbe.'

'Thank you, sir.' The constable saluted and stepped back.

Lestrade checked the interior of the motor. A 1907 Lanchester, later model than his own and in better condition. The canvas roof was pulled back. It was a glorious day and he was already at this early hour regretting the Donegal. Yesterday had been good, too. That would explain the absence of roof. The deceased lay slumped in the driver's seat, her head against the passenger's door. She had been an attractive woman, aged about fifty. Well dressed. No gloves. Her nails were well cared for, but one of them was broken and recently. She was wearing driving habit, her broad, veiled hat lying on the seat beside her. Her eyes were still open, staring sightlessly at the overspreading cedars. Dark red blood ran the length of both sides of her face and had drenched her shoulders and coat. More had trickled down from the head wound to give her pallid features a mask-like appearance. Looped casually around the steering wheel was a length of twine.

Lestrade checked the vehicle again. As Crabbe had said, no signs of damage, no skid marks. There had been no collision.

'Do we know who this lady is?' he called to the waiting constabulary.

'No, sir,' Crabbe answered, 'we've been checking on that all night.'

Lestrade looked at the dead face again. Who was she? Where had she been going? Was it a journey into the unknown?

Chief Inspector Walter Dew knocked at the door of No. 39 Hilldrop Crescent. With him stood Sergeant Mitchell, a new man on the Force, a dab hand with the ladies, but given to bouts of depression. His mother had been frightened by a Seventh Day Adventist while she had been carrying him and that seemed to say it all.

An attractive maid opened the door.

'*Oui?*' she said.

Mitchell looked at Dew.

'Frog,' said the chief inspector. For a man who had never been further west than Tintagel he prided himself on his literary and linguistic talents.

'Can I 'elp you?' she asked.

A more attractive, boyish young woman appeared. 'Yes, gentlemen?' she asked.

'I am Chief Inspector Dew. This is Sergeant Mitchell. We'd like to see Dr Crippen.' Never a mincer of words was the chief inspector.

'I am Miss Le Neve, the doctor's housekeeper,' she announced, 'I'm afraid Dr Crippen is at his place of work.'

'I see,' said Dew. 'Would you mind accompanying us there, madam?' It was an old trick Lestrade had taught him. Don't give them time to think. Worry them. Watch them. Wait.

The Yard men and the housekeeper caught a Number 14 to Albion House and she led the way to the dingy third-floor office. In the gloom, a little man with a torch strapped to his head looked up at them. Miss Le Neve introduced them and quietly sat in a corner while the doctor levered away at a patient who lay gasping and gurgling in the chair. There was a ripping noise and a scream and Dr Crippen held up the recalcitrant molar with the air of a man who has found gold. Both Dew and Mitchell, whose collective stomachs had the consistency of a jellyfish, paled visibly.

'Next!' Crippen shouted, as the bleeding patient hobbled off, lighter by a tooth and a sizeable fee.

Another masochist entered and allowed himself to be pinioned in the bloody leather chair.

'I suppose I'd better tell you the truth,' Crippen smirked.

Mitchell looked away as the doctor applied the forceps with renewed vigour.

'Yes, that would be better.' Dew sensed a collar.

'I made up the stories about Belle's death. As far as I know, she is alive.'

He placed a knee on his patient's chest and tugged. 'Give me a hand here, Chief Inspector, would you?'

Dew jerked his head in Mitchell's direction and the sergeant screwed his courage to the sticking place and gripped Crippen round the waist. There was another crack and both men hurtled backwards against the wall. Another patient crept away, sadder, wiser, broker.

Dr Crippen dictated a statement and Sergeant Mitchell wrote it down. At lunchtime, while Mitchell went out in search of another pencil and Miss Le Neve returned to Hilldrop Crescent, Dew and Crippen went to a local restaurant, where the chief inspector wrestled for the first time in his life with the joys of spaghetti. Then they returned to Crippen's house and the search began.

They caught the Number 41 back to the Yard.

'Well, Mitchell?' Dew knew how Lestrade probed the tiny minds of his subordinates.

'Not too bad, sir. That tooth pulling turned me up.'

Why, wondered Dew, did they all answer that way? 'Do you have any ideas on the case?'

'Well, it's obvious, sir. His wife's run away, hasn't she?'

'What about her gowns in the wardrobe?'

'Er . . .'

'I'll tell you what about the gowns in the wardrobe. She stole them.'

'Stole them, sir?'

'Why else would a man like Crippen invent stories of her death? Pride, Mitchell. Pride. Mrs Crippen was a dubious character, Sergeant,' Dew was getting into his stride as they lurched along the Embankment, 'she had a number of aliases. Belle Elmore, Cora Crippen, Kunigunde Mackimot . . . Mackamo . . . Well, you know. That's suspicious in itself. All the same, these chorus girls. She was helping herself to goodies of all kinds. He found out about it. They had a row and he kicked her out. Or she left of her own accord. Done all right though, hasn't he? That housekeeper, eh?'

'He didn't kill his wife, then?'

Dew laughed. 'Kill his wife? You've got a long way to go, Mitchell. When you've been in the business as long as I have, you get a nose for villains. Oh, Crippen may be a lousy dentist, but he's innocent as the driven snow.'

Lestrade strolled that evening on Box Hill. The scarlet sun gilded the bracken and gorse and the sheep munched regardless on the lush grass. He looked at the woman beside him. She was Fanny Berkeley, twenty years his junior, tall, radiant, a breath of fresh air on this Surrey hillside. And the streets of London seemed years away.

'Are you going to tell me or not?' she asked him.

He chuckled. 'You're a policeman's daughter,' he reminded her, 'you know I can't.'

'Exactly.' She squeezed his hand and shook it with irritation. 'And it's *because* I'm a policeman's daughter that I'm asking.'

Lestrade sat down on the short, sheep-cropped turf. He pulled a cigar from his waistcoat pocket and instinctively she lit it for him. He puffed a while. 'Why aren't you married?' he suddenly asked.

'No one asked me,' she smiled into the distance of enclosed fields and sleepy hamlets. 'And you're changing the subject, Sholto Lestrade.'

He deftly flicked the guano off his cuff, only to have it land on his shoe. That he consigned to the grass with as little fuss as possible. 'All right,' he said, 'I'll break the habit of a lifetime. What sort of woman wears those trousers?'

'Trousers? Do you mean harem pants?'

'I suppose I do. Baggy things, gathered at the ankles.'

'That's right. They're usually silk.'

'Probably.' Lestrade was not at his best on fabrics.

'How old is this person?'

'Fiftyish.'

Fanny shook her head. 'Unlikely. Harem pants, like bloomers and mutton chop sleeves a few years ago, are essentially the hallmark of the young. I, for example, wouldn't be seen dead in them.'

'There you have it,' Lestrade said.

'What?' Realisation dawned. 'Ah, the body in the Lanchester,' she said.

He nodded.

'She was wearing harem pants? Pa said . . .' and she swallowed the words.

'Go on,' said Lestrade, 'what else did the Chief Constable of Surrey say?'

'Oh, Sholto,' she said, mimicking him, 'you know I cannot divulge . . .'

'Your Pa and I go back a long way,' he told her. 'I remember him when he still had bumfluff – beggin' your pardon, Miss Berkeley,' and he bent his knees in the time-honoured tradition of the copper-on-the-beat.

'The Caddis Case, wasn't it?' she said.

'Good God, it was,' Lestrade laughed, 'I'd almost forgotten that one. Come on, then, what's Tom Berkeley's theory?'

'Pa hasn't got one. He says he doesn't keep dogs and bark himself. He leaves that to detectives like you.'

'Well, he may be right,' said Lestrade. 'My bark's a lot worse than my bite these days.'

'That's not what I've heard,' and she looked at him wide-eyed until he laughed. He cuffed her playfully with his bowler and perched it on the back of his head. 'A middle-aged woman, then,' Fanny went on, 'wearing clothes that are too young for her, driving an automobile – alone.'

'Get to the point,' he urged her.

'Fast?'

'I've no idea what speed she was doing,' he said.

It was her turn to hit him. 'No, I mean doesn't that add up to a fast lady? Her touch on the throttle is irrelevant.'

'Perhaps it does. But I'm not so sure about the irrelevance of her touch on the throttle. The car had stopped when she died.

And it was out of petrol.'

'That's always happening to me,' Fanny admitted.

'Damn,' he said. 'I thought you'd say that.'

'What?'

'I was hoping there was something sinister in that. I'd forgotten what appalling drivers women are.'

She pulled a face.

'By the way, if you drive, does that make you a fast lady?'

She turned to him and laid her head on his arm. 'Sholto Lestrade, you've known me for nearly twenty years. You mean to say you don't know.'

He stood up and pulled her to him. 'No,' he said. 'I don't. But that doesn't mean I can't find out.'

Their heads bent towards each other; the tired old detective and the chief constable's elegant daughter, whom no one had ever asked. She held him steady in her gaze and he held her steady in his arms. Their lips touched once, softly, and he let her go.

'Fanny Berkeley,' he said, 'I am fifty-seven years old. My back aches and my feet hurt. Tell me what I'm doing here.'

'You're doing what you always do, Sholto Lestrade,' and she took his hand, 'you're working on a case.'

The day that Lestrade walked with Fanny Berkeley on Box Hill, Miss Eliza Barrow moved into the top floor apartment of No. 63 Tollington Park. The Seddon children helped her with the possessions she had while Frederick Seddon, their father and her landlord, watched the frumpish spinster potter in and out of the less-than-palatial rooms. One thing she allowed no one to carry was a black-painted iron box, clearly heavy and clearly full. By nightfall, Miss Barrow was rocking gently in the chair by the empty grate, cradling what looked to Seddon like a bottle of gin.

'Settling in, Miss Barrow?' he asked.

She sat bolt upright, startled, and noticed his sharp cold eyes on her bottle.

'For my chest, Mr Seddon,' she said. 'My asthma.'

'Of course,' he smiled, 'if I could trouble you for the rent?'

'Rent?' She seemed taken aback. 'Ah, yes. Yes. In the morning, Mr Seddon, if you don't mind. I've had a rather trying day.'

Seddon had rarely smiled so often in his life before and twice in as many minutes was a positive strain.

'Aye.' He allowed his native Lancashire to break through. 'Let's say the morning, shall we? Goodnight, Miss Barrow.'

'That's 'im,' the constable on the rooftop called to a colleague perched on a weather vane. That one signalled with a complex series of waves to a third across on a church steeple. This constable pressed his stopwatch and waved to a couple on the roadway around the corner. These two linked arms and stood in the middle of the road as the Lanchester hurtled around the bend. The driver snatched at the handbrake and cursed loudly as the rim of the windshield hit him in the forehead and the car slewed to one side, narrowly missing a waiting horse.

'Now then, sir,' said a constable to the driver, 'are you aware of the speed at which you were travelling?'

'No,' came the reply. 'Are you?'

'I have reason to believe you were travelling at a speed likely to cause an accident, sir.'

'If you two hadn't been behaving like bollards, there wouldn't have been any problem. I might have killed you.'

'Quite so, sir. And that sounds 'orribly like an admission to me, don't it to you, Constable Williams?'

'It do, Constable Glynn. It do. And I don't care for the use of the word "bollards". Officers of the law goin' about their lawful duty deserve rather more respect.'

Williams reached forward to open the door, but the driver was quicker. He grabbed the policeman's wrist. 'Touch this car and you're a dead man,' he warned.

'Oh, is that so?' Williams lunged, but the driver forced the door into the constable's knees and he went down. Glynn rushed to the attack, only to meet the driver's boot in the pit of his stomach. While the constables struggled upright, the driver got out of the Lanchester and held up a card.

'I am Superintendent Lestrade of Scotland Yard,' he told them. The constables blinked at the card in astonishment. Then they sheepishly came to attention. 'I am taking this vehicle back to London for forensic testing in connection with a murder enquiry, gentlemen. Your prints all over it might well put you on the gallows.'

'Blimey,' gulped Williams, 'we're sorry, sir.'

'So am I,' said Lestrade. 'Put some butter on those knees, Constable. But good work on the speed. Your trap almost came off. And at least you couldn't nab me for kerb crawling!'

'All right, Walter. Put it all together. What have you got?' Lestrade buried his moustache in the morning tea.

'One . . . .' Dew had resorted to the policeman's final aid – his fingers '. . .Mrs Crippen has gone to America or so her husband says. Two . . .' he prowled Lestrade's office ' . . .he is clearly enjoying a liaison' – and he allowed himself a self-satisfied smirk at his grasp of language – 'with his housekeeper, Miss Le Neve.'

'Three?' Lestrade prompted him.

'Ah yes, three. Three, Dr Crippen and Miss Le Neve appear to have gone. His business partner told me he had wound up his business interests. And here's the stinker, sir. Crippen sent out for some boys' clothes.'

'Boys' clothes?' Now Lestrade was intrigued. 'Crippen hasn't a son?'

'No, sir. No children at all.'

'And Miss Le Neve?'

Dew looked shocked at his guv'nor's inference. For all he was a hard-bitten copper, he was still a man of his class and a Victorian at that. He couldn't keep up with the pace of the new Georgians.

'Hilldrop Crescent?' said Lestrade. 'Islington, isn't it?'

'Yes, sir.'

Lestrade downed his tea. 'Well come on, Dew. We've got some digging to do.'

And so it was that Lestrade, Dew and Mitchell entered the cold, dead house in Hilldrop Crescent. The French maid had gone. Dust had not yet gathered on the broad aspidistra leaves. Lestrade's head ached from the jarring blow in the dead woman's Lanchester and he didn't really have the time for this. But there was a smell about Dr Crippen he didn't really like. He'd never met the man, but he knew that Dew's theory about Cora Crippen's light-fingered habits was sadly wide of the mark.

'Where shall we start?' Mitchell's voice was a staccato whisper in the hall.

'What are we looking for?' asked Dew.

'I'd settle for a cellar,' said Lestrade.

'Isn't it a bit early, sir?' Mitchell's attempt at levity was not appreciated.

The Yard men found the electricity switched off, so Mitchell groped around in the kitchen for some matches. By the light of a solitary candle they reached the uneven cellar floor. It was dank and acrid down here for all it was July above.

'We've looked here before,' said Dew.

'Pass me that poker, Mitchell,' Lestrade ordered and he began to prod the loose flagstones. One by one, they came away and Lestrade reached his hand into the dark void below. He took his bowler off and his jacket and rolled up his sleeve. Mitchell and Dew stood frozen. A few more leverings with the poker and the most nauseating stench rose from the cellar floor. Mitchell gagged and vomited into a corner. Dew visibly rocked back on his heels. He had never been the same since finding the corpse of Mary Kelly on her deathbed in the dark, dead days of the Ripper.

'Mitchell,' said Lestrade quietly. 'If you can't stand the smell, get out of the cellar.'

'I'm all right, sir.'

'Right, then,' said Lestrade. 'Pass me that candle.' He lowered the guttering flame into the darkness. He saw the tangled mess of bleached hair and the stinking heap of human flesh; all trace of bone had gone.

Lestrade knelt upright. 'Gentlemen,' he said, the candle throwing lurid shadows on his face, 'meet Mrs Crippen.'

'Yes?' the grim-lipped young man looked up from the mess on the table.

'Er . . . Chief Inspector Dew,' the newcomer announced, trying not to look at the shapeless heap under the lamp's glare.

'Well?' The young man continued to stand, scalpel poised.

'You are . . .?' Dew ventured.

'Waiting,' he answered.

'No . . . I mean, are you Doctor Pepper?'

'No, I am Bernard Spilsbury. May I be allowed to continue?'

'Yes, yes, of course.' Dew felt as green as the walls of the mortuary, 'I just wondered . . .'

'Yes, of course you did. I never make conclusions until I have finished my work.'

'It is a matter of urgency, sir.'

Spilsbury sighed. 'It always is.' He had come a long way from the anxious, neurotic, spotty youth from Leamington. He no longer suffered fools gladly. Walter Dew least of all.

'Very well,' he said. 'What we have here' – he stirred it a little with his scalpel – 'was once a female. Overweight. Bleached hair. Ovaries removed some time ago. Look.'

Dew tried to do so while closing his eyes.

'Operation scar in the lower abdomen.'

Dew opened his eyes. Even now he didn't know which way up the body was.

'Cause of death – and you may not quote me on this yet – hyoscine poisoning.'

'Ah.' Dew tried to look informed. It fooled no one, especially Spilsbury. It was even possible that Cora Crippen was not taken in.

'Traces of it all over the place. She would have ingested it in tea, perhaps coffee. With plenty of sugar it would be virtually undetectable. She would have become delirious. In twelve hours or so she would have been paralysed and dead – in that order.'

Dew tried to smile, but he felt his gorge rising and made for the door.

'Then she was cut up,' Spilsbury called after him. 'Most of the head is missing.'

Inspector Stockley Collins had been at the centre of the Fingerprint Room for more years than he cared to remember. Since the first appointment of Edward Henry, he had been a fingerprint fanatic. Since the Stratton case his lonely nights, often by candlelight, with brushes and powders, had been vindicated. But on the dead woman's Lanchester he drew a blank.

'Gloves, sir,' he told Lestrade. 'Smudges on the wheel and dashboard. But all the prints here are the same – the dead woman's. Do you know who she was yet?'

'Philomena Marchment. Forty-eight years old. Family, none traced at present. Friends – precious few, it seems, though I've yet to check them.'

Lestrade lit a cigar, heedless of the signs telling him not to.

'All in all,' he sighed, 'I know less about her than Dew does about the bits on Spilsbury's slab.'

'Yes, apart from the games thing, it does look thin, doesn't it?' Collins agreed.

'Games thing?'

'The diabolo string.'

'Diabolo string?' Lestrade was beginning to sound like an echo.

'This.' Collins produced the coloured twine that had been wrapped around the steering wheel. 'It's from the diabolo game. You remember – about three years ago – it was all the rage. Everybody had one.'

'You're right,' said Lestrade, 'I even bought my daughter one.'

'I don't want this put around, sir, but I . . .' Collins checked that they were alone ' . . .I once found Sir Edward playing with one.'

'Tsk, tsk,' Lestrade shook his head, 'if you were taller, Collins, I'd kiss you.'

'Useful bit of gossip, eh, sir?' Collins looked pleased with himself.

'Not the Lord Love Us business – though it's all good stuff to store up – no, Collins, diabolo. Can you get me one?'

Collins looked a little sheepish. Then he ferreted in a nearby drawer. 'As a matter of fact . . .'

'Ah,' Lestrade's face creased in a wry grin, 'show me how it works. You're obviously an expert.'

'It's relaxing, sir. After a hard day.'

'Yes, of course.' Lestrade humoured him.

Collins placed the wooden peg on the taut string and whirled it around, so that the peg spun like a top and whined with a soporific hum up and down the string.

'Let me try.' Lestrade handled the string. It flopped limply once or twice. 'Story of my life,' he muttered, but he soon got the hang of it.

'It's all in the wrist action, sir.' Collins hovered, adding helpful hints.

'So they tell me,' agreed Lestrade. He concentrated for a moment, getting maximum speed on the string, then jerked it forward, so that the peg hurtled across the room and smashed Collins' glass-plated door. There was a muffled shout from somewhere beyond it and Blevvins appeared.

'You look shattered, Sergeant,' said Lestrade. 'Sorry about that, gentlemen.'

'This piece of paper, sir,' Blevvins quickly recovered his sangfroid, 'it's from the *London Illustrated News*.'

'Paper?' Lestrade's mind was still on the killing power of the wooden plug.

'The newspaper advertisement we found in the Lanchester. It's—'

'An advertisement for diabolo. Yes, I know.'

Blevvins' face fell.

'Never mind, Sergeant. Good work, anyway.'

'This one?' Collins produced the complete page from his diabolo box. They matched perfectly. 'They put them in each box of the new ones,' he explained, 'they were so proud of it. It was supposed to be the perfect thing for ladies to do while gentlemen repaired the—'

'Lanchester,' all three men chorused.

'At least we know our murderer is an advertising agent's dream,' said Lestrade. 'Tell me, Collins, were these plugs always made of wood?'

'I believe some were metal, sir.'

Lestrade nodded. 'Hard enough to smash a skull,' he said, almost to himself. 'Come on, Blevvins. You'd better let the doctor pick those bits of glass out of you. I might even buy you a cuppa.'

'Thank you, sir,' said Blevvins, 'I could murder a cup of tea.'

And there was something in the glint in his eye that told Lestrade he probably could.

The *Daily Mail* had carried the story for days. 'The Chase of Crippen'. And when the nonsense and the silly season of stories had gone – he was really an exiled Crown Prince on the run; he had drowned himself in somebody's garden pond; he had been eaten by tigers in Regent's Park – the strong probability remained that he and Miss Le Neve had gone to Belgium. Lestrade couldn't understand why there. Froest was furious that Dew had let them go at all. Dew himself looked up the Yard atlas to find out where it was.

Then the observancy of Joe Public came to the Yard's assistance. A Captain Kendall of the SS *Montrose* had reported an odd couple on his ship bound for Canada. The man had been short, nervous and very attentive towards his teenaged son John. He'd cracked his walnuts for him and held his hand. The boy had seemed deaf. At least, he didn't seem to answer to his name. And there'd been something girlish in his make-up. . . .

So it was that Walter Dew, who had never been further west than Tintagel, screwed his courage to the sticking place and boarded the SS *Laurentic* at Liverpool. He wore Lestrade's pea-jacket and sailor's cap and, despite the habitual green he developed, hoped to pass as a pilot when he caught up with the *Montrose*. Sergeant Mitchell went with him, metaphorically to hold his hand, but he spent most of his time actually holding the hands of the pretty wardresses whose job it would be to take charge of Miss Le Neve. Long before they had reached the Bar Lightship, Dew had finished the tripe sandwiches so lovingly prepared by Mrs Dew and the eight little Dews. And homesickness was added to seasickness.

It was on Sunday, the last day of July, that the little party boarded the *Montrose* in the St Lawrence Seaway. Dew was doing his best to control the wobble in his legs. Mitchell pulled himself with effort from the wardresses. On the deck of the *Montrose*, a little man with rimless spectacles walked with his odd little legs strutting out each side.

'Good morning, Dr Crippen,' said the pilot, 'I am Chief Inspector Dew of Scotland Yard. I believe you know me.'

Crippen stood still, then threw up his arms with a curious reflex. Mitchell thought he was going to jump over the side and rushed forward, but Dew held him back.

'Good morning, Mr Dew,' said Crippen quietly.

The chief inspector charged his man and Mitchell handcuffed

him. Dew went below to the cabin where 'John Robinson' sat on the bunk, reading. His suit was very ill-fitting – the boy's outfit Crippen had ordered before winding up his affairs in England.

'Miss Le Neve?' he asked. 'I am Chief Inspector Dew.'

Odd how that simple statement brought out different reactions in people. Frank Froest had repeated it many times, as though in disbelief. Harvey Crippen had thrown up his arms in terror – or resignation. Ethel Le Neve screamed and fainted. Sergeant Mitchell wasn't surprised. It was the effect he assumed Dew had on all women.

After three weeks in Canada, when Dew shared the reputation of the scarlet-coated Mounties of having 'got his man', the little party sailed back on the *Megantic*. Dew had sent a telegram back to Lestrade – 'Handcuffs, London. Crippen and Le Neve arrested. Dew.'

For a brief but fleeting moment, Lestrade was impressed.

By moonlight, Dew and Crippen walked on the deserted deck. They had become oddly attached over the past days, and not merely by handcuffs. Dew began to feel almost sorry for the man.

'Why hyoscine?' he had asked him.

'It's a depressant,' muttered the quiet doctor. 'Cora made incessant demands on me. When she had no gentlemen friends. She had a . . . voracious appetite, Inspector. Voracious.'

'What did you do with her bones?'

'I burnt them.' Crippen shuddered at the memory of it. 'I cut up her body and burnt her bones in the grate. It's funny,' and he chuckled his quiet, brittle laugh, 'I made two mistakes, Mr Dew. I am supposed to be a doctor, but I reckoned without the march of science. I miscalculated the effects of quicklime on Cora's body. And . . .' he pointed to the crackle of the radio the other side of the cabin wall past which they walked '. . . I reckoned without the Marconi machine. A wonderful instrument, eh?'

'It is indeed,' Dew agreed.

Crippen stopped. 'I don't know how things will go,' he said. 'I want to ask you if you will let me see her. I won't speak to her. She's been my only comfort for the past three years.'

His large eyes were brimming with tears. It was nearly a month since the guilty lovers had last seen each other. Dew took him to his cabin door and signalled the wardresses to put Mitchell down and bring Ethel Le Neve to the door of hers. They gazed at each other across the corridor. There was silence. Walter Dew, in love with a woman himself, turned away. Not for the first time, he told himself he had a rotten job.

Shots in the Dark

Life began to crowd in on Lestrade. Death began to crowd in on him even more. He had two unsolved – perhaps insoluble – murders on his plate, even without the lady in the Lanchester. Her name was Philomena Marchment, a divorced lady of private means whose antics had shocked polite society some years ago when it was rumoured she had ousted Mrs Keppel as the favourite confidante of the late King. Lestrade himself had gone to her town house – the legacy of a particularly juicy divorce settlement made on her by Sir Clive Marchment, the great white hunter. A sleepy little cottage in the Surrey village of Virginia Water would have to wait until he could get out of London.

Lestrade was a little surprised to find the door at No. 74 Portman Square opened by a tall, angular figure whose sex seemed rather in question. The figure wore a Homburg hat and a man's suit, lightweight linen to match the heat of August. The superintendent introduced himself and was ushered in.

'Do you smoke?' the creature asked in a dark brown voice.

'Cigars,' said Lestrade.

'Thank you.' The figure held out a long, pale hand and proceeded to stuff Lestrade's cheroot into a diamond cigarette holder. 'Light?' it asked.

Lestrade fumbled for a lucifer.

'I am Isadora,' the figure said.

That ought to have made it clear to Lestrade, but pretentious names had never been his forte.

'I am – or rather was – Phil's companion. How did she die, Superintendent?'

Lestrade was shown into a large and comfortable drawing room.

'I believe she was killed by a game, er . . .'

'Madam.' It was as though Isadora sensed the superintendent's confusion. 'Call me madam. A game.' She blew smoke rings to the panelled ceiling. 'You intrigue me, Mr Lestrade. Let me see now – death by Halma? Murder by Monarch? Oh no, it must be Bobbies and Thieves, surely?'

'You seem, madam, if I may say so, unscathed by your late companion's death.'

'Do I, Mr Lestrade?' Isadora poured herself a large brandy from the tantalus on the table. 'I will be frank with you, Superintendent. I have scant regard for men in general and policemen in particular. I was . . . very fond of Phil. Fond enough to want the murderer brought to book. I have shed my tears, Superintendent. My grief is my own affair. It is private. My vengeance must perforce be public.'

Lestrade assessed his current sparring partner. Not unattractive in a mannish sort of way, but the straight, short-cropped hair under the Homburg and the casual way with smoke and drink tended to undo all that. He was getting old, he told himself again. He couldn't cope.

'What game?' She brought him back to the present.

'Diabolo,' he told her.

'Diabolo? How?'

'Imagine the peg to be of steel rather than of wood,' he said. 'Imagine it spun from a tautly held string. The tension would give it the impact of a slingshot. Very nearly that of a bullet.'

Isadora closed her eyes briefly and gulped down her remaining brandy. 'David and Goliath,' she said.

'Do you have a diabolo set, madam?' he asked her.

'What?' She seemed far away. 'Oh, no. I suppose I played like everyone else when it was the rage. A little passé now, don't you think? I've taken up golf.'

Lestrade winced. Next she'd be entering for the 1912 Olympic Games.

'Of course, I ran in the Olympics.' She blew her cigar smoke in a matter-of-fact sort of way. 'No one suspected.' She poured herself another drink. 'Rather fun really – to show you men how to do it.'

'How long have you known Mrs Marchment?'

'Miss!' Isadora was indignant. 'Phil may have retained the bastard's name, but Mrs is a shackle, Superintendent. A nominal one, I grant you, but a shackle as surely as those of steel you clamp to the ankles of suffragists.' She relented a little. 'Nearly three years.'

'And you lived here with her?'

'Is that remark intended to be offensive?' she asked him.

'No, madam. Unless of course you have something to hide.'

'Hide, Superintendent? Certainly not. I am not ashamed of the fact that Phil and I were lovers. And you must know you cannot touch me for that.'

Lestrade wasn't sure he wanted to touch Isadora for anything.

'The one useful thing that vile old hag of a Queen-Empress did for us was not to acknowledge our existence. Her total ignorance of true beauty has given the Sisters of Lesbos a free rein.'

'Sisters of Lesbos, madam?' Lestrade smelt conspiracy.

'An Order I founded some years ago, Superintendent. Men are not allowed.'

'Was . . . Miss . . . Marchment a suffragette?' Lestrade probed.

'Oh,' Isadora rolled her eyes heavenward, 'what a word. Coined by that bigot Harmsworth in his nasty little rag. The term is "suffragist", Superintendent. And in answer to your question, yes, she was.'

'Militant?' Lestrade pursued.

'If by that you mean did she hit policemen with a brick concealed in her handbag, then no. But she was a staunch believer in the cause of downtrodden womanhood. We buried her in the green and purple of the Order.'

'The Sisters of Lesbos?' Lestrade sought clarification.

'The Women's Political Union,' Isadora explained.

'Were there any . . .' and he hesitated to suggest it '. . . men in Miss Marchment's life?'

She lowered her cigarette holder and blew smoke through her nostrils. She looked rather like the dragon must have looked to St George, Lestrade thought.

'I'll forget you said that,' she said.

'Madam, I . . .'

'I really must be going now, Superintendent. I was in fact on my way out when you arrived.'

Lestrade stood up with her and his tipless nose reached her chin.

'And Mr Marchment?' he said.

'God knows,' she said. 'Or more probably the Devil.'

'You are not being very helpful, Isadora,' he said to her.

'Good heavens, am I to be accused of obstructing the police in the course of their enquiries?'

Lestrade sighed. 'Madam,' he said, 'has it occurred to you that we are on the same side, you and I? I may be a man' – for a brief moment he sounded unsure. 'I may even be a policeman' – even that caused him moments of doubt – 'but if you can overlook these facts, you will find that I am as anxious to catch Miss Marchment's killer as you are. Perhaps even more so.'

She looked down at him. It was a truce, not a surrender.

'Very well,' she said. 'He lives in the Albany.'

They had called it *the* Albany a few years ago – a palatial residence on the right side of Piccadilly. It had gone through a number of names – Sunderland, Piccadilly, Melbourne – Sergeant Dickens recited them all as he and Lestrade jolted in the hansom around the Circus. Latterly, it had divided into apartments for gentlemen of private means. Those gentlemen had decided that 'The Albany' had given it the air of a public house. In fact several of them had been employed on a part-time basis throwing out drunks who refused to leave the magnificent entrance until they were given a drink. Curiously enough, these same gentlemen had been visited recently by Sergeant Blevvins of Scotland Yard in the pursuance of his duty. Now that *was* curious. Thomas Portnoy, found hanging in Clement Danes' steeple and Clive Marchment, husband of Philomena Marchment found dead in her Lanchester, *both* lived at the Albany. Lestrade mused to Dickens on the coincidence. And when they alighted and Lestrade waited for Dickens to pay, the hansom driver leaned over and scrutinised the pair.

'Excuse me,' he said in his truculent Cockney, 'are you two policemen by any chance?'

Dickens looked at his feet. Was it that? Or his helmet-shaped head that had betrayed him?

Lestrade had no such qualms. 'Who wants to know?' He could be as truculent as any Cockney.

'I was wondering,' the growler went on, 'whether you gentlemen are officers of Scotland Yard.'

'And if we are?' Lestrade asked.

'Nothin'.' The growler took up his reins and whip. 'Only you'd know Mr Edward Henry,' he said.

'*Sir* Edward,' Dickens corrected him and as he said it he heard Lestrade's intake of breath. He felt his metaphorical stripes ripped from his sleeve.

'Edward who?' Lestrade tried to probe the growler further.

'Edward Henry,' repeated the cabbie. 'He's a very good friend of mine. Very good. It's a small old world, ain't it?' and he cracked his whip to jolt the old hack into action.

The Yard men watched him go.

'What was all that about?' Dickens asked.

'I don't know, Sergeant, but I'll be whispering in future when

I travel by hansom. Didn't get his number, did you?'

'Better than that, sir,' Dickens grinned, 'it's all those years poring over the small print in encyclopaedias. I got his name.'

'And?'

Dickens looked confused. 'And his number, sir.' He was triumphant.

'No, I mean what *is* his name?' Lestrade humoured the man.

'Alfred Bowes,' said Dickens.

Lestrade consigned it to his memory too and they entered the Albany.

Sir Clive Marchment's man was a giant and silent African, who stood solid and black in the doorway, dangling with leopard skins and hair. Lestrade and Dickens looked at him and then at each other.

A barked command from somewhere behind the huge figure made them both jump. The African bowed to them and gestured to the end of a long corridor, the walls of which were adorned with the stuffed heads of every animal known to man. Few of them were known to Lestrade, however, and all that was written below each was an incomprehensible place name, he assumed, and a date. He was particularly impressed by a white rhinoceros, whose murderous horn protruded from the dusty, leathery nose of the monster. Impressed because he hadn't seen it until it hit him in the mouth and he entered an ante-room with a swollen jaw.

'Ugly brute, isn't he?' a voice called.

Lestrade looked at the African. 'Yes,' he concurred through aching teeth.

'Not him, the rhino.' A tanned, middle-aged man in khaki shirt and jodhpurs strode across the tiger rugs that littered the enormous hearth. Here a fire roared and crackled. Lestrade and Dickens began to feel the perspiration trickle under their boaters.

'Sorry about the heat,' their host said, whisking away flies with what appeared to be a yak's tail, 'but when you've lived in the tropics, August in England can be damned chilly. Don't you agree, Mr ... er ...?'

'Lestrade, sir. Superintendent Lestrade, Scotland Yard. This is Sergeant Dickens.'

'You and your man like a drink?' Their host snarled something guttural to the African, who vanished as silently as he had come and reappeared with a tray of brandies. 'Magnificent, isn't he? Zulu. How old would you say he is?'

Lestrade looked the negro up and down. 'Thirty?' he guessed. Dickens knew better than to disagree with his guv'nor.

'He's sixty-three.'

Lestrade's eyes widened. This shiny black with muscles like a drayhorse was six years older than he was.

'He fought with Cetshwayo at Isandhlwana,' their host went on. 'God knows how many of the South Wales Borderers he brought down. It would make your eyes water to see what he can do with an assegai.'

'I don't doubt it, sir, but I fear we have other business. You *are* Sir Clive Marchment?'

The khaki hunter drained his glass. 'I am,' he said. 'And you've come about my late and unlamented wife.'

'Unlamented, sir?' Lestrade accepted the gestured offer of a chair and began to fan himself with his hat.

'Oh, come now, Superintendent. Philly and I parted fourteen years ago. Apart from a brief exchange of mutual hatred in some ghastly courtroom, I haven't seen her since. I understand that harpy she lived with identified the body. She's certainly seen it more recently than I have. Another drink?'

Lestrade declined. 'So you know Isadora?' he asked.

'I knew of her. I had two or three foully offensive letters from her in the early days. You know the sort of thing – all men are beasts, etc., etc. A pity someone didn't kill her too.'

'Sir?' Lestrade began to smell a rat, but in this heat it was probably his own socks.

'I do read the newspapers, Superintendent,' Marchment

explained. '"The Police Suspect Foul Play" and don't tell me a superintendent and a sergeant from Scotland Yard visit the ex-relatives of all motor-accident victims. Philly was murdered' – he wandered to the window – 'but I'm damned if I know why.'

'What sort of woman was she, sir?' Lestrade asked.

'God, what an impossible question.' Marchment laughed. 'My ex-wife was a shrew, Superintendent. Oh, intelligent, clever even, but bitchy. She was a poseuse. You name the new fad, she took it up. Cycling, smoking, Votes for Women. Stereotypical. I'm not surprised such women are murdered.' He fixed his flinty eyes on some imagined distant object and raised his hands. 'Wait till you see the whites of their eyes, then, click,' and he let fly with a deadly index finger as his imaginary quarry sailed through the air to lie bleeding in the dust.

'Did you approve of your ex-wife's suffragist interests?' Lestrade pursued the point.

'When we lived together she was only flirting with the movement. It was in the days before those maniacal Pankhursts appeared on the streets. But then my wife flirted with lots of things, Superintendent – men, women. I suppose she was trying to prove something. She was a picker-up of unconsidered trifles, a saver of souls, a champion of lost causes. God knows what the latest one was.'

'Among her friends,' Lestrade changed tack, 'can you think of anyone who disliked her?'

'Enough to kill her? No. Except perhaps Imtali here.' He gestured at the Zulu.

'Oh?' Lestrade searched the vacant, black face for an emotion. He found none.

'He is inordinately fond of me, Superintendent. If he thought that anyone was about to hurt me . . . Sergeant, are you armed?'

Dickens looked blank. 'I have a truncheon, sir,' he said.

'May I see it?' Marchment asked.

Dickens looked at Lestrade, who nodded. The sergeant fumbled in his pocket and jerked out the leather-bound cosh.

Before he realised what was happening, the Zulu had snatched it from him, whirled Dickens off the floor and was holding him up against the wall with the truncheon jammed against his throat. Dickens was choking, his feet kicking inches from the animal rugs. Lestrade was upright, his brass knuckles ready to go for the African's kidneys, when a few gentle words from Marchment caused the Zulu to drop the sergeant. Dickens crawled back to his chair, nursing a ravaged neck.

'Sorry, Sergeant,' Marchment poured him another drink, 'but you see what I mean? If I hadn't intervened, Imtali would have killed you.'

'Could he have killed your wife, Sir Clive?' Lestrade put the knuckles away.

'Imtali speaks no English, Superintendent. I do not discuss my marital affairs with my bearer, especially in Swahili. Tell me, was Philly's neck broken?'

'No,' Lestrade answered.

'Then Imtali is not your man. He tends to snap spines.'

Dickens could vouch for that.

Lestrade changed tack again. 'Did you know Mr Thomas Portnoy?'

'Portnoy? Here at Albany? Yes, I did as a matter of fact. He lived below, on the third floor. Didn't care for Imtali's bongos.'

'Drums,' Dickens rasped by way of explanation for Lestrade.

'He was forever grumbling. Sending bumptious little notes.'

'And what did you do about Portnoy's complaints?'

There was a silence. Even the flat tigers on the floor seemed to be straining for the answer.

'I hanged him in St Clement Danes,' said Marchment.

Dickens stood up, ready to reach for the handcuffs, but Lestrade intervened. 'You must admit, Sir Clive, that your position is an odd one. Two people have met deaths in recent weeks. One was your ex-wife, the other a near neighbour. That sort of coincidence must make you almost unique.'

'Or guilty,' croaked Dickens.

Marchment remained supremely cool in the roasting heat of his trophy room. 'Gentlemen,' he said, 'I am a killer by profession. Every dead thing you see around you I killed. And when I kill, I do it with a gun. Something like this perhaps.' He pulled from an umbrella stand a high-powered rifle with sights and adjusters. He threw it to Lestrade. The superintendent had never really been at home with guns. They were not exactly regulation issue at the Yard. He held it gingerly.

'Not like that, man.' Marchment snatched it back, swung it onto his chest, cradled the carrying strap over his arm and nicked back the bolt. The rifle came up level with Lestrade's head. 'This thing would stop an elephant at four hundred yards,' he said. 'At this range, Superintendent, there'd be literally nothing left of your head.'

Lestrade gently deflected the gun's muzzle with one finger.

'What do you make of this, Sir Clive?' He produced a smashed lead plug from his pocket.

Marchment lowered the rifle and examined it. 'Difficult to say,' he murmured. 'Badly corroded. Been in water for a while?'

Lestrade nodded.

'It's probably an automatic bullet. Mauser, I'd say.'

'Mauser?' Lestrade repeated.

Marchment growled at the huge Zulu, who bowed and vanished, reappearing in seconds with a mahogany case. Marchment flipped open the lid to reveal a pistol. 'Broomhandle Mauser,' he said, handing it to Lestrade. 'It would be my guess your pellet came from a gun like that.'

'There are those – Frenchmen mostly – who believe that it ought to be possible to say precisely which gun fired a particular bullet. Do you think that's possible, Sir Clive?'

'Balderdash,' was the White Hunter's professional opinion. 'Especially with a slug as smashed as that.' He paused. 'Is that what killed Philly?' he asked.

'No, sir.' Lestrade pocketed the evidence and returned the pistol to its case. 'These guns,' he said, 'do I assume they are of German manufacture?'

'The best ones, yes, but you find them everywhere. Lots of officers here have them, not to mention civilians. Does that get you anywhere?'

'Probably not,' said Lestrade. 'Thank you for your help, Sir Clive. If we need to contact you again . . .'

'I am bound for the Gold Coast next month, Superintendent. If you wish to clap me in irons, you'll need to do it before then.'

Dickens coughed his way out of Albany. Lestrade dodged the lurking rhinoceros and they hailed a cab.

'Penny for your thoughts, Dickens,' Lestrade whispered, lest it was Alfred Bowes who sat above them on the box.

'I was just wondering if a broken larynx can heal by itself, sir,' Dickens growled.

'Big lad, the blackamoor, wasn't he?'

'You might say that, sir.'

'Big enough to haul Thomas Portnoy up to the belltower at Clement Danes.'

'The Ashanti knot!' Dickens' exuberance caught his throat anew and he regretted it.

'Congratulations, Sergeant. You're coming on.'

'So you think the Zulu killed Portnoy because he complained about his drumming?'

'More likely he sensed that Portnoy had crossed his master. You saw how sensitive he could be . . .' Lestrade smiled benignly at his injured lieutenant.

'So we went to investigate one crime and ended up solving another?'

'I'm not so sure it's as simple as that, Sergeant. For instance, a twelve-foot Zulu wearing leopardskins carrying a struggling bell-ringer under his arm would probably give rise to the odd observation, don't you think? Even at dead of night in the Strand. Even so, we'll keep an eye on Robinson Crusoe and his Man Friday. There may well be more to them than meets the eye.

Lestrade had not taken any leave for more months than he cared to remember. The hot summer of 1910 was blistering but brief. And autumn came all too soon with gales and rain. On such a day, two very attractive ladies arrived at the Yard and much to the amusement of Inspectors Elias Bower and John Kane, not to mention Sergeant 'Buildings' Peabody and innumerable constables, Superintendent Sholto Lestrade was carried bodily past them all out into the courtyard, where Sir Edward Henry's tethered horse proceeded to defecate inches from the superintendent's shoes as he scrambled into a waiting chaise.

'No Silver Ghost today, Letitia?' he asked the elder lady.

'Harry's in that, being Something in the City. He'll join us later for dinner. Flageolets suit you?'

Lestrade was about to protest that he didn't care for Spanish sadism, when Emma cut in, 'But first, Daddy, tea at the Astoria. You look dreadful. When did you eat last?'

They munched their way through a veritable heap of cream cakes and sundries while the orchestra in the Palm Court serenaded them.

'Well,' sighed Lestrade, surfacing from his umpteenth éclair, 'my favourite two ladies in the whole world,' and he put an arm round them both. 'This has been nice.'

They all laughed. Then Lestrade became serious. 'Letitia, how's Ivo? I meant to write . . . You know how it is.'

She looked down. 'I know,' she said and held his hand. 'Ivo's better. Much better. He's back at Eton for the Michaelmas term. His memory's fully restored. Except for the accident. He can't remember a thing about Binky's yacht.'

'And Rupert?'

Letitia's lip quivered for just an instant. 'Rupert has gone, Sholto. We've come to accept that. . . . Now' – she sniffed back her tears resolutely – 'I have to get to Liberty's before they close.' She stood up. So did Lestrade. 'No,' she said, 'I think your daughter has something to say to you.' She smiled at them both and swirled away.

Lestrade looked at his little girl. Where had the years gone? he wondered. It wasn't long since he had held her to his chest that dreadful night her mother had died. How she reminded him of Sarah now, her bright grey eyes, her golden hair.

'Daddy.' She shook his arm.

'Sorry,' he said. 'I was far away.'

'About Rupert . . .' she began.

'Darling, I got nowhere,' he said. 'Vavasour, Oates, Hook, they couldn't help. It's true I never reached Hobsbaum. He was out of the country for months. I suppose he's back now. . . . Emma, I tried. Letitia seems to have accepted it. Why can't you? Rupert and Ivo were swept overboard by a freak wave. They tell me that kind of thing can happen.'

'I know, Daddy. And you're right. It just seems so . . .'

'Cruel?' he looked steadily into her eyes.

She nodded.

'The world, my girl,' he said, 'is a cruel place.'

'You tried Jamie Snagge, I suppose?' she said, helping herself to more tea.

'Snagge?'

'Yes, he was on Binky's yacht that day.'

'Was he? You didn't mention him.'

Emma laughed. 'No, and I'll bet no one else did either.'

Lestrade looked puzzled. 'No, as a matter of fact they didn't.'

'I'm not surprised. Jamie is rather a non-event. Ballard says you have to listen very hard in a room to hear his breathing. It's the only way you know he's there.'

'Ballard?'

'Ballard Hook,' she reminded him, feeling a blush on her cheek.

'Ah, yes. Your lieutenant.'

'Commander,' she corrected him.

'Promotion?'

'Yes, last month. Jamie serves with Ballard on the *Achilles*. I'm afraid he's rather quiet and rather dull. Secretive, really.'

'All right.' Lestrade was prepared to humour his daughter for one last time. 'Where might I find your Mr Snagge?'

'Ah, that's the problem. The *Achilles* sailed for the Mediterranean last week. She won't be back before Christmas, I'm afraid.'

'Was that what you had to tell me?' he asked. 'About Snagge?'

'Not exactly.' She felt her heart pounding. 'It's about Ballard. . . .'

'Yes?'

'Er . . . there was a burglary. At Ballard's parents' house.'

'Oh?'

'Yes. Nothing much taken. Some family silver, a family tree . . .'

'All very familiar, then?' Lestrade pinched a sugar cube when he thought no one was looking.

'Daddy, you're making fun of me,' Emma pouted.

'And you're not being straight with me, young lady.' He wagged a finger at her. 'Since when is a superintendent at the Yard interested in some provincial jemmy job? What else about Ballard Hook?'

She smiled coyly under drooping lashes. 'He . . . oh, Daddy, he's asked me to marry him.'

Lestrade sat back in his chair. He'd been preparing for this day for years. Emma Bandicoot-Lestrade lived with Harry and Letitia, but she was his daughter. When the time came *he* would give her away, give *his* consent. It would be Lestrade walking down that aisle with the loveliest girl in the world on his arm. He may have been preparing for it, but he wasn't ready.

'I see,' he said.

'No, Daddy, you don't.' She held his hand. 'When you saw Ballard, what did you see? A dashing young naval officer? A brave man? A loyal friend? He's all those things of course, but he's more. Much more. He's . . . he's . . .'

'The man you love?' Lestrade filled in the missing words.

She nodded. 'There were four men in my life,' she said. 'You, Uncle Harry, Ivo and Rupert. Rupert's gone . . . and now Ballard has taken his place. Not as a brother, like Rupert, but, yes, as the man I love.'

He looked across the table at her. 'What do you want me to say?' he said.

She pulled herself upright in her chair. 'You are my father,' she said, 'and whatever Mrs Pankhurst says, I will do as you say. If you say I cannot marry Ballard Hook, then . . . so be it.'

Lestrade remained motionless, unblinking during what was obviously a rehearsed speech. His daughter had got round him before. With subtle wiles like hers, she didn't need the muscularity of the suffragettes to win him over. He leaned across to her and took her hand. 'When the *Achilles* returns from the Mediterranean, I think I'd better have a word with Commander Hook, just to make sure his intentions are honourable.'

'Daddy!' she screamed and flung her arms around his neck. Frosty eyes swivelled in their direction. Macassared heads turned. Only the Palm Court Orchestra carried on playing. They had seen it all before.

The country cottage of Philomena Marchment was a little less than idyllic by the end of October. Lestrade had been dragged screaming into Sir Edward Henry's coronation arrangements and that had kept him busy planning procession routes and working with an opposite number in the City Force. What though he told himself several times a day this was not the work of a superintendent of Scotland Yard? Then of course there was Walter Dew, who had always had problems with the long words in his reports. The Crippen case promised to be *the* case of the decade, and Dew was tending to chase his own tail without much success. It was Lestrade who came to his rescue. And so it was later than he intended that the superintendent came to peruse the contents of a modest little labourer's cottage at the far end of Virginia Water with a fine view of Windsor. He obtained the key from the village hall and checked the house from stem to stern. More harem pants in the wardrobe, a lot of literature of the nefarious feminist kind. And no other clues. Then Lestrade found her letters, bundles of them tied in pink ribbon at the back of a drawer. They were addressed to Phil and signed simply 'J'. Had Lestrade not met Isadora, he would automatically have assumed that 'J' was a man. Now, he was not so sure. The endearments were tempestuous, the prose purple. But it *could* have been written by a woman. He wished now that he had read Sir Richard Burton's translations in more detail. Perhaps the boffin of the Yard could make something of the handwriting. On the other hand, Lestrade would ideally have liked to have solved the case before they planted him in his box.

> *I imagine us, darling Phil, locked in the embrace as we were when last we met, our lips and arms entwined, lovers in the dark . . .*

He checked the postmarks on his way back to the Yard. London. Not much help. Still, they might repay further work. They might yet tell him who 'J' was.

'There's a lady to see you, sir,' Peabody told him at the outer desk.

Fanny Berkeley sat waiting for him.

'Hello, Sholto,' she said.

'Fanny,' he threw his bowler expertly onto the hat-rack, 'this is a pleasant surprise. Dickens,' he bellowed. 'Tea!'

The sergeant shuffled off to do his master's bidding.

'I was hoping for supper,' she murmured.

Lestrade paused and looked at her.

'You can't just wander back into a woman's life,' she said, 'and leave without a word.' She crossed to him, placing her hand on his as it rested on the desk. 'You need protection, Mr Lestrade. If I remember our walk on Box Hill, even the birds have got it in for you. I can save you from all that.'

'You'd need a pretty wide hat!' Lestrade chuckled.

'How's the Marchment case?'

'Sshh,' Lestrade leapt to the door, 'not here, Fanny. It's more than my job's worth. But there are some letters I'd like you to look over later.'

'Over supper?'

He twirled his moustache for a while. 'What would your father say to his little girl having supper with a lecherous old policeman?'

'Tut,' she scolded. 'He's a lecherous old policeman himself.'

'Sir!' Fanny crashed sideways as the door burst open.

'Blevvins,' Lestrade was calm, 'that is the second time you have knocked over a lady in my office.'

'Oh, I'm sorry.' Blevvins threatened to break Fanny's arm by yanking her upright. 'It's murder, sir.'

'Working with you? Yes, Blevvins, but I'll survive. I'm not sure about Miss Berkeley, however. Fanny, are you all right?'

'May I dust you down, ma'am?' Blevvins sensed the chance of a lifetime.

'No, you may not,' Fanny and Lestrade chorused.

'It's a corpse, sir. At the Bioscope. You'd better come.'

Lestrade shrugged. 'Sorry about supper,' he said. 'Some other time?'

She smiled. She had been brought up a copper's kid. She'd heard that one before.

The cinematograph theatre called the Bioscope stood in Shaftesbury Avenue. It was dusk when Lestrade got there and uniformed constables held back the surging crowd outside as he alighted from the station wagon. He entered the theatre, Blevvins at his elbow, which gave the superintendent no comfort whatever.

'Lights!' Lestrade shouted.

An electric switch clanged and the rows of seats were thrown into sharp silhouette against the screen.

'What are they showing?' he whispered to Blevvins.

'*The Great Train Robbery*. Have you seen it, sir?'

'My dad worked on the case,' Lestrade answered.

'Sir?'

'Never mind, Blevvins. Before your time.'

Lestrade's gaze came to rest on the single head with the bowler hat in Row F, Seat 13. 'Unlucky for some,' he murmured. He sauntered down the aisle till he came level with the victim. A man of about thirty, slumped to the right, well dressed, slim. It was his face that held Lestrade's gaze. The mad, staring eyes, the fixed grin with the thin lips pulled taut against bared teeth.

'I didn't know there was a funny bit in the *Train Robbery*,' Blevvins observed.

Lestrade ignored the tastelessness of the remark. 'Who found him?' he asked.

'Some bloke sitting next to him. He's in the back with the manager.'

'Hello!' A voice caused both men to turn. A waddling figure emerged into the half-light. 'Ah, you must be in charge of the case.' The new arrival clearly aimed this at Lestrade.

'No, sir. I am Sergeant Blevvins. *This* is Superintendent Lestrade.'

Both men looked oddly at Blevvins.

'William Hepplewhite. Theatre manager. This is dreadful. Just dreadful.' Mr Hepplewhite proceeded to dab his profusely sweating brow with a handkerchief.

'Warm, are you, sir?' Blevvins could make a hiccough sound menacing. 'Nervous, perhaps?'

'Tell me,' Lestrade ushered Hepplewhite away from the distressing figure, he also wanted him away from the corpse, 'what happened?'

'We were about ten minutes into the show,' he said, 'when there was a scream. Well, frankly we're used to that. I fear the invention of the cinematograph is a godsend for men with straying fingers.'

'You assumed it was merely a little slap and tickle?'

'Until people started shouting and screaming everywhere. I thought then someone was exposing himself.'

'What did you do?'

'What we always do. I get a bucket of water ready.'

'Bucket of water?' sneered Blevvins. 'I'd get a pair of bricks and . . .'

Lestrade raised a hand for silence.

'Then I saw . . . that.' Hepplewhite jerked a perspiring head in the direction of the corpse. 'It was . . . horrible. May I sit down?'

Lestrade helped the manager into one of his own chairs.

'The rest was chaos. The theatre must have emptied in seconds. I'm amazed no one was hurt. I called a constable on his beat.'

'Who?'

'Name of . . . er . . .' Blevvins attempted to read his notes in the dim light. 'Anyway, he's in the foyer.'

'All right. Mr Hepplewhite, come with me. I want to talk to the gentleman who was sitting next to the deceased. And to this constable. Blevvins' – the sergeant snapped to attention – 'touch anything in here and there'll be two murders to investigate. Am I making myself clear?'

'As crystal, sir.'

Lestrade left, but got no further than the double doors when an elderly lady jabbed him in the groin with a knitting needle.

'Is this your case, sonny?' She grimaced up at him.

Assuming the old girl had found some lost luggage, Lestrade tipped his hat and made to pass on.

'Miss Fitzgibbon,' Hepplewhite whispered. 'Our organist.'

'Charmed, madam.' Lestrade had other business.

'I saw it all, sonny,' she shouted.

'Saw . . . ?'

'. . .it all,' she repeated.

'May we use your office, Mr Hepplewhite?'

Here waited the constable and the neighbour of the recently departed. The bobby gave Lestrade his report and the neighbour knew no more than that the deceased had munched nuts throughout the performance and had suddenly slumped sideways; he assumed with an attack of indigestion. Indeed, he had been about to offer him one of Carter's Little Liver Pills when he realised the futility of the gesture.

'And you screamed?'

'No, sonny, I did.' Miss Fitzgibbon entered the conversation for the first time. 'You see, my organ goes up and down . . .'

Lestrade could believe that.

'. . .and as I was rising to accompany the chase of the sheriff's posse, I saw the murdered man fall sideways. This gentleman did indeed offer him something.'

'You saw all this in a darkened auditorium?' Lestrade was incredulous.

'I've been playing in theatres for fifty years,' she told him with pride, 'Dan Leno once told me he'd never heard a *vox humana* like mine.'

Lestrade assumed that went without saying.

'I've seen things that no decent woman should have to witness,' she scowled at Hepplewhite, 'and more!' Lestrade was stopped in mid-interrogation.

'I'm sure that is so, Miss Fitzgibbon, but I'm afraid Scotland Yard cannot be responsible for the habits of cinema-goers.'

'I mean, I saw the murderer.'

Eight eyes focused on the diminutive crone of the oscillating organ. Lestrade leaned forward, deciding that his best policy was to humour the old faggot.

'Can you describe him, ma'am?'

'But of course. Moments before the uproar, when everybody was running in all directions, a tall young man sitting five or six rows back got up and left the auditorium. He walked quickly to the door without looking back.'

'And what did he look like?'

'Rather like Mr de Milo, though not so broad, with a hint of Mr Clavell. His walk of course was pure Henry Irving.'

'You mean he had a limp?' Lestrade had followed the last part of the conversation.

'No, I mean he had towering grandeur!' Miss Fitzgibbon raked him with her squint.

'Mr de Milo and Mr Clavell . . .?'

'Film actors,' Hepplewhite explained.

That didn't help Lestrade at all. The first and last film he had seen had been the late Queen Empress' funeral. He couldn't find much of a plot.

'Tell me, Miss Fitzgibbon, what was this man wearing?'

'A dark coat, a Homburg hat and something bright . . . here.' She waved a hand vaguely at groin level.

'A fob watch?' guessed Lestrade.

Miss Fitzgibbon let out a basso profundo which implied that she didn't know.

'A fob seal?'

Da Capo.

'Where were his hands?'

'The same position as yours, sonny, on the ends of his arms.'

Hepplewhite shook his head sadly.

'I mean, did he place them in his pockets?'

'As a matter of fact, he did, though I don't remember which one.'

'What are you getting at, Superintendent?' the manager asked.

'Perhaps nothing. Miss Fitzgibbon, may this constable take you to the Yard for a statement?'

'Do I get a cup of tea?'

'Most certainly,' Lestrade assured her.

'Come on then, sonny,' and she linked her arm through the constable's. He took care to avoid her knitting needles.

Lestrade dismissed the neighbour of the deceased, having ascertained his name and address, and returned with Hepplewhite to the dark of the auditorium.

'You know of course that she's as mad as a hatter, Superintendent?'

'Who?'

'My organist, Miss Fitzgibbon.'

'Certifiable?'

Hepplewhite nodded. Lestrade was crestfallen. He had hoped to wrap this one up quickly. It was autumn and he had murders piled up from the spring. Blevvins was whistling loudly when they got back, whiling away the time by finding dog-ends under the seats and collecting the tobacco to roll one enormous cigarette of his own.

'Not on duty, Blevvins,' Lestrade reminded him wearily.

'Yes sir. Sorry sir.' The sergeant dropped the contents of his roll onto Hepplewhite's floor.

'How are you at organs?' Lestrade asked him.

'Er . . . I must have missed that lecture, sir.'

'No doubt. Get down there and sit by the thing. Mr Hepplewhite, can you operate it for us?'

The manager scuttled away to operate levers. Lestrade counted back from the corpse, five, six rows and sat down. To his astonishment, the auditorium was filled with the strains of 'I Do Like to be Beside the Seaside' and the reeds, gilded and floodlit, rose from the floor with a demented Blevvins leaping about on the keys like a man possessed.

'Thank you, Mr Paderewski!' Lestrade roared above the row, and sergeant and organ fell silent. 'Can you see me, Blevvins?'

'Perfectly, sir,' he answered sheepishly. The sergeant watched as Lestrade put his hand to his mouth, appeared to cough and got up. He watched his guv'nor stride to the corpse and tilt the head forward, peering down in the half-light to the collar.

'What is it, sir?'

'You've seen this film, Blevvins?' Lestrade gestured at the screen behind them.

'Yes, sir. Twice.' Blevvins crossed the auditorium to join him.

'Would I be correct in assuming that *The Great Train Robbery* is an exciting adventure?'

'Oh, yes, sir. Lots of shooting and killing and—'

'So Miss Fitzgibbon, the organist, would have been playing loudly?'

'Well they did when I saw it at the Pictorium. Deafening it was.'

'But not so deafening as to drown a gunshot?'

'Sir?'

'Think, Blevvins. The organist told me that she saw a man sitting where I was just now, get up and leave as the pandemonium started. If that man was our murderer, how did he do it? At long range?'

'A gun!' Blevvins was warming up.

'Too loud. Even above Miss Fitzgibbon. Too loud. And what about people to his right and left? Wouldn't you be a teensy bit surprised to see a member of the audience cocking a pistol at the screen, however carried away he had become by the action? Think again.'

'Bow and arrow, sir?' Blevvins was faithful to the new genre.

Lestrade didn't pause in his stride. 'To be accurate, you'd need to stand up to shoot. A *little* bit obvious, perhaps. Anyway, Miss Fitzgibbon says our man put one hand in his pocket as he left. You can't hide a bow as easily as that.'

'What, then, sir?' Blevvins was a sergeant. He had exhausted the possibilities, run the gamut of his imagination. It had taken less than a minute.

Lestrade coughed again in that curious way.

'Night air, sir?' Blevvins was unusually solicitous.

'Night air, be damned. A blowpipe, man.'

Blevvins' jaw fell slack.

'The only film I've seen was Queen Victoria's funeral, but with it was a reel on the Indians of Peru, or somewhere else in Africa. They use blowpipes to hunt, Blevvins. Little tubes of bamboo or something with a hollow centre. A dart inserted at one end, tipped with a virulent poison, a quick blow and hey presto!' He tilted the head down again and pointed to a small hole below the dead man's hairline, caked with dark blood.

'We'll need the coroner to tell us what sort of poison, but it was quick. Look at his face.'

'A blowpipe.' Blevvins tipped his bowler backwards. 'Well, I'll be blowed.' It was a singularly fatuous thing to say, but Lestrade was used to it. 'Are we looking for a pygmy then, sir?'

'Yes, Blevvins,' Lestrade humoured him, 'two, in fact. One, the one with the white face and Homburg hat, standing on the shoulders of the other to give the impression of a normal-sized man. But keep at it, Blevvins. You're getting better.'

A Bloody War

Lestrade looked for the thousandth time at the wall in front of him. In the spring a great deal of regulation green paint had shown through. Now there was no green at all. Just a mass of notes, memos, ideas, flights of fancy.

'I want answers, John. It's only because of the coronation that Lord Love Us isn't breathing down my neck. But I'm starting to get anxious looks from Frank Froest.'

'Does he think you might touch him for a bob?' Kane ventured.

'I'll forget you said that, John,' the superintendent said, puffing slowly at his cheroot. 'Look at it,' he was back to the wall again, 'we've ground to a halt on all of them.'

'That's the best thing about the British Public,' Kane soliloquised. 'Commit a murder under their noses and they don't see a damned thing.'

Lestrade nodded.

'It's like this book I've been reading—'

'What?' Lestrade sat upright.

'This book. It's about this man—'

'Yes, yes. Of course,' Lestrade leapt to his feet, 'that's it. The missing link!'

Kane looked around him. 'I thought it was Blevvins' day off.'

'What have we got, Inspector? It was staring me in the face all the time, for months, and I didn't see it. It's a terrible thing, getting old, John.'

'I'm sorry, sir, I don't see.'

'Arnold Truscott, the corpse in the cinema. What did he do?'

'Stop a poisoned dart?'

'No, no, for a living, man.'

'Er . . .' Kane consulted the wall. 'Civil servant. A clerk in the Albert Dock.'

'And what did he do for a hobby?'

'Wrote short stories.'

'Under the name of Rudolph La Rue. Percy Hinchcliffe – the body on the beach—'

'A writer . . .' Realisation began to dawn.

'Thomas Portnoy, dangling in the bell ropes?'

'A writer of religious tracts.'

Lestrade was nodding now, tying together the warped threads.

'Where does that leave us?'

'If I remember my mathematics, John, with a common denominator. We're looking for one man, Inspector. And he's getting bolder by the minute.'

'You think there'll be more?'

'Yes, I do. Unless we stop him first.'

'What about Philomena Marchment?'

'Thank you, John, I thought you'd bring her up.'

'She doesn't fit, does she?'

'At the moment, no. Although we must assume she wrote letters. The only woman. No connection with the printed word. Well, she may have something entirely different. We'll leave her out for the moment.'

'What do we know about our man then, sir?'

'You tell me,' said Lestrade.

'Well, if we can trust Miss Fitzgibbon's account—'

'Which of course we can't.'

'Oh?'

'You remember – she behaved most peculiarly when she made her statement. Kept muttering "Beecham's Powders, Beecham's Powders".'

'I thought that was Blevvins' influence.'

'Not this time. He was with me at the Bioscope.'

'What then?' The end of Kane's tether was quickly reached.

'Method?'

'Ah. Diverse.' Kane began to chew his pencil. 'Let's see. Hinchcliffe was shot, though I'm damned if I know how. If Clive Marchment is right about that bullet, it came from a pistol. That means close range. Yet no one we've spoken to mentioned a boat with a swimmer. Unless . . .'

'Yes?'

'Unless Hinchcliffe was trying to swim the Channel at night.'

'Or . . .?'

Kane shook his head. There was no 'or'.

'But we know he's powerful,' Kane tried to salvage something of his reputation, 'Thomas Portnoy weighed thirteen stone.'

'And he has a knowledge of poisons. Curare is not common. I didn't find that one in the Brigade case.'

'And he had a knowledge of South American practices too,' Kane was warming up, 'the blowpipe.'

Lestrade nodded. 'And there it ends, John. He vanished like a thief in the night. But now we've made the connection, we're halfway there. Get on to some publishers. Ask Walter Dew to go with you. I hear he's writing a book himself.'

Kane chuckled. 'Well, he's got the title. That's taken him three months.'

Lestrade clicked his tongue. 'I hope I was never as disrespectful when I was an inspector,' he said, knowing perfectly well he had been. 'What's it called?'

'*I Caught Crippen!*' Kane collapsed in shrieks of laughter.

'Did he now?' Lestrade joined him. 'Well, I hope he'll mention it was my poker that cracked those bricks on the cellar floor. Close the door on your way out.'

The day that Inspector John Kane began to pound his beat around London's publishers the black flag was hoisted briefly over Pentonville Prison. The prison doctor checked the twirling body and pronounced it dead. The warders cut it down and laid it in the cheap pine coffin. One of them took the photograph of the boyish girl and her handful of letters and threw them in. They screwed down the lid and lowered into the ground all that was left of Hawley Harvey Crippen.

No policeman in the short dark days at the end of 1910 could afford to be away from his trade for long. Days earlier, the relative calm of the capital had been shattered by what had come to be known as the Houndsditch Murders. Superintendent Patrick Quinn of the Special Branch had had a field day. The perpetrators of the bloody deed were said to be foreigners. It therefore followed that in the eyes of Special Branch men everywhere they must be anarchists, bent on subverting the State. *The People* informed the public that Mr Churchill, the Home Secretary, required 442 constables to protect him whenever he appeared out of doors. Mrs Pankhurst looked on that as a victory in itself and was not in the least deflated when Superintendent Quinn was at pains to point out in the press that the actual number was only 439.

Lestrade went with the others from the Yard to the solemn funeral procession just before Christmas. Pedlars mingled with shoeblacks, who in turn mingled with rather elderly errand boys. They all looked rather familiar to Lestrade as Quinn's men. And if they hadn't fooled him it wasn't likely they would fool determined anarchists either.

'Rum do, eh, Sholto?' Inspector Wensley of Froest's squad found him in the black-coated press of the silent people. 'Bentley, Tucker, they were good lads, the City boys tell me. Did you know it took Constable Choat four hours to die? Eight bullets in him, he had.'

'Any leads, Fred?'

'Well, Quinn rushes around arresting everybody with a funny

name. I wonder he hasn't felt your collar yet.'

'Well, it's early days.' Lestrade stamped to relieve the cold.

'I think we could have done without Winston bloody Churchill.' Wensley gestured to where the Home Secretary and his lady wife walked grim-faced in the cortège. 'Going in?'

Lestrade looked up at the solid grey of St Paul's. 'We'll be in there soon enough, Fred, you and I. Let's see if we can find a coffee shop open. You're buying.'

They waited until the last of the procession had moved up the stone steps and had vanished inside. The organ thundered, louder and more evangelical than anything Miss Fitzgibbon could muster. The black-gloved constables of the Metropolitan Police stood guard on the great Cathedral while their City brethren prayed inside.

'So what happened?' Lestrade wrapped his frozen hands around the cup.

'Don't you read the papers?'

'Come on, Fred. Don't be coy. This is Sholto, your ol' mate. You still owe me one from the Ripper Hunt.'

'Blimey, talk about the long memory of the law!'

'That day when the Commissioner . . .' Lestrade began loudly.

'All right, all right. You've made your point,' Wensley fanned the air with desperate hands, looking furtively around, 'you'll have to get round Patrick Quinn for the details. All I know is that a clump of bobbies went to investigate peculiar noises in Exchange Buildings.'

'That was the sixteenth?'

'Yes, Friday night. Bloody cold. They found a house full of foreigners – Eastern Europeans, they reckon – who opened up on them.'

'I got that from the *Gazette*. What then?'

'We have reason to believe . . .'

'Careful, Fred, you're beginning to sound like a policeman.'

'Oh, God, not that!' Wensley began to cry into his coffee. Then, suddenly serious, 'We think they've got automatic weapons.'

Lestrade stiffened. 'Say that again.'

'We have reason to believe . . .'

Lestrade cuffed the younger man playfully round the ear. 'Mausers?' he asked.

'Russians, Poles, Serbo-Croats. I suppose there could have been some Mausers among them.'

'No, no, Fred,' Lestrade humoured him, 'a Mauser is a pistol.'

'Oh, a *Mauser*.' Wensley covered up. 'Very possible. Very possible.'

'And you got one of them?'

'We did. It was the next day. I was at the Leman Street nick when a call came through. Said he was a doctor and there was a man dying in Grove Street. Gunshot wounds.'

'Ah.'

'I took a few of the lads. I don't mind telling you, Sholto, I was shitting myself.' Wensley had a deathless turn of prose. 'It's going up those stairs. Narrow. One way up and one way down.'

'What did you find?'

'George Gardstein, deader than a doornail. Gunshot. And not pretty.'

'One of your boys?'

'No. We reckon he was hit by one of the others.'

'Others?'

'There was a woman with him. Gave her name as Sara Trassjonsky. The trouble is that all these goys have aliases as long as your pego.'

'Thank you, Inspector. I didn't know the rumour had got round.'

'But there are others. Special Branch is looking for about a dozen. It's funny, Trassjonsky said something odd. 'Course, I haven't told Quinn.'

'Course not,' Lestrade understood, 'what was it?'

'She said "Peter wanted it. Getting hot for him. Needed peace."'

Lestrade lit a cigar and poked one into Wensley's mouth. 'Which you took to mean?'

Wensley shrugged. 'You know these goys can't understand a bloody word half the time.'

'You'll have to let Walter Dew have a go at her. You know his rapport with foreigners.'

Wensley choked on his cheroot. 'I hear you've got to make an appointment to see him these days after the Crippen thing.'

'So they tell me. Who's Peter?'

'Ah, Superintendent Lestrade, you haven't been reading your bulletins from on high,' Wensley crowed.

'After the forty-third page from Lord Love Us on the coronation plans, I tend to doze off,' Lestrade admitted.

'Well, on page forty-four of the last three, there's been mention of one Peter Schtern, alias Peter Piaktow, alias Piaktoff, alias The Frenchman, alias—'

'Yes, all right, I get the picture.'

'That's very droll, Sholto.'

'What is?'

'I was going to say alias Peter the Painter. He's the kingpin of the whole bloody gang of them.'

'What did this Sara Tramsjobsky mean – "He needed peace"?'

Wensley pondered. 'Well, I'm guessing of course . . .'

'So what's new?' Lestrade asked.

'I think the Houndsditch shootings were a blind. A diversion for something else.'

'Any idea what?'

Wensley shook his head and wrung his hands like a character in the book he'd once read. 'I'm only an 'umble inspector, guv'nor. You superintendent blokes are the ones with brains. All I know is' – he blew smoke to the ceiling – 'we're going to hear from Peter the Painter again.'

Christmas seemed to come early that year. Lestrade snatched a day with the Bandicoots at Bandicoot Hall. But there was more to the festive season this year. Something had to be faced and Lestrade faced him in the library, surrounded by the books Grandfather Bandicoot had bought by the yard and of which Harry had read not one line. Commander Hook, tanned and magnificent in his blue and gold, stood to attention watching Lestrade roasting his backside gently.

'You sent for me, sir?'

'At ease, man,' said Lestrade, 'this isn't a court martial,' although inside he felt it was and the sword tip pointed at *him*. 'Drink?'

'Thank you, sir, no.'

'You're not making this easy, are you, Mr Hook?'

'Sir?'

'Tell me, Commander, what are your prospects?'

'Well . . . I've sailed my last voyage, sir. At least for a while. I earn one pound thirteen shillings a day as Naval Commander, although I have recently been appointed to Lord Fisher's staff.'

'The First Naval Lord?' Lestrade was anxious to prove his grasp of current affairs.

'It's called First Sea Lord now, sir. And I believe Lord Fisher resigned from that post last month.'

'I see,' Lestrade walked about a bit, 'a desk job, then?'

'Naval Intelligence, sir. I can't say more. You understand?'

Lestrade nodded. He was not at ease with intelligent men, especially those who were so much younger than he was.

'Emma has told me of your plans,' he said.

Hook looked disconcerted for the first time.

'She . . . ought not to have done that, sir.'

Lestrade looked at him. 'I haven't been much of a father to

that girl,' he said, and held up his hand as Hook looked to be about to interrupt. 'When her mother died, I didn't know how to cope. A policeman's lot . . . well, I turned to Harry and Letitia.' Lestrade chuckled. 'Perhaps you should be having this conversation with them.' He was serious again. 'Do you love my daughter, Ballard Hook?' he asked.

'With all my heart, sir,' he said.

Lestrade extended his hand. 'You're her choice,' he said. 'I won't go against that.' And they shook hands. Lestrade broke away. 'One more thing; shop, I'm afraid.'

'Sir?'

'You'd better call me Sholto, Ballard. Otherwise there'll be more ranks in the family than the whole bloody army. Jamie Snagge.'

'Yes?'

'Friend of yours, isn't he?'

'Yes he is, after a fashion. My Number Two at the moment. Charming fellow. Why do you ask?'

'He was on Hobsbaum's yacht when the Bandicoot boys went over. You didn't mention that.'

Hook thought for a moment. 'Didn't I really? I'm sorry, I thought I had. That's rather the sort poor old Jamie is. Rather nebulous if you know what I mean.'

Lestrade didn't, but he wasn't going to let his future son-in-law know that. 'Where could I find him now?'

'The poor lamb's on duty over Christmas. He'll be on the *Achilles* until the middle of next month. At Plymouth. There's . . . er . . . no news of Rupert, I suppose?'

'None. But Emma asked me to look into the whole business. When I've seen Snagge, that's the last of it.'

'Binky any help?'

'I spoke to him on the telephone,' said Lestrade with some distaste. 'As everybody else has confirmed, he was below at the time. All the same, there's something about the accident . . . I don't know, perhaps it's just a little girl's sense of loss.'

'I'll take care of that now, with your permission, sir ...
Sholto.'

Lestrade smiled and nodded. Hook bowed and left. The
superintendent stared into the crackling flames and took to
drink.

The body of Leon Beron lay under the furze bushes on Clapham
Common. The legs were folded neatly and the head and face
were drenched with his blood. Constable Mumford, shivering
in the cold of the New Year, stumbled over him. Now
Mumford was a shrewd copper and he noticed that the toes of
Beron's boots were caked in mud. The body had been dragged
some distance. And he had not been robbed. Mumford noted
the time on his cheap half-hunter. Ten-past eight. It was the start
of another raw day. New Year's Day, Sunday, First of January.
Topers were creeping quietly from the nearby hostelry, hoping
the copper wouldn't notice them as he appeared to have his
hands full with one drunk already.

It was Alfred Ward's case, but as he searched the body in
Mumford's wake, and the tobacco pouch, the two paper bags,
the halfpenny and the half-eaten ham sandwich came to light, he
passed it to Fred Wensley, the renowned expert east of St Paul's.

'This is Leon Beron,' Wensley told him. 'Pimp, landlord,
fence. He's a Russian Jew.'

'He's a dead Russian Jew now.' Ward looked up at him from
his position crouching over the corpse. 'What do you make of
the face?'

'Not pretty, is it?'

'How was it before?'

'Not pretty,' Wensley confirmed. 'Mind if I bring the guv'nor
in on this?'

'Lestrade?' Ward stood up. 'I heard a rumour he'd retired.'

Wensley chuckled. 'Wishful thinking, old man. Mumford,
get a van.'

* * *

They circled the remnants of Leon Beron that evening, Sholto Lestrade and Frederick Wensley. They had uncrossed his legs and the body had been stripped and washed. Lestrade reflected, not for the first time, on the transient nature of man. There were three deep gashes in the chest, the work of a long blade, broad, single-edged, he guessed. The centre of the head, above and below the hairline, was blackened and crushed, but it was the cheeks that held the attention of both men.

'Looks like the letter "S",' Lestrade mused, twisting his head from side to side to see it from all angles. 'You're the expert, Mr Venzel.' He gave Wensley the name the Jews gave him. '"Schmuck"? "Schlemiel"? How's your Yiddish?'

'Great minds,' said Wensley. 'I'm sticking my neck out here, Sholto, but I'm wondering if it's not "S" for "spic".'

'You've got me there, Fred.'

'Spy,' Wensley translated. 'Double agent, traitor.'

Lestrade looked at him. 'One for Superintendent Quinn, then?' He grinned.

Wensley glared at him. 'Oh, no,' he said in his West Country lilt. 'Patrick Quinn's not getting his hands on this one. I've got a few ideas of my own.'

'Oh?'

'I've known Leon Beron for years,' he said. 'All right, he's a Russian Jew, but he's not Peter the Painter. Not even a member of a Society, so far as I know. Alfred Ward talked to a witness this afternoon. A Mrs Deitch, who said she saw Leon earlier in the company of somebody who sounds familiar. Can I take a look at the Register?'

'What is it about you, Fred?' Lestrade switched off the lights. 'I don't see you for months on end and suddenly you're tied to my tail.'

'All in a day's work, Sholto,' Wensley grinned.

The Yard men ascended the spiral staircase that led from the makeshift morgue in the basement, their voices echoing through the corridors of the night.

'Good God,' another voice hailed them at the top of the stairs. 'Not enough crime in the City for you, Fred?' and the sentence was punctuated by a sneeze.

'Gesundheit, Frank,' Wensley returned.

'No need to be offensive,' snorted Froest good-naturedly and paunched his way past Lestrade. 'Any joy on the Bioscope job, Sholto?'

'I'm juggling so many balls at the moment, I ought to be in a circus,' Lestrade sighed. 'Who's got the Register?'

'Peabody.'

'Right. Goodnight, Frank. Don't do anything I wouldn't do.'

Sergeant 'Buildings' Peabody was dozing over his cocoa when Lestrade and Wensley descended on him.

'That's him!' Wensley shouted.

Cocoa and sergeant went everywhere as Peabody woke up.

'So sorry, Sergeant,' Lestrade beamed with the warmth of a crocodile. 'Did we wake you? What is it, Fred?'

'I knew that Mrs Deitch's description rang a bell. You aren't the only one with a memory, Superintendent. The man with Beron was one Morris Stein, alias Moses Tagger, alias Steinie Morrison. He's a ticket of leave man, Sholto. That's where I'd seen him, reporting to his local nick, as he had to under his licence.'

'What was he in for?' Lestrade asked.

'Burglary and theft,' Wensley checked the Register, 'released in September. Ah ha!' he suddenly cried, threatening to reawake the recumbent sergeant, but there wasn't much chance of that. 'According to this, he was in Whitechapel first, but then moved to Lavender Hill where he worked as a baker.'

'Ten minutes from the Common.' Lestrade nodded.

'I'll ask Alfred to put out a notice on him.'

'Watch yourself, Fred,' Lestrade looked under the tall man's armpit, 'he carries a gun. The Register never lies.'

'There's a lot of it about. 'Night, Sholto – and thanks.'

Lestrade closed the book and watched his old friend bundle his way out into the freezing night. He sipped what was left of the snoring Peabody's cocoa. He wasn't sure. The 'S' on the cheeks. Steinie Morrison? Perhaps. What sort of murderer left his initials on his victim? The Register's description talked of a broad, handsome man, well over six foot tall, who habitually wore sharp clothes and a wide-awake. You'd notice a man like that. If Morrison was going to kill Beron, would he allow himself to be seen in his company? It was too pat. Too easy. He knew Fred Wensley for the good copper he was. But he couldn't go along with him this time.

As if to comfort the sleeping desk sergeant, Lestrade dropped the Register loudly on his way out.

By that January, Lestrade would have admitted, had Emma asked him, that the last thing on his mind was the death of Rupert Bandicoot all those months before. At Christmas, the Bandicoots had been in good spirits and if Letitia had shed a tear at the empty chair, Ivo was almost his old self. The term at Eton had helped after the initial solemnity and memorial service that betokened the passing of Professor George Holliday. But if Lestrade had pushed it to the back of his mind, his daughter had not. And accordingly, on another biting morning in January, Commander Ballard Hook turned up at the Yard with Lieutenant Jamie Snagge, the last of those aboard Binky Hobsbaum's yacht that fateful winter's day.

'I apologise, Sholto, for arriving unannounced like this, but you know how insistent Emma can be.'

'Think nothing of it.' Lestrade arranged for tea in his customary delicate manner by shouting in the ear of Sergeant Dickens. 'Mr Snagge,' he extended a hand, 'thank you for coming.'

'Oh, c-couldn't miss a few days in t-town, what? Rather t-topping, this, S-Scotland Yard, what?'

Lestrade fixed him with a beady eye of too many years' experience. He glanced at Hook to check if this man was real.

The commander's moustache twitched in a gesture that Lestrade knew was disguising a giggle.

'When Rupert Bandicoot and George Holliday were swept overboard,' Lestrade got to the point to save further embarrassment, 'where were you, Mr Snagge?'

'Ah,' Snagge shifted uncomfortably in his seat, 'it was r-rather a long time ago, S-S-S-Mr Lestrade.'

'To the best of your memory, then,' Lestrade persevered.

'W-well, if I remember r-rightly, I was in the f-f-f—'

Both Lestrade and Hook found themselves craning forward, willing the man to get it out.

'. . .foredeck,' he managed. 'B-b- Hook here and the – b-b-b–lads were aft.'

'And Holliday?'

'With them.'

'Was anybody else on deck?'

'P-possibly. That a-a-arse Vavasour was lounging around s-somewhere.'

'Can you tell me,' asked Lestrade, beginning to doubt whether Snagge could, 'what happened?'

'Well, it w-w-was rather o-odd, really . . .'

But Lieutenant Snagge got no further, because Sergeant Blevvins crashed into the office, miraculously without knocking anyone over.

'Yes, Blevvins?' Lestrade's eyebrow reached a critical level.

'It's a message from the Home Secretary, sir. Sidney Street. You're to come at once. He says he's got a bloody war on his hands, sir!' And then, uncharacteristically, 'Oh, begging your pardon, gentlemen.'

Lestrade snatched up his bowler and Donegal, briefly checking that his Apache knife with the brass knuckles was in its usual place.

'Gentlemen, I'm afraid we'll have to resume some other time.'

'Sholto, I've a cab waiting below. Mind if we tag along?' asked Hook.

Lestrade hesitated.

'A–actually, B–B–Hook, I really must be going.'

'Ballard,' said Lestrade. 'If what I suspect is happening in Sidney Street really *is* happening, it's no place for civilians.'

'Ah, but there I have you, Sholto. I may be in mufti today but I'm categorically not a civilian. Come on, I may be of some help.'

They parted company with Snagge at the side entrance and Lestrade clambered aboard Hook's hansom.

'What was he going to say?' Lestrade whispered, glancing up and behind to see who the growler was.

'Jamie? God knows,' laughed Hook. 'You'd better ask him again.'

Lestrade wasn't sure he had the time. 'Emma told me he was a shy retiring type, that's why none of you had mentioned him.'

'Yes, I've been thinking about that. I did mention him. When we first met, shortly after it happened. But he is shy. All that bluster and stutter. It's his way of coping. Mind you, some of the chaps make it hell for him in the Ward Room, but I think, between you and me, old Jamie is rather deeper than you'd suppose.' He broke off to yell to the driver, 'Come on, cabbie, there's a guinea in it for you if you get us there before nightfall!'

The cab lurched in response and Lestrade found himself hanging on for dear life.

'Oh?' He tried to continue the conversation.

'Well, these foreigners, you know. Still waters . . .'

'Foreigners?'

'Yes, Jamie's mother was Austrian or something. He of course was privately educated. Been all over the world, South America, Africa. Her second husband was Count von Some-body or Other, Austrian Ambassador. Jamie's real father died before he was one. Did you know, for instance, that Jamie is rather a womaniser on the quiet?'

Lestrade tried to stop himself hitting the rim of the cab with his teeth too often.

'I wouldn't have said he was the type.'

'That's what I mean,' Hook said. 'Still waters ... Mind you, we don't know who she was, but there was a woman in his life recently, an older woman, apparently. Some say she was an old flame of the late King. They broke it off a while ago, but he was upset recently. He got some news in Gib on our last Mediterranean voyage. He wouldn't tell us what it was, but I believe it was something to do with her. He's also, would you believe, under that idiot exterior, a crack shot.'

Lestrade looked up. 'Is he now?'

The cab horse shrank back on its hindquarters as the growler reined in. Lestrade and Hook were confronted by a line of bobbies halting all traffic.

'Mr Lestrade,' a sergeant of the Metropolitans recognised him, 'Mr Churchill's compliments, sir. This way.' He paused at Hook's presence.

'It's all right, Sergeant,' Lestrade said, 'this gentleman is with me.'

The little knot of rushing men hurtled down the human corridor made by the officers of the City Force. The crowd beyond them swayed and muttered in the flurrying snow. There must have been hundreds of them. On the corner where the Rising Sun had thrown open its first- and second-storey windows and out of which people hung and pointed, a line of Scots Guards stood in their khaki and check.

'I see what Churchill means about a war,' said Hook.

'Where is the Home Secretary?' Lestrade asked the sergeant.

'This way, sir.' The three men picked their way between the soldiers and ran across Sidney Street to the far side. A body of City men with Fred Wensley in their midst saluted Lestrade. From behind a wall to their left a voice called, 'Lestrade?'

'Sir?' The superintendent knew it to be the voice of the Home Secretary.

A moment later Winston Churchill hopped over the crumbling masonry that formed the yard between Sidney and Wolsey

Streets. He shook Lestrade's hand. 'Remind me when this nonsense is over to build a few more public conveniences in these streets. Terrible to be taken short, isn't it? It was the same at Omdurman. Thanks for coming, Lestrade. Who's this?'

'Er . . .' Lestrade was a little nonplussed. To bring a non-policeman into the firing line was not exactly legal.

'Ballard Hook, sir,' the commander shook Churchill's hand, 'Royal Navy.'

'Navy, eh? Don't tell me you've come to lodge a complaint about my attack on the Naval Estimates?'

Hook laughed. 'Not this time, sir.'

'Good. Lestrade, Wensley here will explain. I want to get a better look.'

'Keep your head down, sir!' Wensley called as the top-hatted Home Secretary and a couple of constables scurried to the other side of the street. This time a burst of gunfire rang out, scattering the crowd behind the line. Heads vanished from the windows of the *Sun* and screams were punctuated by bullets. An officer of the Scots Guards bawled orders to his men and they flung themselves to the wet pavements, Lee-Enfields cocked and ready.

'Look at that,' Wensley shook his head, 'thinks he's at bloody Omdurman again.'

'What's the score, Fred?' Lestrade asked.

'Anarchists,' Wensley told him. 'Almost certainly the Hounds-ditch lot. They're barricaded in Number a hundred – that house there.'

'How many?'

'God knows. I've tried counting puffs of smoke, but it's useless. John Mulvaney's over there somewhere trying to stop the Guards from shooting people. I reckon there are at least six in the house. Not to mention half the Woolwich Arsenal.'

'What are they firing?' Hook asked.

'Automatics.'

'Are your boys armed?' Lestrade asked.

'If you can call it that. Churchill gave the go-ahead. The best we've got is a Webley.'

'What happened?'

'We got a tip-off. Usual thing. Foreign accent on the line, to say the Houndsditch mob were in Martin's Mansions. Mulvaney and I came round and got the landlord and his family out. Our chums are on the first floor, we think. There is only one staircase up. It's narrow and it's straight. I remembered Bentley and Choat. No problem getting a coffin down those stairs, I thought. So we waited.'

'And?'

'And I never cease to be amazed by the stupidity of our sergeants.'

'I'll drink to that,' Lestrade concurred.

'Two of them, would you believe, started throwing gravel at the window! The anarchists threw lead back.'

'Anybody hurt?'

'Sergeant Leeson. It's bad. I don't think he'll make it.'

'And since then?'

Wensley spat viciously into the gutter. 'It's developed into this circus. I reckon there must be seven hundred coppers here, Sholto. And there's never one around when you want one. Not to mention the Army. You know Churchill's ordered up field pieces and shells, don't you? The bloody Horse Artillery are on their way.'

Lestrade chuckled. 'Well, I'm disappointed, Fred. I should have thought that a frontal charge by the Twenty-first Lancers down the street here . . .'

'Do I detect something less than enchantment with your chief, gentlemen?' Ballard Hook was clearly amused.

'It's his obsession with the military,' complained Wensley. 'There are a few thousand Welshmen at Tonypandy who didn't thank him for that.'

'I've known Churchill since he was a cadet at Sandhurst,' said Lestrade. 'He's a good man. But I'm not sure he's had his finest hour yet.'

'What do we do?' Hook was anxious to get involved.

'We stop it before anybody else is hurt. Oh God, no!' Lestrade withered against the doorway, but the stout wood would not yield.

'Lestrade! What are you doing here?'

'Superintendent Quinn, what a surprise!'

'Who's this?'

'Commander Hook,' said Lestrade.

Quinn's face fell. 'Commander?' He was nettled.

'Royal Navy, sir,' Hook reassured him.

'Ah, I see. Special Branch.' Quinn positively puffed out his chest. 'Now then, Lestrade, what's it all about?'

'Well, you see that house there, Quinn, the one with the shots ringing out from it?'

'Don't condescend to me, Lestrade. You know exactly what I mean. Why are you here?'

'I happened to be passing,' Lestrade beamed, 'along with the rest of London by the look of it.'

'Lestrade!'

'All right, Paddy me boy, keep your shillelagh on. I had a summons from the Home Secretary.'

Quinn bridled.

'May I suggest,' Lestrade whispered in his ear, 'you get Mr Churchill down to the other end of the street for his own sake. It's getting a bit hot around here.'

'Suggest?' Quinn roared. 'To Churchill? Are you mad?'

'Who's in the house, Quinn?' Lestrade asked.

Quinn looked from side to side. He even checked inside his own coat. 'I am not at liberty to divulge . . .' he began. Wensley stamped angrily and turned away.

'Damn your protocol!' hissed Lestrade, anxious not to rattle still further the wavering policemen at his elbow. Shooting matches in the middle of a Stepney morning were hardly commonplace.

'All right, all right. We're not sure who's in the house, but we've been watching a number of anarchists for months.

Russkies, Yids, Poles, you name them, we've been watching them.'

'Why?'

'Why?' Quinn was flabbergasted. 'Because they're foreign, Lestrade. They're bent on the destruction of civilisation as we know it. And because the Right Honourable Home Secretary persists in allowing them to come into the country in droves.'

'Anybody in particular?'

Again, Quinn checked the vicinity for Ears. 'Joe Levi known as Josef the Jew. Yoshska Sokoloff. Yoserka Duboff. George Gardstein – he's dead, we know that. Fritz Svaars. And that's only the men.'

'Who's their leader?'

'Damned if I know,' Quinn admitted, 'but my guess would be Peter Piaktow, alias Schtern.'

'Peter the Painter?' Lestrade asked.

'Yes. What do you know about him?'

Probably more than you, Lestrade thought. 'Only what I read in the papers,' he said.

'We don't know what he looks like, but we'll get him one day. It might be today.' He glanced behind him to the dark, shattered windows of Martin's Mansions.

'Superintendent Quinn!' Churchill's voice hailed him from across the street.

'Coming, sir.' Quinn turned to Lestrade. 'Keep out of my way,' he hissed, 'I don't want amateurs under my feet,' and he ducked under Hook's arm and bobbed across the street.

'Strike you as odd,' Lestrade said to Hook, 'that the Head of the Special Irish Branch should be called Patrick Quinn?'

Before Hook had time to react, two shots rang out, ricochetting around the suddenly silent street. There was a scream and Quinn went down clutching his leg. There was an embarrassing pause before any copper would run the gauntlet of fire to get the injured detective out of it.

Again, the Guards opened up with a hail of fire power,

causing Quinn to flatten himself to the wet tarmac.

'You were saying, Sholto?' Wensley said.

'You know this area better than I do, Fred. How can we get to that house?'

'Hawkins Street,' said Wensley. 'Runs off to the right. But they'll have every entrance covered.'

'What about the roof?'

Wensley hadn't thought of that. 'Worth a try.' Wensley checked his revolver. 'I'll get you one of these, Sholto.'

'No thanks,' said Lestrade. 'I wouldn't know what to do with it.'

The three men slid along to the next doorway, wondering which would hit them first, the anarchists' bullets from the front, or the Scots Guards' from behind.

'Mr Hook,' said Wensley, 'I don't think you should be here, sir.'

'Nonsense,' said Hook. 'Come on, gentlemen; last one in Number a hundred is a cissy!'

'At least take this.' Wensley slapped a pistol into Hook's hand and they moved in the direction of Hawkins Street. Bullets whined across the area, driving diagonally into the bricks above Lestrade's head. He flung himself into the wall at the corner of Hawkins Street as another shower of brickwork decorated his bowler.

'They're damned good!' commented Hook, crouching beside Lestrade.

'They're not trying.' Wensley joined them. 'They haven't hit anybody in two hours.'

'Quinn?' Lestrade reminded him.

'Like I said,' said the West Countryman sardonically, 'they haven't hit anybody in two hours.'

'What now?' Hook too checked the chamber of his Webley.

'Who authorised that?' They heard Churchill's voice shouting behind them. But the Yard men and the commander had come too far to worry about orders now.

'There's an alley across there.' Wensley pointed to the black hole that faced them. 'And a fire escape. It'll get us onto the roof of one-o-two. How we get inside a hundred from above, God knows.'

'Ballard, can you use that thing?' Lestrade pointed to the revolver.

'Well, I'm no Jamie Snagge, but I'll have a go.'

'All right. I make it two windows of Number a hundred that can still see us. Give us some covering fire while we cross the street.'

'Say the word,' said Hook. 'Inspector Wensley, do you have any more ammunition?'

''Fraid not, Mr Hook. Six shots is all you get.'

'Well,' Hook grinned, 'let's hope there are no more than six of them in the house. At your signal, Sholto.'

'Ready, Fred?'

Wensley nodded.

'"For what we are about to receive ..."' muttered Lestrade. 'Now!' and he launched himself for the alley. He heard the crash of gunfire. The anarchists'? Hook's? Wensley's? He couldn't tell. He felt the wind whip his flying Donegal and his bowler spun God Knew Where. He somersaulted into the darkness. A man of his age shouldn't even be out in weather like this, let alone rolling around dodging bullets. Fred Wensley landed heavily beside him.

'All right, Sholto?'

Lestrade gasped an answer that brought a blush even to Wensley's hardened cheek. Ballard Hook bounced off the wall seconds later.

'What ho!' he grinned. 'Topping, what?' and he jerked himself upright.

'There's the fire escape,' Wensley pointed, still on his knees.

'And there's the fire!' hissed Lestrade. All three men looked on in horror as smoke billowed from the upper windows of the anarchists' house. Flames followed, licking the black brickwork fiercely as they leapt for the sky.

'It's a smoke screen,' said Hook. 'They'll be coming out behind it. Come on!' He dashed for the fire escape but the smoke here was thick and black and he dropped back.

'We'll do better at the front,' said Lestrade. 'Fred, with me.'

The Yard men hurried round the corner, keeping their heads down. The manic clanging of bells and whinnying of horses behind them heralded the arrival of the fire brigade. Brass helmets flashed among the blue of the Force and the check cap bands of the military.

'Let it burn down,' Churchill gave the order. 'Scots Guards at the ready.'

The muzzles of one hundred guns came up to the level, trained on the black shell of the building known as Martin's Mansions, crumbling in the inferno.

'I've never seen fire work so fast,' Wensley told Lestrade as they reached Sidney Street again. There was a ripping noise, followed by a crash as part of the building fell away, showering the nearest watchers with sparks.

'Hook!' the Yard men chorused and scrambled back through the bevy of constables for the alley.

'If anything has happened to that boy,' said Lestrade as they ran, 'my daughter will never forgive me. Hook!' he shouted. The alley was a corridor of smoke and flame. 'No one could have got out that way,' he said.

Wensley tapped his arm and pointed. In the sheet of flame that faced them, a blazing figure stood and tottered for a moment. 'Ballard . . .' Lestrade's voice was almost inaudible. The body seemed to crumble before their eyes and a sickened cry arose from the crowd at their backs. It rolled at Lestrade's feet and he jumped back.

'It's a dummy!' he said.

'That'll be one of Fleischmann's,' Wensley told him in a matter of fact sort of way. Lestrade looked at him quizzically. 'Lives on the ground floor of Martin's Mansions,' he went on. 'He's a costumier.'

Lestrade glared daggers at the inspector. They were beaten

back by the smoke again, driving them towards Sidney Street. It did not take long. The winter winds whipped the flames into a frenzy and as the firemen closed in to begin sifting the debris, a wall fell and crushed six of them. Two charred corpses were carried out, one hit by bullets. Through the blackened, flaking skin, Wensley recognised Fritz Svaars. The other man he did not know.

'Well, Sholto, you were right,' he said, 'the cavalry have come to the rescue.'

He pointed to where the Horse Artillery had drawn up at the end of Sidney Street.

'Not much point in unlimbering, really,' a voice said behind them.

Lestrade spun to see the grinning, scorched face of Ballard Hook. He found himself gripping the sailor's arms despite himself. 'We thought you were dead,' he laughed.

'So did I,' Hook told them. 'The fire escape gave way and I was pinned behind it. Thanks for this, Mr Wensley.' He returned the pistol. 'Everybody all right?'

They crossed to where Patrick Quinn lay on a stretcher, still directing operations as Churchill prepared to leave.

'Lestrade,' said the Home Secretary. 'You went forward without orders.'

'Yes, sir,' said the superintendent. 'Rather like a certain war correspondent I remember some years ago. What was his name now . . .?'

Churchill laughed. 'The difference is' – he tapped Lestrade on the lapel as he left – '*I* got a medal.'

'How are you, Quinn?' Lestrade looked down at him. 'Nothing trivial I hope.'

Quinn sneered. 'Look at this lot.' He pointed to the veritable armoury that the firemen were bringing out of the smouldering shell that was No. 100.

'What's this?' Lestrade crouched beside the stretcher.

'Don't touch it!' screamed Quinn, believing Lestrade to be going for his leg.

The superintendent picked up one of the pistols. 'What's this?'

'It's a gun, Lestrade.' Quinn had never rated Lestrade highly, but this was imbecility at its worst.

'Is it a Mauser, Sholto?' Wensley crouched beside him.

'That's what I like about you, Fred. Your glimmer of intelligence. To be precise, a Broomhandle Mauser.'

'You've seen one before?' asked Quinn.

'Once,' said Lestrade. 'It's the most powerful hand-gun in the world. Beats anything we've got.'

'What's it all about, Sholto?' Wensley stood up with Lestrade. 'This thing with Mausers?'

'A long shot, Fred, a long shot.'

'What about the other body, Wensley?' Quinn asked.

Wensley shook his head.

'Peter the Painter?' Quinn ventured.

'Next time, Superintendent,' said Wensley grimly. 'Next time.'

The Published and the Damned

The gentlemen of the press had a field day with Sidney Street. Why hadn't the police attempted entry from the roof? Why hadn't the fire brigade flooded the anarchists out? Who let all those damned foreigners in in the first place? And why didn't Winston Churchill resign?

'The *Chicago Police Review* says that very few fat men are guilty of serious crimes,' was Sergeant Dickens' contribution to the day.

'They obviously don't know Froest,' grunted Blevvins. 'His whole bloody existence is a serious crime.'

'How did the Guv'nor make out with that Jewboy?' Dickens asked him.

'Morrison? Said he was a fly bugger. Sharp. Wide. You know the type. I offered to lend Lestrade my knuckle crushers, but he said he could manage. If you ask me, he's going soft.'

'Couldn't break him, then?'

'You know the Guv'nor, Charlie, better than I do. It's Ward's case. And he passes it down to Wensley, who asks Lestrade to have a go. You'd have thought *somebody* could have got something from him.'

'He's got more form than you've had hot dinners, that Steinie Morrison. He also had a gun when Wensley picked him up.'

'I hear Mr Venzel took four blokes to get him. There'd have been none of that nonsense if I'd been there.'

'You enjoy your work, Reggie, don't you?' Dickens observed.

'Let's just say when His Excellency the Home Secretary gave the go-ahead on guns, I offered up a silent prayer. Here we are, spilling our guts on the London streets while the bloody public moans about police inefficiency. And what help do we get from the Bench, eh? Look at this bloke who Morrison's up before – Mr Justice Darling – I ask you! You'll get no justice from a bloke with a name like that. He'll probably smack his wrists and make him stand in a corner. By the way, where *is* the Guv'nor? I haven't had to make tea all morning.'

'Round in St Martin's Street, at Macmillan.'

'Who are they? Bookie's runners?'

'A publishing house, you nincompoop. Come on, Reggie, you're four years my junior. Shame to get out of the habit. Put the kettle on, will you?'

Lestrade entered the premises from the bold façade of St Martin's Street and padded his way through the plush carpets that graced the floors of the hall and waiting rooms. He was ushered into an upper-storey room that looked over the National Gallery. Below he noticed briefly a pale woman wandering sadly along its steps. Sarah Rose, her mind gone, sighed and waited still for her George. But she would never meet him there – he was with the only real love of his life, in Southend.

'I am Frederick Macmillan.' A suave middle-aged man with a pencil moustache met him at the door. 'You must be Superintendent Lestrade. I have of course read many of your exploits in the *Strand Magazine*' – this last was delivered in a whisper – 'though for professional reasons, I am only allowed to mention *Macmillan's Magazine* in this building.'

Lestrade took the offered chair.

'How may I help, Superintendent?'

'I'm not sure, Mr Macmillan. For some weeks now I've had men wearing out shoeleather trying to locate a certain publisher. I think you are that publisher.'

'If it's about the Bentley Purchase, that was a long time ago and perfectly legal,' Macmillan was quick to assure him; 'and I'm afraid we haven't a single copy of Morley's *Gladstone* left. You should have seen us eight years ago. Where you're sitting now were piles of The Book up to the ceiling . . .'

'As much as I'd love to stroll down memory lane with you, Mr Macmillan, I have rather more pressing business.'

'Ah.'

'May I ask if these names mean anything to you?'

Lestrade passed to the publisher the list that had haunted him for months. The names that were etched into his heart – Percy Hinchcliffe, Thomas Portnoy, Arnold Tasker.

'Why, yes, they do.' Macmillan rang a bell on his desk. 'They have all written for us at one time or another. And . . .'

'And?'

'And they are all dead, Mr Lestrade.' Macmillan was to the point.

'There is a further link between them, sir. They were all murdered.'

Macmillan did not blink. 'Then I think you'd better talk to our Mr Irons,' he said.

A pretty young secretary entered and curtseyed. 'You rang, sir?'

'Yes, my dear.' Macmillan flirted with her. 'Is Mr Irons in this morning?'

'Not until this afternoon, sir.' She bobbed out again.

'Who is Mr Irons?' Lestrade asked.

'Haverstock Irons, one of our readers. He handles the genre we know as Mystery. Arnold Tasker wrote exclusively for him under the nom de plume of Rudolph La Rue. But you knew that.'

Lestrade nodded.

'What of Percy Hinchcliffe?'

'Miss Artois.'

'Was that his nom de plume!'

'No, no,' Macmillan smiled, 'Percy Hinchcliffe wrote in the

genre we call Romance, Superintendent. I wooed him from Mills and Boon. Our gain, their loss. Miss Artois is the Reader who specialises in romantic tales.'

'I understand he was also a playwright?'

Macmillan waved that aside. 'Trivia,' he said. 'He did write some trite nonsense which ran for four nights at the Garrick. There was more merit in his essays. He was a passionate advocate of human rights. And more latterly the Peace Movement, of course.'

'The Peace Movement?'

'Oh yes. I understand there's quite a coterie of literati involved.'

Lestrade hadn't expected the Italian connection.

'Do you think we'll have a European War, Mr Lestrade?'

'It hadn't really occurred to me, sir,' the superintendent confessed.

'It's occurred to the Kaiser. Did you read in *The Times* the other day that the man himself said "Nerves will win the next war." I only hope it isn't the last. He worked with Stead, of course.'

'The Kaiser?'

'No, no. Hinchcliffe. He was a crony of W. T. Stead, the journalist.'

That rang no bells for Lestrade at all, but he committed the name to memory. He would ask Dickens when he got back to the Yard.

'Would you care to talk to Miss Artois?' Macmillan suggested. 'She may shed some light on the problem for you.'

'Would that be possible?'

'Yes, of course.' Macmillan rang the bell again and the same curvy secretary bounced in.

'Ah, Mabel . . .'

'Florence,' she corrected him.

'Yes, of course. Would you show this gentlemen to Miss Artois' office. Mr Lestrade, if I can be of any further service . . .'

'You have been most helpful, Mr Macmillan. I shall know where to come.'

They shook hands and a younger Macmillan emerged from a cunningly concealed panel once the policeman had gone.

'Well, Frederick?'

'You heard him, Maurice.' The elder Macmillan lit a cigar. 'He doesn't know anything.'

'And the Tenniel plates?'

'Maurice, we bought those Tenniel plates from old Bentley, fair and square. I really don't know why you're so obsessed with them.'

'I know there was nothing dishonest. All the same, we ought really to have returned them to old Tenniel's family. You *are* familiar with the laws of copyright, Frederick?' Maurice lit a cigar too.

'Just stash them away in a vault somewhere and forget about them, Maurice. Superintendent Lestrade isn't interested in your feeble little collections. He's after bigger fish altogether.'

Florence, the secretary, also known as Mabel, was a very flighty young lady. She wiggled her pert little bottom in front of Lestrade all the way along the corridor and then squeezed as close as she could to him in the lift.

'Warm for March, isn't it?' she said, thrusting two enormous, corseted breasts up at him.

'I hadn't noticed.' Lestrade extricated himself from behind one of them. 'Miss – er . . .'

'Fox. Florence Fox. Thirty-six Wenceslaus Court, E.13.,' she blurted out.

Lestrade smiled. 'Tell me, Miss Fox – Miss Artois: would you say she's a good judge of character?'

'She's a cow.' Miss Fox's face fell. 'Stuck up, she is. She don't like me. I've only had this job for two weeks. And already she's got it in for me. But Mr Macmillan's ever so nice. He lets me sit on his knee, you know.'

'And Mr Irons?'

'Yerr! I wouldn't want to sit on his knee. He's mad as a hatter, he is. Talks to hisself. I wonder Mr Macmillan keeps him on, I do.'

She reached across Lestrade's chest to unlock the door and shivered as she touched his lapels. 'Ooh,' she sighed, 'you'll think me ever so forward, but I've got this thing for older men.'

'Really?' Lestrade squeezed past her into a foyer. 'Where do you keep it?'

She tapped him with a playful slap. 'Oooh, you are a one. Here we are.' She knocked on the door. 'Don't forget, thirty-six, Wenceslaus Court.'

'I'll try not to,' he said.

'Come,' a voice roared from within.

'Superintendent Lestrade to see you.' Florence hovered in the doorway.

'Thank you, Lucy,' the voice said.

'Florence,' the secretary corrected her, winked at Lestrade and exited.

'Jemima Artois.' The reader advanced on Lestrade in a swirl of pink and feathers. She held her hand out towards his lips. Lestrade shook it.

'Miss Artois, I am from Scotland Yard.'

'Ah, how romantic.' She pulled him to her. 'Please call me Jemima.'

'Miss Artois, I am conducting a murder enquiry.'

'Murder?' Miss Artois clutched her false pearls with a cadaverous hand. 'How very, very disturbing. Will you take tea?'

In a weak moment, perhaps to clear his throat and mind of Miss Fox's cheap scent, Lestrade agreed. The green concoction with the floating leaves which appeared before him he was totally unprepared for, but he downed it manfully as the capacious leather chair enveloped him.

'Tell me what you know of Percy Hinchcliffe,' he said.

'Ah, dear Percy,' Miss Artois flicked aside a rope of pearls, '*flowers for Miss Courtney.*'

'I beg your pardon.' Lestrade had lost her drift.

'His first work, Superintendent. It was called *Flowers for Miss Courtney*. He was kind enough to dedicate it to me.'

'Did he have any enemies?'

'Enemies? I really don't know. He was a mild man. Good and sweet. A little eccentric, perhaps, as all writers are . . .'

'Yes, I've heard that,' Lestrade said. 'Did his books sell?'

'Very well. They made him comfortably off, I believe.'

'Is it your job to choose works of fiction, Miss Artois?'

'Jemima,' she reminded him. 'Of the romantic kind, yes. Tell me, do you read romances, Mr Lestrade? Perhaps you are familiar with *Lady Pakenham's Carbuncle*?'

'Nothing would induce me, madam,' Lestrade assured her. 'Wouldn't your selection of a writer lead to jealousy among those you had not selected?'

'Well . . . I suppose so, yes. But that is professional jealousy, Superintendent. Surely it could never lead to murder?'

'You don't deal with Mystery books, Miss Artois?' Lestrade smiled.

'Well, I must bow to your superior experience, Superintendent. But it would be impossible to compile a list of those disappointed in the publishing world. Macmillan is of course a *very* prestigious firm. We have our reputation.'

'Do you have copies of Mr Hinchcliffe's books?'

'Indeed I have.' She rummaged with sparkling-ringed fingers along the shelves that lined the office. 'Here are the five he wrote for us.'

Lestrade weighed them in his hands. 'May I borrow these, Miss Artois?' he asked.

'Oh, you're going to look for clues. How very, very exciting.'

'Would that it were, ma'am,' he said, and thanked her for her help. 'I'll find my own way out.'

In the foyer on the ground floor, Lestrade heard a voice he knew. He was just congratulating himself on having evaded the welcoming bosoms of Miss Fox when the voiced hailed him. 'Sholto Lestrade!'

The superintendent whirled to see a short, beetle-browed man with thick-lensed glasses. He was a good deal balder than when they had last met.

'Rudyard Kipling!' he said. 'How stands the Empire?'

The poet shook the policeman's hand warmly. 'Well, Sholto, for the time being. But with all this talk of paying our Members of Parliament, God knows for how long.'

'Yes,' agreed Lestrade grimly, 'they'll be talking of paying policemen next.'

'Rudyard, my dear chap!' Frederick Macmillan appeared at Kipling's elbow. 'That girl will have to go.'

'Girl?' Kipling shook the publisher's hand.

'Samantha Fox, my new secretary.'

'Florence,' Lestrade corrected him.

'Yes, that's right. Samantha Florence. She distinctly told me Thomas Hardy was here.'

'So that's why you were hiding,' Kipling chaffed him. 'Freddie, I'd love to talk now, but Lestrade and I are old friends and we haven't met for years. May I call after luncheon?'

'Delighted, my dear fellow. I had thought of red leather . . .'

'Lovely,' beamed Kipling and ushered Lestrade out of the door.

'Red leather?' Lestrade asked him.

'They want to bind my *Mowgli*,' Kipling explained.

'High time someone did,' Lestrade agreed and allowed the poet to pay for his lunch.

They reminisced on this and that, although Lestrade had precious little experience of that recently, what with his age and his old trouble.

'I wrote a poem for you, you know,' Kipling told him over coffee and brandy.

'For me? Rudyard, I didn't know you cared!'

Kipling chuckled. 'It was after that business at Roedean. I called it "The Sons of Martha".'

'I didn't tell you my mother's name was Martha.'

'God, was it? Well, I'm damned. No, I was referring to the

Biblical Martha. Some people have duty thrust upon them, Lestrade. They shoulder their own burdens and everybody else's.

> "It is their care in all the ages to take the buffet and cushion the shock.
> It is their care that the gear engages; it is their care that the switches lock . . .
> As in the thronged and the lighted ways, so in the dark and the desert they stand,
> Wary and watchful all their days, that their brethren's days may be long in the land . . ." '

'That's funny,' Lestrade smiled.

'Not intended to be, Sholto.' Kipling was a little hurt.

Lestrade sensed it. 'No, no. Not funny. Odd. Coincidental if you like. I had a letter from the late King before he died.'

'Preferable to one after, I would have thought,' Kipling observed. 'What did it say?'

'Not a lot, really, but he asked me to look after his people, "as I had always done" he said. It was rather touching really and rather similar to your poem, don't you think?'

'Yes,' Kipling mused through the cigar smoke, 'yes, I do. Anything to do with your being at Macmillan?'

'Macmillan?' Lestrade returned to the present. 'Oh, no. That was something else entirely.'

'And you're not going to tell me what, are you?'

'As ever,' Lestrade smiled grimly, 'my lips are sealed.'

'I don't know whether I quite trust publishers, Sholto.' Kipling quaffed his brandy. 'Except American ones.'

'You trust *them*?'

'Of course not. I am *sure* I don't trust them. Do you think I am certifiably insane?'

'Does the name Marienbad mean anything to you?' Lestrade asked.

'Marienbad? It's a spa town in Bohemia. Popular with the

County set. In need of Glauber's salts then, Lestrade? It must be the Stilton!'

'The King mentioned it in his letter. I thought nothing of it until now.'

'Wait a minute, there was some fuss there, wasn't there, a couple of years ago? During the late King's visit. I don't remember what now, except that as usual most of it was hushed up. Well, these Bohemians . . . Lord, look at the time. I may not trust publishers, Lestrade, but I've learned not to keep them waiting. Byron treated them as tradesmen, you know.'

Lestrade didn't know. He wasn't even sure he knew who Byron was, but time and business were pressing. He and Kipling hailed a cab for St Martin's Street and parted company in the plush foyer. Lestrade promised to call at Batemans again when he could and Kipling promised to call at the Yard. Perhaps he might do a recital at the next Police Revue.

Lestrade's next quarry, Mr Haverstock Irons, Reader of Proofs, was as elusive as ever. His personal staff were extraordinarily tight-lipped about him, so Lestrade courted the attentions of Miss Fox of the Forward Manner. He found her hurrying out of a broom cupboard with a junior clerk, still with the pencil in position behind his ear. She was a little ruffled, her hair awry and her breasts even more impressive now that she had not had time to entrap them properly behind her corset. Flustered she may have been, but she did impart to Lestrade the little bit of gossip he had been hoping for. When Mr Irons was in 'one of his moods', he was to be found, it was rumoured, in a little den in Greek Street. Lestrade knew the very one and caught a cab immediately.

Chief Inspector Walter Dew was of course the Oriental Expert. Were his collars and cuffs not starched by Mr Foo himself? And were his sexual exploits not the stuff of legend from Leman Street to the Yard itself? And would not Mrs Dew be had up for murder in the first degree if she ever found out? Dew, however, was elsewhere, working on the first page of his autobiographical opus. No doubt, for professional and ambitious reasons, he would have fully applauded his guv'nor's visiting Mr Irons. Here, after all, was a chance to place his name in type for all eternity. In the event, Lestrade was alone.

He cut through the dingy courtyard flanked by the seedier bordellos. Behind him and to his left was the Bioscope Theatre where Arnold Tasker had met his end. Perhaps the man Lestrade sought could shed some light on that one for him. Time, he sensed, was running out. The sunlight of mid-March vanished as he turned a corner. He cradled the brass knuckles in his hand as he splashed through the puddles on the uneven flagstoned ground. At the brass balls of the pawnbroker he stopped, pulled the bell ring on his right and waited.

A yellow face looked at him through the iron bars of a grille. Lestrade nodded and flashed a roll of notes. The grille slid back and a small, frail Chinaman ushered him in to the almost total darkness.

'I would like a smoke,' Lestrade said.

The little man clapped his hands and from the darkness two burlier Chinamen appeared. One rummaged in his left hand pockets, the other in the right. The brass knuckles flashed out and the Chinaman flicked out the deadly blade. He grinned silently, his teeth flashing white in the semi-darkness. Lestrade wondered in what form it would be returned to him and was relieved when it was hilt-first. His superintendent's card was blowing aimlessly in the gutter outside where he had dropped it and he hoped no one would find it, at least for a little while.

He peeled off first one five-pound note, then another. This case was costing him an arm and a leg. 'A friend of mine recommended you,' Lestrade said to the yellow men. 'Mr Irons.'

'We have no names here,' said the first Chinaman in a fractured guttural growl. He snatched the proffered notes and led Lestrade through a maze of pawnbroker's goods to another door, framed by heavy velvet curtains. Beyond this the smoke hit him like a wall. Acid. Dense. He hung his Donegal and bowler on a hook and sat down on a pile of cushions. In the centre of the floor, as his eyes became accustomed to the gloom, an ornate Chinese pot was placed. Extended from it into the shadows a series of pipes coiled and twisted like lethal snakes. One of these was passed to Lestrade. He adopted the cross-legged pose, took the curiously wrought lip into his mouth and inhaled. So far so good, he thought. Just like smoking an ordinary Meerschaum. It burned his eyes a little so he closed them and began to see the whole room bathed in a soft, golden light. He heard music, too, a low piping broken by the tinkle of chimes, wind-blown. He puffed again and his head became lighter. The room began to swim in his vision. He gripped the brass knuckles tightly to maintain his grip on reality. He shuffled sideways along the cushions until his shoulder touched that of the next smoker.

'Haverstock Irons?' he murmured.

'Not when I'm smoking,' came the distant answer.

Lestrade got up and resumed the search. The face in the darkness did not fit the description given to him by Miss Fox. She was probably not very reliable, but he had no other source on which to pin his hopes. He stumbled over something in the smoke and a gong sounded, deafening to his estranged ears.

'Haverstock Irons?' He crouched beside a second.

'I can see little cockroaches. Hundreds of them,' came the happy, sleepy reply. Lestrade checked the tube from which this one was smoking and wondered what was in it.

'I am Irons,' a soft voice behind him said.

He turned to see a pair of slippered feet and Oriental silk robes in a shadowy recess. The pipe he had was longer than some of the others and it meant that the smoker was plunged still further into darkness. Lestrade couldn't see the face at all, try though he might.

'My name is Lestrade,' he said. 'Please do not be alarmed. I am from Scotland Yard.'

He expected a rush for the doors, a flash of light, the sudden arrival of shrieking Orientals brandishing curved scimitars. Instead, there was a long, low chuckle.

'Well, well, well,' Irons mused. 'A policeman with a habit. How very, very naughty. If I were a criminal, Mr Lestrade, I could make myself a rich man out of you. Smoke?'

'Thank you. I roll my own.' He watched the shadows for eavesdroppers to their conversation. He could see nothing, no one. Not even his confidant here in the corner.

'*Papaver somniferum*,' Irons droned, 'the Opium Poppy. When the world becomes altogether too crass, Mr Lestrade, I retire to its welcoming arms. A smothering of leaves, a pulse of scarlet . . .' He paused. 'Don't tell me old Freddie Macmillan's found out about me? The miserable old bastard has shopped me to the peelers. Well, I can't say at the moment that I give a tinker's damn about that.'

'No, Mr Irons, Mr Macmillan didn't tell me you were here.'

'Who then?'

'I am not a liberty—'

'Ah, but who is, Inspector?'

'Superintendent.'

'Quite. Who is at liberty? Not you with your forms in triplicate, your procedures and your bloody idiot of a Home Secretary. Not me with talentless buffoons hammering at my door crying for Fame and Fortune—'

'Actually, it was Miss Fox, Mr Macmillan's new secretary.'

'Ah, yes,' Irons spat in the corner, 'Isabella. Her pitcher hath been too often to the well, Lestrade. A worse trollop than Anthony.'

'No doubt she's been blessed in an administrative way.' Lestrade sought to defend her, though he didn't know why.

'Ashes, ashes,' Irons murmured. 'Bitter and grey, and as dark as sin . . .'

'Rudolph La Rue.' Lestrade came to his purpose.

'Dreadful.' Irons spat again. 'He has the talent of my left testicle. They are both woefully underused.'

There were shufflings and coughings in the darkness. The glow began to dim in Lestrade's vision and his flesh began to crawl.

'He is dead, Mr Irons,' he said. 'Rudolph La Rue, writer of mysteries, was murdered.'

'The only mystery about him is why I ever selected his rubbish in the first place. Ah,' he chuckled, 'I remember now,' he caressed the pipe lovingly, 'the noxious weed,' he said, 'I was under its influence when I read Mr La Rue's first story. Unaccountably, people actually bought them. Well, there you are. I've never understood the appalling lack of taste that marks the great British public. Of course, I blame Wilkie Collins—'

'Why should anyone want to kill Arnold Tasker?'

'You've obviously never read anything of his.'

Lestrade waited while the headless figure puffed once more on the pipe.

'I can understand why someone should want to see Phil Marchment dead, of course.'

Lestrade emerged like a man out of a dream.

'What?' he said dumbly.

'No, La Rue, Tasker, call him what you will, was a peasant.'

Lestrade gripped the silken sleeve to pull the man towards him, but Irons shrank back, invisible, elusive. 'Marchment,' Lestrade rasped, unaware of the growing unease around him, 'you said "Phil Marchment". What of her?'

'She was a defender of lost causes,' Irons slurred. 'Her latest was the Peace Movement.'

'The Peace Movement?' Lestrade's brain whirled. 'Was La Rue involved in that too?'

'As La Rue, no, but as Tasker he wrote essays denouncing the Kaiser, condemning the arms race.'

'What about Percy Hinchcliffe?'

'You'd have to see Fanny Artois about him.'

'Did he write anything about peace? About the German threat?'

'Yes, of course. Good God, man, you're the Law. What do

the great British public pay you for? When I heard that these people died, I naturally assumed someone was on to it.'

Both men were shouting now, Lestrade scrabbling nearer, Irons backing away. The superintendent felt his arms being hauled upright. A naked foot caught him high in the ribs and a second in the pit of his stomach. He went down, gasping and as his head bobbed up he saw his own brass knuckles flash before him, snatched by lightning yellow hands from his pocket. The blade clicked out, silver and still. He stopped, fighting for breath, and flinched as the blade bit deep into the floor an inch from where his nose had once been. He rolled sideways, aware of two solid, sweating figures above him.

'Are you all right, Mr Lestrade?' a voice called from the cushions.

'Mr Irons? Where are you?'

'Over here.' A powerful hand gripped Lestrade's. 'We obviously cannot talk here. The natives are getting restless. Come to Macmillan tomorrow at ten. I'll be there.'

The hand fell away as Lestrade was hauled upright again. A yellow nose pressed against his. 'You go now. You trouble,' came the broken snarl. Again the knuckles were jammed into his pocket. The Donegal and the bowler were flung at him and he was kicked out into the afternoon alley.

It took Lestrade a full ten minutes to recover himself. The fresh air worked with the opium fumes to drive a hammer into his head and he found himself staggering along Greek Street until he collided with a blue coat that looked vaguely familiar.

'Oh dear, oh dear,' said the constable, 'been imbibing a little too freely, have we, sir? Come along, then, let's see if we can dry out, shall we?'

Lestrade shook himself free. 'I am Superintendent Lestrade,' and heard his voice echo down a long tunnel of its own making. 'Get me six more men, Constable, and come with me.'

'Well, I am Sir Edward Henry,' the constable replied, 'and I've got a better idea. You come with me.'

'For God's sake, man, there's no time to lose.' Lestrade fumbled for his superintendent's card and then remembered having to lose it before he entered the Den.

'Now then, sir, don't upset yourself.'

Lestrade wasn't sure he could manage what he had in mind now, what with the opium and the pain in his ribs and his proximity to retirement, but desperation drove him on. He aimed a careful right cross at the constable's jaw and sent the man sprawling. As he hoped, the bobby blew his whistle to summon assistance and Lestrade hurtled off in the direction of Leicester Square.

'Oi!' A second copper arrived. 'I want a word with you!' but Lestrade kept going. People were scattering in all directions. Shoppers, babies, perambulators, dogs, all fled to left and right in their attempt to escape from the path of this deranged lunatic who was rushing through them. When Lestrade glanced back, there were four coppers in his wake, and at that point, he doubled back, dodging one, shoulder barging a second, only to be brought down heavily by the third and fourth.

'You're under arrest, sir,' one of them said, sitting on his chest. 'We've got another bloody Steinie Morrison here, lads. Get a barrow.'

From nowhere a hand cart arrived and Lestrade was strapped securely to it.

'Don't I get an umbrella?' he growled.

'My, my. We are familiar with police procedure, aren't we, sir? Afraid our friends are going to see us all trussed up like a chicken? Well you should have thought of that before you started going berserk and cutting up rough. No umbrella for you, my lad.'

People poked Lestrade with their umbrellas, however, as he was wheeled past them. Reeling as his brain was, the rest was doing him some good. Beyond Shaftesbury Avenue, the little group of policemen, arrested and arresting, came face to face with a sergeant who visibly paled. In place of the avuncular

'Well done, lads,' which they expected, they got instead the rough edge of the sergeant's tongue and a short, sharp, effective tirade which Lestrade considered good enough to consign to memory for future use.

'Don't you know a superintendent of Scotland Yard when you see one?' He began unbuckling the straps, when Lestrade stopped him.

'Thank you, Sergeant, I think I'm safer where I am. I'm certainly faster. Back to Greek Street, lads, on the double, and we'll say no more about the unfortunate events of the last few minutes, shall we?'

They swung wide on the corners, the uniformed coppers pushing Lestrade like some crippled old general insisting on leading from the front. Passers-by stopped agog at the spectacle. But Lestrade had to get into that opium den before his prize got away. In Greek Street, it was shoulders to the door and the timbers eventually cracked and split under the collective force of the Force. Lestrade was grateful that the mood of the Houndsditch murders and of Sidney Street had not dampened the ardour of the copper on the beat. In the event, nothing but an empty pawnbroker's shop waited for them beyond the door. Lestrade, now free of his arresting harness, made for the second door, brass knuckles in place over his fist.

'See if there's a bull's-eye back there,' he barked to the man at his elbow. The sergeant and one other crashed through the curtains, coughing and spluttering in the smoke.

'I thought we'd closed this place down once,' the sergeant croaked.

'It's hard to keep a good den down,' Lestrade observed. 'Watch yourselves, lads. There ought to be a few Chinamen here, pretty handy with their feet.'

Anatomically, it sounded odd, but nobody took any chances. They waited until the constable who had found a bull's-eye came in, then advanced on the darkened room in line abreast, truncheons at the ready. They stumbled and cursed over cushions and one of them kicked the hookah in the middle of the floor.

'Watch that,' Lestrade warned him. 'The stuff in there will turn your boots white.'

'Superintendent!' The copper on the left of the line had found it. Lestrade snapped his fingers and the bull's-eye shone full on a prone figure thrown back on the cushions. Lestrade turned him over and recognised from Miss Fox's description the grey, dead face of Haverstock Irons.

'Damn,' Lestrade muttered.

'Who is he, sir?' the sergeant asked.

'He *was* my hope,' Lestrade sighed, straightening, 'perhaps my last. Sergeant, check the building. And get some light and air in here. We're closing this place down for good this time.'

It was late that night when Lestrade stood in his shirtsleeves in the Bow Street Morgue.

An attendant, dribbling mucus, shuffled behind him. 'Will this take long, only I've got to lock up, see?'

'Not long.' Lestrade circled the corpse, naked now. Stripped of the Oriental robes and robbed of speech and life, Haverstock Irons looked small and old.

'You didn't keep your appointment,' Lestrade found himself whispering. He checked again the puncture marks in the neck – a jagged hole, badly administered with a needle he guessed. Poison. Opium, probably. In different circumstances, had Lestrade not gone back to Greek Street, it might never have been noticed. An old degenerate succumbing at last to his vile habit. Would anyone mourn him? Not Rudolph La Rue, certainly.

Lestrade heard the sniff and shuffle behind him and turned to go. As he did, he patted the small, shrivelled hand. The attendant had already switched off the light. Lestrade held the hand in the dark.

'Switch it on again,' he said quietly.

The long-suffering attendant did so. Lestrade held the hand tighter, as though shaking it.

Very touching, the attendant thought, but he had a long way to trudge on a torrential night. But it wasn't fondness that held Lestrade there. It was the grim realisation that the man whose hand he had shaken hours earlier in the darkness and stupor of the Greek Street den was not Haverstock Irons. His brain whirled. He had been talking to Irons, certainly. All the information he had pointed to that. And then the Chinamen had grabbed him. And when he got back to Irons ... The voice seemed the same. Or was it? He still hadn't been able to make anything of the face. But the hand ... the hand was broader, meatier, the grip altogether that of a more powerful man.

In the stillness of the Bow Street Morgue, with only the dead and the damned for company, Lestrade knew he had met his man. He had shaken hands with Death itself.

The Under the Pier Show

Suddenly it was summer. A blistering June that boded well for the coronation. Sir Edward Henry, Head of the Criminal Investigation Department, was going to the Delhi Durbar, though not, as the rumour ran, because of the colour of his skin. In the meantime, he was fanning himself with his straw boater in the airless hell-hole that was his office. Before him, squarely on the carpet, stood Superintendents Lestrade and Quinn.

'Let me see if I understand you then, Lestrade,' Henry was saying, 'you've got four corpses on your hands. Methods of disposal vary from a blow dart in a Bioscope Theatre to an injection of opium. The salient point seems to be that all the victims were members of the Peace League. So we are looking for a war-monger?'

'It would seem so, sir.'

'Then you must work with Quinn here. It's clearly his territory.'

'With respect, sir—' Lestrade protested.

'You don't know the meaning of the word!' snarled Quinn.

'At least I don't go around getting myself shot in the street,' Lestrade riposted.

'Gentlemen!' Henry intervened. 'I suggest we'll get nowhere bickering among ourselves. May I remind you that this is the month of His Majesty's coronation? London is teeming with foreigners; any one of them might be suspect. Frankly, Lestrade, you can thank your lucky stars that the country is gripped by the excitement of the coronation. It takes people's minds off little things like your failure to stop this madman. Now, Quinn, unwrap that cotton wool brain of yours and give me your best guess.'

There was a silence which surprised neither Henry nor Lestrade.

'All right, then, your *only* guess.' Henry poured himself a brandy. He made no attempt to offer one to his subordinates.

'Mormons,' said Quinn. The strain of thought had cost him dear, judging by the look on his face.

Lestrade crumpled inwardly.

Henry's teeth almost bit through the glass. 'Yes,' he said eventually, 'I got the Home Secretary's memo on that. Is that the best you can do?'

'I *have* been in hospital, sir,' Quinn offered by way of excuse.

'Yes, overnight, wasn't it? Back in January?' Lestrade was anxious to set the record straight.

Quinn scowled at him. 'Nevertheless, I have been busy with the East End anarchists. Peter the Painter—'

'I realise all that, Superintendent. But let's be frank, shall we? You and I both know that the Painter is no longer in the country. You've missed him. Now, concentrate on essentials. Which is the nation most likely to threaten us?'

Another silence.

'Germany,' said Lestrade.

'I was about to say that,' Quinn snapped.

'Exactly,' Henry threw a copy of *The Charivari* across his desk, '*Pax Germanica*.' He pointed to the armed and vicious double-headed eagle, ignoring the tiny Dove of Peace. 'We are looking war in the face, gentlemen. And if anybody can stop this war, it's the Peace League. Somebody's killing them.'

'But who, sir?' Quinn asked.

'That's for you and Lestrade to find out,' Henry told them. 'But I want no more shootings in London streets, Quinn. And I want no more corpses dangling in bell towers or sprawled in opium dens, Lestrade.' Sir Edward Henry rose to his full height, approximately level with Lestrade's tie pin. 'You will work together, gentlemen. And you will get results. Do I make myself clear?'

'Perfectly, sir,' the superintendents chorused, and they left the room. When they were clear of the door, one went to the right, the other to the left. They continued to work closely together, two floors apart.

'Mormons,' said Lestrade to Sergeant Jones.

'Mormons,' Jones repeated, giving his brain time to focus, 'actually called the "Church of Jesus Christ of Latter-Day Saints". Founded by one Joseph Smith and five others in eighteen thirty in New England, America. In eighteen thirty-one they moved to Ohio and thence further westward, ever followed by persecution, particularly after their polygamous pronouncements in eighteen forty-three. There were riots thereafter and Smith and his brother were shot—'

'Yes, all right, Sergeant. Thank you.' Lestrade was, as usual, sorry that he had asked.

'May I ask why you want to know, sir?' Jones poured some tea, pre-empting his guv'nor's request.

'Mr Churchill apparently has a bee in his bonnet about them. And Mr Quinn is convinced our man is one of them.'

'Perhaps one of his wives will shop him then, sir,' Jones chuckled.

'You know, Sergeant, there are times when you remind me of your late departed father, the Inspector of River Police . . .'

'Thank you, sir,' Jones beamed.

'. . . and it scares me witless. But for once you've given me an idea. I haven't time for tea now. I'm off to Virginia Water' – he gulped nonetheless as he made for the door at the cup the sergeant had brewed for him – 'which I suspect is what this is made of. If Quinn looks in, you haven't seen me.'

* * *

'It's a bit thin, Sholto,' the Chief Constable of Surrey was saying.

'I was just thinking how nice it was, Tom,' Lestrade commented.

'Not the bacon, man.' The chief constable reached for more fried bread. 'Your theory about the Peace League. After all, you've only got the word of a self-confessed addict, now deceased. What's to say it isn't all in his mind? He was a thriller writer, wasn't he?'

'Reader rather than writer.' Lestrade tackled his eggs head on. 'What do you think, Fanny?'

'I think it's odd you stayed at The Farnham rather than coming here last night. What were you thinking of?'

Lestrade looked at Tom Berkeley. 'I needed to clear my head,' he said. 'Dear friends though you both are, there are times when I need to be alone.'

She poured him more coffee. 'What if you're looking at one victim?' she said.

'Sholto's already said, dear, *four* victims.' The chief constable reached for the toast: 'Any marmalade?'

'Under your nose, Pa. That's not what I meant. Explain to him, Sholto.'

'Er . . .' Lestrade busied himself searching for the butter.

'Men!' Fanny Berkeley said. 'Just you wait until we women are on the Force!'

'Fanny!' roared her father. 'Please! I'm having my breakfast!'

'What I mean is' – she refused to be browbeaten – 'what if our murderer intended to kill only one victim? And what if the others were merely blinds, to throw you, Sholto, off the scent?'

Lestrade nodded. 'So who would the real victim be, Fanny?' he asked her.

She ran a manicured finger around the rim of her cup. 'Philomena Marchment,' she said.

'Ha!' Berkeley guffawed. 'Just like a woman. Trust you girls to stick together.'

'Why her?' Lestrade asked.

'Why are you back in Surrey?' she countered.

Lestrade smiled. Had he known the word *touché*, he would have used it.

'All right,' he said, 'there *is* something about her I can't put my finger on.'

'Latterly, from what I've heard, most men couldn't,' observed Berkeley.

'Don't be vulgar, Father,' Fanny scolded him. 'It suits you. I've been thinking about those letters, Sholto, the ones written to Philomena.'

'Ah.' Lestrade finished his coffee. 'And?'

'From a man, definitely. Younger than her, I'd say. A rather shy young man.'

'Shy? I thought those passages were rather purple,' Lestrade mused.

'Have you never been in love, Sholto Lestrade?' Fanny asked him.

He looked at her for a long moment. Was that a blush in her cheek? And what an odd question. She knew his past. Sarah, his wife. Others she may have guessed at.

'Yes,' he said, 'I have.'

She couldn't return his steady gaze. 'Men write things in letters they wouldn't dare say to a woman's face. The same is true . . .' she paused, glancing up at him ' . . . of women to men.'

'But the letters spoke of . . . shall we say, encounters.'

'When a man is in love . . .' Fanny went on. 'What about your Dr Crippen?'

'I thought he was Walter Dew's Dr Crippen.' Tom Berkeley downed the last of his coffee. 'Fanny my dear, don't bore Sholto with your scatterbrained theories all day.' He tugged the napkin from his collar. 'I must be off. The Lord Lieutenant's invited me for a shoot. Wouldn't care to join us, Sholto?'

'Thanks, Tom, but no. The last time I went shooting, somebody nearly blew my shoulder off.'

'All right. Have fun, you two.'

Tom Berkeley disappeared to the waiting de Dion.

'Well,' Fanny tucked her father's napkin into his ring, 'I still haven't managed supper, but at least I've had breakfast with you.'

He chuckled. 'Fancy a drive?' he asked.

'Virginia Water?' She raised an eyebrow.

Lestrade shook his head, laughing. 'You know, I'm not sure your old man's right at all. You'd have made a damn good copper, Fanny Berkeley.'

They took the chief constable's trap with its yellow wheels and piebald hackney and sped along the leafy lanes to Philomena Marchment's cottage. Naked boys splashed each other in the lilied lakes past which the trap rattled, Lestrade keeping a tight rein. He hadn't driven for some time and it had to be said that a horse was a very different kettle of fish from his Lanchester, lovingly encased in mothballs and lavender bags at his home.

The thatched cottage remained unsold, and time had taken its toll. The windows hung open, like gaping holes in a toothless jaw, the thatch hung limp and bedraggled in the morning sun. Ivy had forced its way up and through the mellow bricks. The gate swung on its rusty hinges as Lestrade helped Fanny down from the seat.

'What do you hope to find, Sholto?' she asked him. 'After all this time?'

He leaned on the tattered hedge. 'Inspiration?' he said. 'I don't know. When you've turned over every stone, Fanny, and nothing has crawled out from underneath, all you can do is turn them all over again.'

He tilted back his bowler. She held his hand and made him smile. Then a sound caught them both. She looked at him.

'Inside the cottage,' he said.

'Rats?' she asked.

'Wait here.' He placed her behind him. 'If I'm not out in five minutes, call a policeman.'

At the door, he heard the noise again. No rat climbed stairs like that. Unless of course it was a hundred or so rats standing on each others' shoulders and wearing boots. A shadow crossed the landing as he peered in. He kicked the lower half of the barn-style door with his boot, but was wrong in his assumption that the top half too was open and fetched himself a nasty one on the forehead. While scrabbling to find his bowler in the undergrowth, a pair of feet swept out of the back door. Lestrade ducked under the water pump and rolled over the picket fence. He hadn't reckoned with the lawn on the far side being lower than it was on this and he fell heavily, checking himself inches short of a stagnant pond, less than pleasant in balmy July. He heard Fanny's voice and realised his quarry must have gone the other way around the cottage. At the gate again, he saw her talking to a man he vaguely knew.

'Mr Snagge?' He brushed the grass seeds from his suit and hair.

'Ah.' The naval officer was clearly embarrassed. 'Mr . . . Mr Lestrade, wh-what a coincidence.'

'Indeed it is,' said Lestrade. 'May I ask what you are doing here?'

'L-looking for property,' he said. 'M-my family l-live not far away and I'd l-like a place in the country for wh-when I'm h-home on l-leave, rather than s-sponging off F-F-Father.'

'That would be the Ambassador?' Lestrade said.

Snagge looked at him oddly. 'D-don't tell me you're after this c-cottage too, S-S-Lestrade?'

'Do you know who lived here?' Lestrade asked him.

'I w-was under the impression that no one did,' he answered.

'I mean formerly,' said Lestrade.

'I b-believe it b-belonged to a M-Mrs Marchment,' Snagge replied. 'W-why?'

'No reason,' Lestrade answered, and, remembering his manners, 'I see you have met Miss Berkeley.'

Snagge bowed, clicked his heels and raised Fanny's hand.

'Ch-ch-ch!' He sounded like the quarter-past six from Victoria. 'Delighted,' he managed.

'Mr Snagge.' She nodded to him.

'W-well,' Snagge grinned, 'I don't th-think this is really what I'm after. Miss Berkeley, it's b-b-been a pleasure.'

'Mr Snagge.' She smiled.

'G-give my regards to B-Ballard, Mr L-Lestrade.'

'Don't you see him these days?' Lestrade asked.

'Oh, d-dear me, no. N-not now he's got his knees under J-Jackie Fisher's table. N-Naval Intelligence, you see. I d-doubt Ballard will see the d-deck of a ship again. Th-that's the way up, don't you know? Not for p-powder monkeys like me of course. But for r-r-ripping chaps like Ballard – w-well, the world's his oyster. Good day!' He tipped his boater and strode off up the road.

'What a sweet man,' said Fanny.

'What was he doing here?' Lestrade asked.

'You policemen!' Fanny scolded him. 'So suspicious! The poor man is looking for a house to buy. What's odd about that?'

'Nothing, except that this house isn't for sale.'

'How do you know?'

'When we found Philomena Marchment's body, I went over her papers with a fine-toothed comb. There were no instructions for the selling of her estate and she had no heirs.'

'That is odd, isn't it?'

'Perhaps, but then,' he helped her up onto the trap, 'Philomena Marchment was an odd woman.'

'Sholto?' she said after a mile or so.

'Fanny.' He didn't take his eyes off the road.

'What is Mr Snagge's first name?'

'Er . . .Jamie, I think. James, I suppose. Why?'

'Oh, no reason,' she said. 'Just womanly curiosity.'

Womanly curiosity was what impelled Emma Bandicoot-Lestrade to accompany Commander Ballard Hook that summer to attend the Naval Review at Spithead. The loving couple called at the Yard to persuade Superintendent Lestrade to join them, but all leave had been cancelled for the month of the coronation and anyway Lestrade was not much company.

'Poor Daddy.' Emma kissed his cheek. 'Ballard said there'd be no point.'

'How astute of him.' Lestrade was more barbed than usual. Perhaps it was the heat, perhaps the haunting aspect of a faceless Nemesis whose hand he had shaken weeks earlier.

'Father!' Emma scolded him. 'That's not nice.'

'Indeed it's not.' He patted her hand. 'Sorry, Ballard. One of those days.'

'I have those, Sholto.' The Commander grinned. 'You won't miss much anyway. I'll be holding Baron Kilverstone's hand all day.'

'Jackie Fisher?' Lestrade asked.

'Yes. Have you met him?'

'No, but I bumped into a friend of yours the other day who I think would like to.'

'Oh, who was that?'

'Lieutenant Snagge.'

'Jamie? Good Lord, where was he?'

'I thought you said his father was the Austrian Ambassador.'

'Yes, so he is,' said Hook.

'Is it customary for Ambassadors of Empires to live in Surrey villages?'

Hook blinked. 'I really don't know,' he said. 'We have the Embassy here in London, of course, but a country seat would have been quite in order, I would have thought. Why do you ask?'

Lestrade waved it aside. 'Oh, no reason. Merely that Mr Snagge was buying property in Virginia Water and mentioned that his parents lived nearby.'

'Well, that is odd,' Hook mused.

'Is it?' Lestrade sensed something.

'What is, Ballard?' Emma joined the conversation, having been intrigued for the last few moments with the menacing eyes of the sergeant in the outer office.

'Well, Jamie's mother I know has a country seat in Yorkshire. I didn't know they were moving south. Still, that's Jamie for you.'

'So it would seem. Ballard, I must be frank and say there are a few things about your friend Snagge I am unhappy with.'

Hook chuckled. 'Aren't we all?'

'I think I'll have to talk to him again.'

'You'll be lucky, Sholto. He left yesterday for the Baltic.'

'The Baltic?'

'That's near—'

'Yes,' Lestrade interrupted the interjection from the outer office. 'Thank you, Dickens. Get on with your ABC. The grown-ups are talking.'

'We must be away, Sholto.' Hook caught Emma's hand. 'Must catch the Pompey train.'

'That's Portsmouth, sir.' Dickens again. This time Lestrade threw his pencil at him.

'Isn't it a shame, Daddy, Sir Edward Henry banning aeronautics for the coronation. Ballard was going to fly over the Abbey.'

'Really?' said Lestrade. 'I didn't know you flew, Ballard.'

'Oh.' The commander was clearly embarrassed. 'Not very well, I'm afraid. Sir Edward was quite right, my dear, bearing in mind my limited prowess at the controls. I'd probably plough into Tower Bridge. Come, dearest, we must away.'

'Er . . . Emma. Please don't think me difficult. But if Ballard is to be with Lord Fisher all day, what of you?'

She crossed back to him, taking him in her arms and smiling indulgently. 'That's not what's worrying you, Sholto Lestrade,' she said, 'it's my being alone in a carriage with a strange bearded man! Don't worry, Aunt Letitia and Uncle Harry are meeting us at Waterloo. We'll be perfectly chaperoned.'

Lestrade felt a little sheepish. She kissed him and the lovers scampered out into the Embankment sunshine. Hook whistled piercingly and Alfred Bowes, Hackney coachman, cracked his animal into motion. He had taken his place, as was his custom these days, in the Rank opposite the circular turrets of the Yard. From that spot, when the sun was at his back, he could make out dim movement in the office of Sir Edward Henry on the first floor. He placed his foot on the brake and kicked the canvas sheeting down over the old Tranter pistol that lay there, waiting for his chance.

'Waterloo, cabbie. Step on it,' Hook called and bundled Emma in. 'Why did you tell your father Letitia and Harry were joining us?' he asked her laughingly.

'If you were the father of a girl, you wouldn't have to ask that question.'

'Perhaps I will be one day,' he said, and kissed her.

Alfred Bowes brought the whip down and hauled his hansom into the path of an oncoming motor cab, cursing and spitting at the driver, who was only too ready to return the compliment.

Lestrade watched them go from his office window and turned to the realities of life. 'Blevvins,' he called. The sergeant of the menacing eyes lurched through the door. He was improving. He had remembered to open it first.

'Sir?'

'How long have you been with me now, Sergeant?'

'Er . . . let me see, sir. Best part of fifteen months, I should say.'

'I'm not sure about the best part, Blevvins, but I'm going to give you a rare treat anyway. Get your titfer. We're going to meet a living legend.'

An Act of God got in the way. As Blevvins turned out the Yard Wagon to take them to the Underground, the heavens opened. By the time they reached Baker Street, water was belching through shattered sewers and the disconsolate policemen sloshed up to their ankles in slime. They made their hazardous way towards the eerie grey of the London skies, slipping on the wet steps and cursing as they trudged.

'July,' muttered Blevvins. 'Bloody hell.'

'Sir, sir!' The urgent cry behind them made them turn to see a saturated Sergeant Jones floundering past irate fellow travellers. 'Mr Lestrade, sir.'

'Don't tell me you've come with an umbrella, Jones. How thoughtful. You really shouldn't have.' He swiped it from the sergeant.

'No, sir,' Jones was gasping for breath, 'though you're welcome of course. It's from Superintendent Froest, sir. A body at Bognor. A mutilated corpse.'

A lady passing at that moment shrieked and fainted, bouncing effortlessly on each step until the rising tide caught her.

'Look out there!' Lestrade called as various men plunged in to fish her out. 'Blevvins, did you touch that woman?'

'Sir?'

'Never mind. Jones, get up top and find some bobbies. Close this station before we have mass drownings on our hands.'

'But the body, sir—'

'Leave that to me.' Lestrade turned to Blevvins. 'You'll have to go on alone to interview Mr Stead. Now, Blevvins, this is important. I'd go myself, but you see how things are. Be polite, Sergeant. You know what to ask.'

'Yes sir,' Blevvins beamed.

'Mess this one up,' Lestrade looked the man right in the chin, 'and I'll have your stripes. Got it?'

'Very good, sir.'

'That I doubt,' muttered Lestrade and left the livid sky of London for a beaker full of the warm South.

Hannah Williams walked with her tall, darkly handsome new husband along the beach at Bognor, gazing soulfully up into his sharp, cold eyes.

'An antique shop, beloved?' she asked.

'Yes, my own heart.' He patted her tiny hand, linked through the crook of his arm. 'Only the cheque from my plantation has been delayed. You can't get the staff nowadays. I'm afraid we shall have to wait ... unless ...' He looked at her out of the corner of his eye.

'Unless what, my sweet?'

He raised his topper to ladies passing with a perambulator.

'Oh nothing, heart. I couldn't trouble you ...'

She stopped. 'The two hundred pounds I have saved,' she shouted.

He clapped a hand over her mouth, fanning the air with the hat lest anyone had overheard.

'Oh, my best love,' he tittered, 'I couldn't begin our long life together with such a debt hanging over me.'

'A debt, George?' Her eyes widened at the mention of the word. 'No, no, my darling. We must share. What's yours is mine and ...'

He placed a finger to her lips. 'Very well,' he said, 'I accept. But only as a loan, mind. I insist. When can we withdraw the cash?' He caught her look and smiled broadly. 'My agents are insisting on a deposit, dearest heart.'

'Well, tomorrow,' she said.

He checked his half-hunter and resigned himself to that.

'Tomorrow it is, my darling.' He encircled her waist with his arm. 'Did I tell you about my town house in Bristol? You'll especially love the bathroom ...'

And he tipped his topper to the anonymous ferret-face below the damp-looking bowler which rushed blindly past in the direction of Aldwick.

Lestrade had sat huddled in a corner of the southbound Victoria train, steam rising from his extremities as though he were a walking Chinese laundry. He was not in the best of moods and his recent stumble over one of the groynes had not helped. If George Williams, also known as George Rose, also known as George Joseph Smith, had glanced back as he walked with his lady-love, he would have seen the little cordon of blue-coated constables ringing the pier. Curious sightseers were milling on the sands, or leaning over the elegant wrought-iron railings to enquire what the trouble was. For nearly a whole day they had been there and the whole town buzzed with more excitement and rumour than it was ever to know again. Each enquiry was met with the same time-honoured response from the gentlemen in blue: 'Move along there, there's a good gentleman,' which rankled a little with the ladies who were curious.

'What have we got?' Lestrade asked the plain-clothed inspector, once everyone had established identities.

'He's hanging up here, sir,' the answer echoed under the dark wetness of the pier, green and vile with the rotting debris of the sea. It reminded Lestrade curiously of the Baker Street Underground he had left behind that morning. The inspector pointed to where the body of Andrew Urchfont McAbendroth dangled obscenely from an angle of the pier supports. His head hung loose on a neck that was clearly broken. His clothes, shirt and trousers hung in shreds and his arms, trunk and legs bore the marks of long, deep gashes on which the blood had set dark and hard.

'Who found him?' Lestrade asked.

'Two fishermen, just before dawn this morning. We've got them at the station now.'

'How did he get up there?'

'High tide.' The inspector pointed to the line of dark green weed that ran level with the corpse's shoulder. 'I've lived here all my life, sir. It's my guess . . . if you won't think me forward, sir . . .'

'In this business, laddie, I've learned that one man's guess is as good as another's. Let's hear it.'

'I'd say he was dragged behind a boat for some distance along a shallow somewhere out there.'

'So those wounds . . .?'

'Shingle, sir. At speed it'll rip a man to pieces.'

Lestrade led the inspector to the sweeter air in the evening sun. 'Tell me about Andrew McAbendroth,' he said.

The story continued over a well-earned pint in the Nye Timber Hotel. The inspector was paying. McAbendroth had been a pillar of the community. A Justice of the Peace and an Oddfellow, in the nicest possible sense of the term. Of Lowland Scottish descent, he had at one time stood for Parliament and was often taken in poor light for the late Mr Gladstone. Unlike that august gentleman, Mr McAbendroth had never, even in his weaker moments, addressed the Queen Empress at a Public Meeting. In fact, he had never addressed the Queen at all. He had, however, been a guest recently at the Lord Mayor of London's Banquet in the Mansion House in honour of the coronation and, it was rumoured, had been nodded to by George V. He had also written the Civic Address from the people of Bognor on the occasion of the Prince of Wales's recent Investiture. No, he was not, as far as the inspector knew, a Mormon and had one wife who had predeceased him by three years apparently of natural causes.

All of this washed over Lestrade as the sea had the corpse of McAbendroth before they had cut him down. What caused him to choke on his beer was the news that the late magistrate had been an active member of the Peace Movement.

'Are you all right, sir?' The concerned inspector slapped the Yard man's back with forceful solicitude.

Lestrade waved the choking fit aside as his face assumed a variety of shades of crimson.

'Who called in the Yard?' he asked.

'I have no idea, sir. I was merely told to await the arrival of a senior detective from London.'

'Do you believe in guardian angels, Inspector Hawkesmore? I'd better have something to wash that down.'

Reluctantly, Hawkesmore flagged down for the third time that evening a waiter on the Nye Timber staff. 'I don't follow you, sir.'

'Think of the odds, man. A body washed up on a beach. The second of its type I've encountered in a few months. I'm working on a case involving a number of victims, all of whom have connections with the Peace Movement. Suddenly I'm called away from all that to investigate what at first seems a total departure. And now you tell me McAbendroth was a member too. Would you call that a coincidence, Inspector?'

'I would, sir.' The younger man sipped the froth from his beer.

'When's your coroner available?'

'Not until tomorrow, I'm afraid.'

'Let's have a closer look ourselves, then.'

'Sir?'

'The late Andrew McAbendroth. Let's find out what made him late, shall we?'

The policemen hurried through the gathering summer night, warm sea breezes lapping across the silver water to their right.

'A series of killings then, sir?' the inspector pried.

'Yes. And forget I said that.' Lestrade patted the side of his tipless nose with his finger. 'This could be bigger than both of us.'

They clattered down the stone steps of the cellar of McAbendroth's rambling, ivy-clad house. The staff were not resident and the inspector had already interrogated them anyway, as soon as the body had been found and recognised. The old magistrate had been in the habit of taking constitutionals morning and evening when the weather permitted. It was simply that he had not come back last evening and his housekeeper, a habitual worrier, had contacted the police.

Now he lay on a table in his own cellar, the green of the gaslight lending an eeriness to the stony Gladstonian features and turning the blood an ugly dark brown. The inspector watched in bewilderment as the superintendent circled the table a few times, tapping the limbs or flicking aside a shred of the garments. He tilted the grey head. It flopped limply to one side. As he surmised, broken neck. Then, under the hairline, something caught his attention.

'Hand me that candle,' he said.

The inspector complied and Lestrade shone the flame against the weed-hung temples. He pulled the pen from his pocket and poked it into the deep, single hole he found there.

'I'd give my right arm to know what caused that,' he said.

'Was it this, sir?' the inspector asked after a pause. He held up a smashed lead pellet. Lestrade took it.

'Where did you find this?' he asked.

'I didn't. One of my men chanced on it this evening as they carried the body up the beach. He was about to throw it away.'

Lestrade slumped back against the wall behind him. 'See that that man gets a citation, Inspector,' he closed his fist on the pellet, 'or at least this,' and he offered the man a cigar.

Three Men in a Bunker

Lestrade spent the rest of that week in Bognor. Among boaters and ice-creams and candy-floss, he felt a little out of place. But he wasn't prepared to knot a handkerchief on his head merely to allay the curiosity of gawping holiday-makers. Hour upon hour, Inspector Hawkesmore's constables combed the beach, looking for something, anything, that could account for Andrew McAbendroth's last hours on earth. All they came up with was donkey droppings, but such was the resourcefulness of the Sussex Constabulary that even these found a use on the roses of one of the sergeants.

The fishermen who found the body could not help much, so Lestrade and Hawkesmore meticulously sounded out the inhabitants of the cottages, villas and hotels along the route the late magistrate habitually took. Nothing. Like the other incidents Lestrade had been checking, no one had seen anything. No one had heard anything. No one knew anything. Not for the first time Lestrade realised the similarity between the great British public and the three little monkeys Frank Froest had on his desk. Evil was indeed something invisible, silent, blind. Whoever the murderer was, he led a charmed life.

As he sped north on the afternoon train, the August sun gilding the sleepy hedgerows, he focused his tired old mind on the facts as he knew them. Six people were dead, all by the same hand. The hand that Lestrade himself had gripped in Greek Street not long ago. Percy Hinchcliffe, writer, eccentric, member of the Peace Movement, shot dead, probably by an automatic pistol. Thomas Portnoy, hanging in his own bell ropes at Clement Danes. Philomena Marchment, killed in her Lanchester by a lethal children's game. Arnold Tasker, alias Rudolph La Rue, novelist, hit from behind in the Bioscope with a poisoned dart. Haverstock Irons, publishing reader, killed by an overdose of opium. And now Andrew McAbendroth, local lion, shot dead, unless Lestrade missed his guess, by a bullet of the same type that killed Hinchcliffe. The link, he remained convinced, was the Peace Movement. All except Philomena Marchment wrote articles about it. Philomena, so Irons had told Lestrade, supported it. A shrewd old bird like Tom Berkeley had found the link thin. A clever girl like Fanny Berkeley thought the other murders were blinds to conceal the actual victim – Philomena Marchment. And those letters rankled with Lestrade too. Who was 'J' and how – if at all – was he involved? What of the man? Was he powerful enough to haul a dead or dying weight to the top of a belfry? He had a knowledge of knots and an acquaintance at least with Africa. He was a good shot and carried a gold fob seal or pocket watch. Lestrade folded the newspaper over his face.

'You're right, Tom Berkeley,' he said to himself. 'It *is* thin.'

Superintendent Frank Froest was not best pleased. He was pacing backwards and forwards like an expectant hippo. Before him stood Sergeant Blevvins, staring straight ahead, unblinking. In two respects, the man was on the carpet. Lestrade entered to have the worst of his fears realised. In the lobby, Sergeant Peabody had told him there was trouble. Lestrade had come to spell that word B-l-e-v-v-i-n-s.

'Tell Mr Lestrade what happened then, Sergeant.'

Blevvins shifted as he realised his own guv'nor was present.

'I began to ask Mr Stead about the Peace Movement, sir, in accordance with my instructions.'

'And?'

'And somehow the conversation got round to Mr Stead's past.'

'Yes?' Froest was a patient man.

'In particular, Mr Stead's book *The Maiden Tribute of Modern Babylon* . . .' Blevvins' formality was cracking. 'He's got a record, sir,' he explained to Lestrade, who was reaching for a chair by way of a crutch.

'What for?' Froest asked.

'Illegally obtaining evidence by illegal means.'

'Illegally?' Lestrade checked, liking to have his facts straight.

'He's a dealer in pornography, guv'nor,' Blevvins went on. 'The most disgusting filth—'

'You saw this "filth"?' Lestrade asked.

'Well . . . no, but I heard—'

'Heard?' Froest swung back into the room from his position at the window. 'Where from?'

'Common talk in the basement, sir,' explained Blevvins.

'The sergeants' nest,' muttered Lestrade. 'No doubt Dickens and Jones supplied you with the facts and you embroidered the rest.'

'He's also a lunatic, sir,' Blevvins tried another tack, 'he claims to have written letters while in a trance, under the pen name of Julia.'

'Julia?' Lestrade repeated.

'Yes. I ask you, a man going around pretending to be a woman. It isn't natural . . .'

'So what did you do, Blevvins?' Lestrade was almost afraid to hear the answer.

'I stuck one on him, sir.'

'What?' Lestrade had turned the colour of Froest's walls.

'Broken nose. Two loose teeth, suspected fracture of the third rib,' Froest offered by way of clarification.

Lestrade rose slowly. 'You did all that because you disapproved of a man's lifestyle?' he said uncomprehendingly.

'Ah no, sir.' Blevvins was a stickler for accuracy. 'The nose and teeth, yes, I must admit, but the rib must have been caused as he went over the balcony.'

'The balcony?' Froest and Lestrade chorused.

'I was interviewing Mr Stead in the upper-storey rooms of his home.'

'What of the Peace Movement?' Lestrade asked, a little superfluously.

'Mr Stead didn't seem to want to continue our little chat after that, sir. I suppose what with his mouth being full of blood and all . . .'

'Blevvins,' said Froest, 'William Thomas Stead is one of the most important figures in the country today. He put journalism on the map, Blevvins. I know that won't mean much to you, but without him there would have been no Gordon expedition to the Sudan, no raising of the age of consent to sixteen and indeed, very little that has happened in this country since eighteen eighty has happened without the influence of Mr Stead. And you call him . . . what was it now? "A lecherous old pervert" and proceed to break his nose.' Froest had turned purple, his fat shuddering with the effort of keeping his hands off the sergeant.

Lestrade put an avuncular arm on Blevvins' shoulder. 'Sergeant,' he said softly, 'are you a thrifty man? Have you put something aside for a rainy day? I hope so, Sergeant, because, you see, it's here.'

Blevvins craned his neck to see the sun dancing on the Thames below. 'No, sir, it's quite . . . oh, I see what you mean, sir.'

'He's your boy, Sholto.' Froest stumped towards the door. 'You do the honours. If I stay here much longer I'll throw up.'

Lestrade sat behind Froest's desk. The chair sank almost to the floor and for a second Lestrade all but disappeared from view. 'Sergeant Blevvins, you are hereby suspended from duty until further notice. You will leave your badge and your handcuffs with Sergeant Peabody on the way out. Any personal effects in your desk or locker are to be removed. All this pending an

enquiry into your fitness to remain an officer of the Metropolitan Police Force.' He dropped the official tone. 'And Sergeant
Blevvins . . .'

'Sir?' The sergeant remained rigidly at attention.

'If I see you on these premises until you are sent for, I'm going
to kick your balls through to the back of your neck. Clear?'

'As crystal, sir.'

'Now get out.'

There was no more to be said.

'Bissus Seddod, Bissus Seddod,' the adenoidal little boy
scampered down the stairs, 'Chickie's dot well.'

Mrs Seddon appeared in the hallway with a cup of tea. 'All
right, Ernie,' she cooed in her soft-spoken Derbyshire, 'I'll see
to Miss Barrow.'

Miss Barrow was having another of her turns. Southend-on-
Sea had not done the trick, neither had the bismuth and morphia
prescribed by Dr Sworn. And as for the sweaty, bony proximity
of little Ernie in bed with her every night, well, Mr Seddon was
probably right. It *was* unnatural and did neither of them any
good. Her room was nauseating. It was rank with the smell of
vomit and diarrhoea and it hummed also with late summer
bluebottles.

'I must get you some flypapers, dear,' Mrs Seddon shouted as
Miss Barrow craned forward to catch the words. 'Have this
cuppa in the meantime.'

Mrs Seddon couldn't bear to stay to discover whether or not
her lodger kept this one down. The stench of the lodger's
problem, coupled with the carbolic sheets hung round the room,
was too much.

'Doesn't the smell bother you, Ernie love?' she asked the
yellow-looking boy as she passed him on the stairs.

'What sbell do you bean, Bissus Seddod?' he asked.

'Never mind!' and she hurried to the shops.

Dr Sworn came again the next day, armed with blue pills and

advice about brandy, because, as he put it so professionally, 'Miss Barrow's motion is so offensive, Mrs Seddon. I wonder your husband stands for it.'

'Oh, he's devoted to her, Doctor. Devoted,' Mrs Seddon assured him.

That afternoon, Mr Seddon showed his devotion by sitting at Miss Barrow's bedside. 'No, no,' he was saying, 'you don't need a solicitor, Eliza. All this talk of death is silly. It's just the weather, that's all. When this hot spell breaks, you'll feel right as rain. Still, I could draw up a will for you.'

'The Bill?' Miss Barrow brushed the flypaper from her face. 'What do we need the police for?'

'No, no, not the *Bill*, dear. A will. You know, a will,' he shouted into her ear-trumpet.

'Very well,' she said, and allowed him to draft a copy in elaborate National School longhand, nominating him, Frederick Henry Seddon, sole executor.

'Thank you,' she said faintly when he had finished, 'thank God, that will do.'

'Indeed,' smiled Seddon, 'that will do nicely.'

Three middle-aged men struggled out of the rough that last day in September. It had been indeed an Indian summer and the golf clubs had never known such trade, not since Kitchener had taken up the sport.

'Here's a chance then, Willie,' said one of them, shielding his eyes with the jaunty cap he appeared to have borrowed from Kier Hardie. 'Ten bob says you can't make the green.'

'Now which is the green?' Willie asked, adjusting his pince-nez.

'That bit down there, with the flag in the middle,' the third informed him. 'Do your best.'

Willie placed the ball on the tee and assumed the position.

'Wider, Willie,' said the watching man. 'Ease back a little. Not too sharp, now.'

Willie's iron whistled through the afternoon and sent the ball hurtling at an angle to disappear in the trees on his right.

'Oohh, he's sliced it.' The third man covered his eyes and crumpled as though the ball had hit him.

'You go on, Arthur,' Willie said. 'I may be some considerable time.'

'Got your sleuthing spyglass, John?' Arthur asked. 'Willie might need it.'

Arthur and John sent their balls winging down the fairway and wandered off in pursuit of them, leaving Willie hacking about in the undergrowth.

'Is it true a policeman did that to him?' John asked.

'So he says; a Yard man, I gather.'

'A Yard man?' John stopped. 'Does Lestrade know about this?'

'Lestrade? Good God, do you mean he's still there? I thought he'd retired.'

'Yes,' muttered John, 'I thought I had, too, but here I am, still treating corns and scarlet fever. Depressing, isn't it?'

'Not as depressing as writing, old boy. Seven hundred and fifty copies a year, that's all. I often wish I'd kept my practice going.'

'Do you ever get to Southsea these days?'

'Oh, occasionally, but life's full, y'know. Oliver Lodge keeps calling for the odd seance.'

'Very odd, if you ask me!'

'Now John, you promised. The Other Side may be nonsense to you, but there are those of us in the scientific fraternity who keep our minds open.'

'Fore!' Willie's cry sent Arthur and John ducking for cover behind a stand of elms. They need not have bothered. The ball plopped harmlessly into the sand of a bunker.

'Not exactly Harry Vardon, is it?' John mused.

'Your shot.' Arthur emerged bravely from cover first. John braced his knees, and hunched over the ball like a vulture laying

an egg. Arthur coughed loudly, causing John to walk about in a
tight circle, then return to the crouch.

'Oh, bad luck,' Arthur crowed as John's ball trickled wide of
the hole. 'Never mind, you're still on the green.'

They glanced back to where sprays of sand over the bunker's
edge were all that bore testimony to the presence of their
comrade-in-clubs.

'He'd better caddie for us next time,' said John. 'I was hoping
we'd get round this course before Christmas.'

There was a sudden roar of engines nearby and a monstrous
black aircraft, struts flashing in the afternoon sun, hurtled over
the Downs towards them.

'Good God!' Arthur shouted. 'What's that?'

'It's a Sopwith,' John called back.

No, it's a Voisin,' Arthur challenged him.

'Whatever it is, it's bloody low and bloody loud.' John did his
best to hold his cap on, but his plus-fours took on a life of their
own, flapping madly in the wind.

'The cheeky blighter's waving,' shouted Arthur as the pilot
turned his machine into the sun again. 'Scorchers on the ground
are bad enough, but in the air I draw the line. Did you get his
number, John?'

'No, old boy, sorry.'

'Well, I'm going after him.'

'After him?' John shouted in disbelief. 'Arthur . . .'

But Arthur had gone, hurtling across the green, brandishing
his Mashie-Niblick like a rapier, hurling insults to the retreating
machine. He called back over his shoulder, 'You'd better give
Willie a hand in the bunker.'

John shook his head at the ludicrous spectacle, reminiscent of
Quixote tilting at windmills, and joined Willie, still playing in
the sand.

'Like this,' he said patiently. 'Swing back and follow through.
That's it.'

Even as he said it he glanced up to see Arthur running back

towards them, still spearing the sky and shouting incoherently. He heard the noise of the returning aircraft, snarling and roaring above the trees. Willie's concentration, such as it was, was broken. He brought the club back for a moment, aware of the aeroplane like a great black bird above him and he saw his friend pitch forward in the sand. The machine tilted away to the low crown beyond the third hole and disappeared from view.

Arthur reached the bunker's rim. 'My God, John.' He sank onto his knees beside the fallen golfer, turning him over. 'What happened?' he asked Willie.

'I . . . I don't know.' Willie still crouched there, in the position in which John placed him. 'I must have hit him with my club. Is he all right?'

Arthur felt neck and wrist with the instincts of the old physician. 'No, Willie, he's not. I'm afraid he's dead.'

It was dark before Superintendent Lestrade reached the Wimbledon Golf Club. Bull's-eyes flickered with the evening breezes as a little knot of plainclothes men crossed the springy turf to the fatal bunker. The police cordon broke and amid muttered comments during which Sergeant Dickens did the honours of introduction, Lestrade knelt beside the corpse.

'I understand he was a friend of yours, sir,' the local sergeant said.

'In a manner of speaking,' said Lestrade, resting his bowler in the sand. 'What happened here?'

'We've got 'im, sir. 'E's in the clubhouse under arrest. Bloke by the name of . . . er . . . William Thomas Stead.'

'Stead?' Lestrade was on his feet. 'I repeat, man, what happened?'

'It seems these gentlemen were playing golf, sir, when Stead walloped the deceased over the 'ead. 'E says it was an accident, of course, but then don't they all? I 'aven't been eighteen years on the Force without 'earing a few big 'uns in me time. And this is one of the biggest—'

'Dickens!'

'Sir?' The sergeant arrived at the double.

'You've got about ten minutes to tell me how this man died. If anyone else touches the body you are to take down his name, rank and number and I will personally see to it that the man is on the streets and out of a job by nightfall. Clear?'

'Perfectly, sir.'

'Sergeant,' he turned to the uniformed man, 'take me to your clubhouse.'

On arrival, there was an air of gloom in the bar. The clock could be heard ticking loudly as the members sat in stunned silence. In the corner, one of them tapped out Elgar medleys on the table with his fingernails until the disapproving eyes of the others reduced him to silence.

'Gentlemen,' the bowler was placed respectfully on the bar, 'I am Superintendent Lestrade of Scotland Yard.'

There was a hubbub as members moved towards him, each with their stories, each with their urgencies. Lestrade raised a hand. 'Dr John Watson was a friend of mine,' he said. 'You may rest assured that I am as anxious to get to the bottom of this as you are. Sergeant, where is Mr Stead?'

'Through 'ere sir.'

'I hope I will not keep you long, gentlemen,' said Lestrade.

'Superintendent,' one of the members hailed him; 'forgive me, I understand that you have your routines, but I was with John when he died. Or at least, immediately afterwards.'

Lestrade looked at the broad features, the narrow, kindly eyes and the walrus moustache. 'Sir Arthur Conan Doyle, I believe.'

Conan Doyle extended a hand. 'It seems odd to meet a man I've been writing about for years,' he chuckled.

'Perhaps libelling is a better word, Sir Arthur.'

'Oh, come now,' Conan Doyle bridled, 'Watson assured me. . . . We assumed you wouldn't mind.'

'No matter,' said Lestrade, 'but we have met before.'

'Really?' Conan Doyle blustered. 'I'm sorry, I'm sure I would have remembered . . .'

Lestrade smiled. 'It *was* a long time ago,' he said. 'In the Sally

Lunn Tearooms in Southsea. And I called myself Lister then.'

'Did you, by George. Subterfuge, eh? That was sneaky.'

'No, Sir Arthur. That was necessary.'

'Look here, Willie didn't kill John, you know.'

'Perhaps you would care to elaborate, Sir Arthur, but not here and not now. Sergeant.' Lestrade pointed to the door in front of which, once the superintendent had gone through it, the burly man placed his elephantine body. No amount of bluster from Conan Doyle was going to get through that.

In the lamp-lit ante-room, filled with cigar smoke, the bearded, worried figure of William Stead prowled the carpet. His nose was still bandaged, but apart from that his encounter with Blevvins seemed to have left him surprisingly intact.

'Mr Stead?' Lestrade ventured. 'I would like to ask you a few questions.'

Stead kept his distance. 'Not from Scotland Yard, are you?' he asked.

Lestrade kept his hands firmly in his pockets and nodded. 'Tell me what happened,' he said, 'in your own words.'

Stead paced the room again. 'I was in the sand-pit – what do you call it – the bunker? I couldn't get the ball out. Arthur and John were very patient with me and John came back to help.'

'And then?'

'I must have swung too wide because John pitched forward beside me. I must have caught his head with the club. God,' he buried his face in his hands, 'it's too awful. Poor John.'

'What happened next?'

'Arthur came over and told me that John was dead. I couldn't – still can't – believe it. I've known John Watson for years. He was like part of the furniture.'

'What did Conan Doyle do?'

'We both left John where he was and ran here to get help. I went back to the body while Arthur waited for the police.'

There was a knock at the door.

'Yes,' called Lestrade, watching the broken man in front of him. It was Dickens.

'May I have a word, sir?'

Lestrade sidled to one corner and whispered with his sergeant. He looked up in surprise, slapped the man on the shoulder and took something from him which he held up to the light. He turned back to the crumpled form of Stead.

'Well, sir, are you a drinking man?' he asked.

Stead looked up in surprise. 'In moderation,' he said. 'Why?'

'I suggest you have a stiff brandy for the road, Mr Stead, and go home. Though I will need a statement from you tomorrow – at the Yard in the morning, if you don't mind.'

'You mean I'm free to go?' Stead blinked uncomprehendingly.

'Why not, sir? There's nothing I can charge you with. A bad game of golf isn't illegal.'

'But . . . John Watson . . . Arthur said it would be manslaughter. He knows about these things.'

'I'm sure he does, Mr Stead. But did he examine Watson's body carefully?'

'Er . . . I don't know. I couldn't say.'

'I don't think he could have. I think in your hurry to get help he missed a vital point. A golf club didn't kill John Watson. A bullet did.' He held up the smashed lead plug Dickens had given him. '*This* bullet.'

Stead slumped back in a chair. 'My God,' he said. 'But who fired it?'

'Sir Arthur Conan Doyle?' Lestrade was feeling more flippant than he had a right to be.

'You're not serious?'

'No, I'm not. Mr Stead, did you notice anything odd while you were playing? Anyone, for instance, lurking near the green?'

'No . . . I don't think so. Unless . . .'

'Yes?'

'No, no. Nothing.'

Lestrade lit a cigar for himself from the oil-lamp's wick. The flame flared suddenly, threatening to burn off his moustache, but he made light of it and turned back to Stead, smouldering a little as he did so: 'Two things, Mr Stead. First, I would like to discuss the Peace Movement with you tomorrow as well as this little affair today.'

'The Peace Movement? Yes, yes, of course.'

'And, secondly, the unfortunate affair of your nose.'

'Ah,' said Stead.

'I feel rather guilty about that. You see, I was on my way to see you, but something detained me and I had to send Sergeant Blevvins instead. I've no wish to subvert justice. God knows, the man had it coming to him . . .'

'You wish me to drop charges?' Stead asked.

Lestrade nodded. 'Let's just say we can deal with Blevvins in our own way, sir.'

'Point taken . . . er . . .'

'Lestrade, Superintendent Lestrade, sir.'

'After what I've been through today, Mr Lestrade . . . That sounds selfish. It isn't meant to. Isn't it dreadful? John Watson is dead, and all I can feel is relief that I didn't do it.'

'A perfectly natural reaction, sir.'

Stead nodded, suddenly very tired and very old. 'Consider the charges against your man dropped, Superintendent.'

'Thank you, sir. We'll see you at the Yard tomorrow.'

Stead went out. Lestrade called Dickens to him.

'Put a man on him, Sergeant. No, better make it two. Plainclothes.'

'Don't trust him, eh, sir?'

'Oh, I trust him implicitly, Sergeant. It's his would-be murderer I don't trust.'

'Sir?'

'Never mind. Just do it.'

'Very good, Sir.'

'Sergeant,' Lestrade collared the giant on the door, 'get your lads to bring the body in, will you? It can stay in this room on a table overnight.'

'Look here . . .' began a member, but a look from Lestrade silenced him.

'Sir Arthur,' Lestrade beckoned and closed the door behind them, 'did you examine John Watson's body?'

'I did.'

'You are a doctor yourself, I understand?'

'I am. Although I must concede I have not practised for a while.'

'What, in your opinion as a medical man, killed him.'

'Well, I assumed . . . er . . . a blow to the head.'

'Caused by?'

Conan Doyle became more assured. 'A golf club. To be precise, a Number Three Iron.'

'Like this?' Lestrade rummaged in a bag in the corner and produced a club.

'No, Lestrade, that is a Niblick. Don't you play?'

'I can't afford the club fees,' Lestrade answered. 'Show me a Number Three.'

Conan Doyle fished one out and handed it to Lestrade. 'Show me how Stead swung the club.'

The good ex-doctor took it in both hands. 'Well, I didn't see exactly, but it was rather like this. Confidentially, you see, Willie isn't very good. Why did you let him go, by the way?'

'Because he hasn't done anything.'

'What?'

'Would have made a good story, wouldn't it? "Death on the Golf Course" – quite a title for you.'

'That's beneath contempt, Lestrade,' Conan Doyle was on his dignity, 'to imply that I would attempt to capitalise on this tragic, tragic accident.'

'But it wasn't an accident.'

'What? But you said—'

'I said Mr Stead hadn't done anything. What about you?'

'What?' Conan Doyle erupted, purple-faced. 'How dare you?'

'There, there, Sir Arthur, watch your blood-pressure. Swing

your club – as you saw Mr Stead do it.'

Lestrade positioned the oil-lamp beside Conan Doyle, approximately where Watson's head would have been in the bunker.

'You see,' he said, 'your Number Three Iron didn't even against it.

'You see,' he said. 'Your Number Three Iron didn't even break the glass, much less smash a skull. Oh, I grant you,' he took the club from Conan Doyle, 'this would make an effective murder weapon, but in the right hands, which were not William Stead's, and at the right angle, which is not in the way you have just demonstrated.'

For a brief moment, Conan Doyle was nonplussed, despite his trousers.

'Ah,' he suddenly said. 'Now I see it. This is all to do with Oscar Slater, isn't it?'

'Who?'

'Come off it, Lestrade. I've been writing for years about him, to the Home Secretary, to the Yard, to the Law Society. He's mouldering in prison now for a murder he didn't commit. Whoever killed Miss Gilchrist, it wasn't Oscar.'

'Don't confuse me, Sir Arthur,' said Lestrade, 'I can only handle seven cases at once. Tell me what happened before Dr Watson fell.'

'Before? Well, let me see. John and I were walking to the green. The eighth hole, it was. John was four under par and I needed a birdie—'

'May we leave your ornithological requirements aside for now, sir?'

'Then that damned Voisin appeared.'

'Voisin?' Lestrade was lost.

'Well, perhaps a Sopwith, then.' No response. 'It's an aeroplane, Lestrade. I've no time for them myself. The damned thing swooped down like a bird of prey, nearly clipping the tree tops. I'm going to write to *The Times* tonight, let me assure you . . .'

'What about the aeroplane?'

'Well, it spoiled my game. John's too. Didn't make any difference to poor old Willie's, of course.'

'What did you do?'

'I gave chase. The blighter was flying so low I thought he was trying to land. I was going to give him a piece of my mind.'

'Then?'

'Then he doubled back. They can turn on a sixpence, those things. Damn good, that pilot Johnny.'

'"Little Johnny Head-In-Air",' murmured Lestrade, feeling increasingly uneasy.

'What?'

'Nothing. What then?'

'Well, the blighter swooped down over the bunker again. I assumed that's what made Willie miss his aim and hit poor old John. Then he flew away.'

Lestrade rose slowly, staring straight ahead. He looked at the smashed lead pellet, still dark with John Watson's blood, cradled in his hand. 'Percy Hinchcliffe,' he said quietly, 'so *that* was how it was done.'

'What?' It was Conan Doyle's turn to feel lost.

There was a knock at the door and the burly sergeant entered. 'Where do you want 'im, sir?' he asked Lestrade.

'Sir Arthur, I would appreciate it if you did not discuss today's events with a living soul.' He looked down at the mortal remains of John Watson: 'Or even a dead one. Can you come to the Yard tomorrow at two?'

'Er . . . yes, of course. What of Watson's housekeeper?'

'Mrs Hudson?'

'Yes.'

'Leave her to me, Sir Arthur. Goodnight.'

'Look, Lestrade, I . . .' Conan Doyle began.

'Yes?'

'Nothing,' and he turned away.

'Here, Sergeant,' said Lestrade, 'on these tables.'

The constables laid the body down and removed the blanket. Lestrade crossed his arms over his chest and closed his eyes.

'Well, Watson,' he murmured when the door had closed behind him, 'so it's come to this. I wonder what the late Sherlock Holmes would have made of this.' He turned and put his bowler on. 'I daresay he'd have said it was Moriarty flying the plane.'

'It'll have to be quick, Alfred,' said Lestrade, emerging from the paperwork.

'Well, sir, it's like this,' Inspector Ward ousted Sergeant Jones from the nearest chair, 'I had a visit the other day from two gentlemen by the name of Vonderahe.'

'Jewish?' guessed Lestrade.

'I didn't look,' said Ward, 'but they had an interesting story to tell.'

'Go on.'

'It concerned a cousin of theirs, a Miss Eliza Barrow, who died recently.'

'Causes?'

'Ah, there you have it. The death certificate seems in order – "epidemic diarrhoea".'

'A lot of it about,' commented Lestrade.

Ward got the distinct impression that his guv'nor's mind was elsewhere.

'The point is the funeral and so on were arranged by Miss Barrow's landlord, a Mr Frederick Seddon.'

'So?'

'So the Vonderahes weren't invited. None of the family were. Seddon swears blind he wrote invitations and has the carbons to prove it.'

'The carbons to prove it?' Lestrade echoed. 'That's odd. What sort of man keeps carbons of funeral invitations? A man with something to hide?' Lestrade was back with his man.

'That's what I thought,' Ward concurred.

'Was she wealthy, this Miss . . . er . . . Barrow?'

'Seddon says not, but she did make a will in his favour shortly before she died.'

'Forgive me, Alfred, but I don't see your difficulty.'

'There's nothing concrete, sir. I think our hands are tied.'

'Epidemic diarrhoea?' Lestrade said, half to himself. 'I wonder. Have you been to Seddon's?'

'No, sir.'

'That's your next step, Alfred. Check out the old girl's room.' Ward made for the door. 'And Alfred . . .'

'Sir?'

'Keep an eye open for flypapers, will you?'

Ward looked confused. 'Er . . . yes, sir.'

'If you find any, see Sir Edward about an exhumation order. And then get hold of Bernard Spilsbury, the Home Office chappie.'

'Why him, sir, particularly?'

'Because he's about the only bloke apart from my good immodest self I'd trust to give us anything like an actual cause of death.'

'Very good, sir.'

Ward and Dickens nearly collided on the landing.

'Mr Churchill is here, sir,' said Dickens.

'Churchill?' Lestrade stood up. 'Straighten your tie, man. It's not often the Home Secretary pays a call.'

'No, sir . . .'

'Well, hop to it, Dickens. Don't keep the man waiting.'

'No, sir . . .'

Lestrade pushed the protesting sergeant into the outer office. A little man with a toothbrush moustache sat in the corner. 'Where is he?' asked Lestrade. 'Where's Mr Churchill?'

'At your service.' The little man stood up, proving to be not much taller than when he had been sitting down.

'Who the hell are you?' snapped Lestrade, having a vague sense that he had had enough for one morning.

'Mr Churchill,' said the little man.

Lestrade checked the calendar. No, it wasn't April the first. He searched the immobile features of Dickens and Jones. No hint of intelligence there.

'All right,' he said, 'I'm game,' and waited for the punchline.

'Superintendent Lestrade,' said the little man, 'I am a very busy man and I understand you require my help.'

'You're ... ah,' Lestrade tried to behave as though nothing had happened, 'Mr Churchill.' He extended a hand. 'Mr Robert Churchill.'

'The same,' said the little man.

'The Home Office's gun chappie,' Lestrade checked.

'I prefer the term "firearms expert",' said Churchill. 'Best of all I would like ballistics generalissimo, but that seems a little pretentious, don't you think?'

Since Lestrade didn't know what he was talking about, he remained non-committal. 'Thank you for coming so promptly. Dickens, tea!'

'Is it with lemon?'

'No, milk and sugar,' said Lestrade.

'Darjeeling?'

'Well, it's brown ...'

'Thank you, I won't. How can I help?'

Lestrade fumbled in his top drawer and placed three twisted lead pellets on the desk. He was startled as Churchill suddenly pitched forward so that his nose almost hit the wood. He surfaced again with an eyeglass jammed in his socket in what appeared to be an excruciating position.

'They're bullets,' he said.

Lestrade was unimpressed. 'Thank you, Mr Churchill. That far I had got.'

Churchill handled them one by one, weighing them in his hands, rolling them in his fingers, examining each one minutely. He even sniffed them in turn, then placed them in his pocket.

'Evidence,' Lestrade reminded him.

'Oh, they're quite safe,' said Churchill, 'I'll be able to give you a more detailed answer when I have examined them under my microscope.'

'I haven't asked a question yet,' said Lestrade.

'You want to know what sort of gun fired these. Am I correct?'

Lestrade nodded.

'Good day.' Churchill lifted his hat.

'Could you manage a guess?' Lestrade stopped him.

Churchill tutted. 'I prefer the word "surmise",' he said. 'Very well – and this is strictly off the record, the wildest of estimates – and I'm sorry it's so vague . . .'

'Yes?' Lestrade waited.

'Probably a Mauser nine-millimetre model, C/98 I'd say. Broomhandle. German manufacture is likely, but perhaps a Far-Eastern copy. Almost certainly used with a wooden rifle butt grip, which, as you know, also serves as a holster.'

Lestrade sat open-mouthed. 'You couldn't be more precise, could you?' he eventually said.

Churchill, who had the sense of humour of the cup of tea Dickens now brought in, tipped his hat again and left.

'So,' Lestrade scalded his top lip on the cup and tried to sound nonchalant, but the scream gave him away, 'it *was* a Mauser. Sir Clive Marchment was right. I'd give my pension to know how many of those there are in circulation.'

'Can't help you there, sir,' Dickens apologised. 'The number of dogs now, I know that.'

'Do you, Dickens?' Lestrade withered him with a glance. 'How singularly relevant.'

Dickens muttered as he turned his back. 'One million, eight hundred and twenty-six thousand, eight hundred and forty-one.'

'What was that, Sergeant?' Lestrade growled.

'I said,' Dickens beamed, 'Mr Stead is here to see you, sir.'

The gentleman of that name, still a little dazed by the previous day's events, entered Lestrade's office.

'Who would want to see John Watson dead?' Lestrade came to the point.

'I haven't a clue, Superintendent,' Stead answered. 'He was a kind, generous man. Less than kind to you, perhaps, in the *Strand Magazine* of a few years ago.'

Lestrade leaned forward. 'Are you suggesting *I* had a motive, Mr Stead?'

The journalist looked horrified. 'Good heavens, no, I ... I believe you're teasing me, Superintendent.' He caught the twinkle in Lestrade's eye.

'I'm afraid I am,' he said. 'Let me rephrase the question. Who would want to see *you* dead?'

'Me?' Stead was incredulous.

'You see, Mr Stead, what happened on the links yesterday was an accident. John Watson was killed by a bullet from an automatic pistol. A bullet which I believe was fired from the aeroplane which flew overhead when you and he were in the bunker. But he was not the target, Mr Stead. You were.'

Stead sat numbed in the chair. 'The Peace Movement,' he said.

'The Peace Movement.' Lestrade nodded. 'Let's talk about it, shall we?'

The Heart of the Mata

Inspector Alfred Ward had never encountered anyone quite like Mary Chater before. Mrs Seddon, whose maid she was, called her eccentric, but that struck Ward as being exceptionally kind. He'd taken Sergeant Peabody with him to give the man a change of air.

'Now remember,' he had said to him; 'you're looking for flypapers.'

'Ah, you'll want Boots the Chemists, sir.' Peabody was ever the resourceful policeman.

'No, man, at sixty-three Tollington Park, not Finsbury High Street. Keep your eyes open and your wits about you, assuming you've brought 'em, of course.'

'She's dead and buried,' Mary Chater had told them. 'You're the umpteenth body who's come pesterin' Mr Seddon about 'er. 'Tain't natural.'

'What isn't?' Ward had asked, smelling a whiff of a confession.

'All you people pesterin' Mr Seddon. 'E done so much for 'er that's gone. 'Ad a lovely set of mournin' cards printed, 'e did. Got 'em cheap. "A dear one is missing and with us no more; That voice so much loved we hear not again; Yet we think of you now the same as of yore . . ."'

'Yes, thank you,' Ward had said, and he and Peabody manhandled her aside to meet the lady of the house. It came as no surprise to either of them to learn that Chater had formerly been a mental nurse.

'She may not be a nurse any more,' had been Peabody's comment, 'but she's still bloody mental,' and he watched her in the kitchen eating potato peelings.

The rest was a matter of routine. Sticky brown flypapers twirled in what had been Miss Barrow's room. Mrs Seddon was decidedly agitated at the presence of the Yard men and she kept urging them to come back later – 'When Mr Seddon will be home.' But by that time Alfred Ward had got his exhumation order from Sir Edward Henry and had made his phone call to Bernard Spilsbury.

And the next day Lestrade received a strange summons. It came, delivered by hand, stamped all over with Admiralty embossings. It was a hand-written note asking him to come at once to the Admiralty and was signed 'Fisher'. Pausing only to reinstate, much against his will, the crestfallen Blevvins, but this time with the rank of uniformed constable, C Division, Metropolitan Police, in charge of water troughs, horses, for the drinking of, he made his way to the seat of the Royal Navy.

It was cold, even for November. The cheers were still ringing in his ears from the Yard where the news had just broken that Sir Winston Churchill had been shuffled in the Cabinet deck to the post of First Sea Lord. Considering the man had spent the best part of the last year condemning naval expenditure, it seemed an odd move indeed, but Lestrade's grasp of current affairs was never immaculate. Anyway, McKenna was Home Secretary now, having apparently done a swap with the aforementioned gentleman. As everyone knew, McKenna had a profound sense of duty. To his left Lestrade saw the Arch they had been littering his way with for the past two years while they built it and he turned into Horse Guards Parade.

He was escorted by a variety of boys in blue, not unlike his own, along a maze of tunnels, if possible more labyrinthine than those at the Yard. Beyond an oak door of formidable proportions he was left to stand in a panelled room hung with portraits of His late Majesty, King William IV, and a galaxy of beribboned admirals. None, however, was more brightly decorated than the one who clumped in through a side door.

'Lestrade?'

There was no mistaking the surly scowl and thatch of close-cropped silver hair.

'Lord Fisher.' Lestrade bowed a little, never quite knowing how low to go when in the presence of aristocracy, but remembering always that this was a self-made man, and he had been born in Ceylon.

'Excuse all this.' Fisher waved to the full dress uniform that hung like a gilded tent around his dumpy frame. 'I'm sitting for a portrait next door. Anyway, it gives my man something to do, polishing the medals. Grog, Lestrade?'

'No, it's Sholto actually, sir,' and even as the words hung on the air, Fisher reached for a bottle and looked oddly at the superintendent, 'but I believe Messrs Conan Doyle and Watson once wrongly gave me the initial "G".'

Fisher coughed, at a loss to know what to do with this conversation, and downed his rum. Assuming it to be a tradition of the Senior Service, Lestrade coughed and did likewise. He felt the steam hiss from his eardrums.

'Are you sure he's our man?' Fisher asked as the click of a door made Lestrade turn. The newcomer nodded. He was in a civilian suit and sported a gilt-edged monocle.

'May I present,' said Fisher, refilling glasses with the air of a man with vast capacity, 'Commodore Harp-Greavesley, Superintendent Lestrade.'

The two men shook hands and accepted Fisher's invitation to be seated. The ex-First Sea Lord unbuckled his sword-belt with some relief and slumped in the ornate chair that headed the long polished table.

'I won't beat about the bush, Lestrade,' he said, 'I asked you here this morning for a purpose.'

'Sir?' Lestrade noticed that the bottom of his glass where the rum had dribbled was rapidly taking the varnish off the table.

'Nigel here is head of NID. Ever hear of it?'

'I don't believe so, sir.'

Jackie Fisher chortled. 'Good. In fact, I'd be damned furious if you had – and worried. Tell him, Nigel.'

'NID stands for—'

'Naval Intelligence Division,' Fisher cut in, 'strictly hush-hush, Lestrade. Take my point?'

'Absolutely,' the superintendent replied.

'You remember Agadir, of course?' Fisher murmured.

Lestrade looked round to see who had come in.

'Back in June,' Fisher reminded him. 'The gunboat *Panther*.'

'Ah, yes.' Lestrade tried to bluff it out.

'It's the Hun, you see, Lestrade. Pray God the country will never know how close we came to war. Tell him, Nigel.'

'We came pretty close to war, Lestrade,' Harp–Greavesley confirmed.

'And there's more,' Fisher went on.

'There usually is,' said Lestrade, who was seriously toying with going out and coming in again.

'What do you know of the Peace Movement?' Fisher asked.

Lestrade sat up in his chair. Bells rang in his rum-fumed brain. 'A little,' he said.

'That's not enough, Lestrade.' Fisher slammed his fist down on the table. 'We have reason to believe that a German agent is in the country doing his utmost to make an Anglo–German war a reality. I want to know what you are doing about it.'

'Perhaps you should have consulted Sir Edward Henry, sir.' Lestrade was cautious.

'Lord Love Us?' Fisher roared. 'He's so wound up in fingerprints and coronation details he doesn't know his arse from his elbow.'

Lestrade was staggered to find that the Yard nickname for his superior had reached the inner sanctum of the Admiralty, but on reflection it *was* less than half a mile away.

'Tell him, Nigel.' Fisher reached for his flat bottomed decanter again.

'Do these names mean anything to you?' Harp-Greavesley handed Lestrade a typewritten sheet. It was a list of the victims whose murderer he had been trailing haplessly now for the past year and a half.

'They do,' he said, 'but there's a name missing.'

'Oh?' said Harp-Greavesley.

'William Stead.'

'Stead is dead?' Fisher asked.

'No, our friend missed him. He got Dr John Watson instead.'

'Who?' asked Fisher.

'Quite,' said Lestrade, 'how did you come by this information?'

'Well, we—' Harp-Greavesley began.

'We have our methods, Lestrade,' Fisher interjected, 'let that suffice.'

'If we'd been able to pool our resources a little earlier,' said Lestrade, 'some of these people might be alive.'

'Good God!' Fisher was on his feet, buckling on his sword again. 'Is that the time? I've an audience with the King in ten minutes. Nigel, I'll leave the details to you. I want this Hun bastard stopped, Lestrade. He is systematically wiping out the very people who can keep us out of war. Do you think I've been building up dreadnoughts all these years just to see them destroyed?'

He stopped at the door. 'Nigel, it couldn't *be* Admiral Beresford, could it?'

'No, sir.' Harp-Greavesley was apologetic.

'No, I suppose not,' Fisher sighed, and he left.

'Walk this way.' Harp-Greavesley made for the other door.

Another naval tradition, Lestrade assumed, and did as he was told. The commodore led the superintendent through a still more intricate network of corridors in the keel of the building. They came at last to a small office, festooned with documents in what appeared to be Chinese or Hindustani. Harp-Greavesley noticed Lestrade's interest.

'Code,' he said, by way of explanation. 'Can't be too careful, you know. Welcome to my Day Cabin.' A uniformed officer had joined them in the office. 'I gather you already know Captain Hook.'

Lestrade could see no Day at all. Not even a window.

'Captain?' he repeated.

Hook grinned broadly, pointing to the extra band of lace on his cuff. 'I think Jackie Fisher signed the wrong chitty. Morning, Sholto.'

'We're very informal here,' said Harp-Greavesley, to explain Hook's levity, 'and I wouldn't want to embarrass Ballard, but he's a first-class intelligence man.'

'So that's where Lord Love Us came from,' Lestrade murmured.

Hook chuckled. 'Sorry, Sholto. All's fair in love and war, you know. I had to keep abreast of your work on this case and feed what I could to Nigel.'

'You see,' said Harp-Greavesley, 'as Jackie Fisher implied, Superintendent, this isn't some elaborate game we're playing. It's for that reason we asked you here, to pool our resources, as you say, and to try to stop this man.'

'Sholto, you've been on the Force for a long time,' said Hook. 'You've seen all types. What do you make of our man?'

'He's generally efficient,' said Lestrade. 'To my mind, he's made only one mistake and that's in missing William Stead.'

'How do you account for that?' Hook asked.

'Difficult shot. I'm no expert – no ballistics generalissimo – myself, but our friend uses a Broomhandle Mauser. I think he killed Percy Hinchcliffe and John Watson the same way, by flying overhead at low level.'

'Risky,' commented Harp-Greavesley.

'But worth it,' said Lestrade. 'Fast getaway. No trace of vehicle.'

'The aeroplane is a new concept, Nigel,' mused Hook. 'Few people have seen one in the flesh. And to most people one type must look much like another.'

'I've lost track of the man-hours we've put in on this case,' sighed Lestrade. 'Checks and cross-checks. We've filled more shoe boxes than Lotus.'

'And what have you come up with?' Harp-Greavesley asked.

'Precious little. Our man is obviously intelligent, strong and a crack shot. He has knowledge of knots and rare poisons. Why do you think he's German?'

'Information from the other side,' Harp-Greavesley answered.

'You've used a medium on this?' Lestrade was incredulous.

'No, no,' Harp-Greavesley was at pains to point out; 'our man in Berlin. He tipped us the wink that a special agent, someone close to the Chancellery itself, had been sent over. His mission was to wreak havoc in Anglo-German relations and to encourage a xenophobic hysteria.'

'Ah.' Lestrade scanned the walls for a dictionary, but he was to be disappointed.

'He seems to be starting with the Peace Movement,' said Hook, 'silencing those whose writings or speeches might avert a war. Nigel will have told you about Agadir.'

Harp-Greavesley and Lestrade nodded sagely.

'One question,' Lestrade said. 'Why didn't you call in Superintendent Quinn? After all, he is Head of Special Branch.'

'You have Ballard here to thank for that,' said Harp-Greavesley. 'We wanted a man of intelligence, Lestrade. Ballard suggested you. I hope it wasn't neo-nepotism.'

They all chuckled, Lestrade, as always, taking his cue from the others.

'In fact, we've already spoken to Mr Quinn,' the commodore went on, 'and elicited what he knew. It didn't take long. One thing, however, emerged from that conversation.'

'Oh?'

'We think our man called himself, a little while ago, Peter the Painter.'

Lestrade was on his feet. 'The Painter?'

'Do you know anything? More than we do, I mean?' Harp-Greavesley caught Lestrade's enthusiasm.

'I don't know what you know. Ballard, when we went to Sidney Street . . .'

'Yes, I know. But we didn't have the connection then, so the Painter was just another faceless anarchist.'

'Quinn and Fred Wensley had him down as a Russian Jew,' said Lestrade.

Harp-Greavesley shook his head. 'If my guess is right, he's a German aristocrat. He needed friends in low places, so he contacted the Sidney Street anarchists. Is there any more news of him?'

Lestrade shrugged. 'There is a Sergeant Leeson who was wounded at Sidney Street who says he's seen the Painter since.'

'And?' Harp-Greavesley pursued the point.

'And we've taken thirty-four men in for questioning. Had to release them all, of course. Not a shred of evidence. One was the Bishop of Bath and Wells.'

'And Leeson?'

'Under suspension, pending urgent medical reports, I understand.'

Harp-Greavesley nodded.

'I was offered a *Mona Lisa* the other day', Lestrade remarked, 'that was supposed to have been stolen by the Painter. That makes the eighteenth *Mona Lisa* the Yard's recovered since August.'

Harp-Greavesley nodded again.

'Gentlemen,' Lestrade got up, 'your revelation has given me a new path to tread,' and, mixing his metaphors, 'I can't of course guarantee a crock of gold at the end of it.'

'We'll try anything,' said Harp-Greavesley. 'I confess, Lestrade, we are at our wits' end here.'

'Very well, then. I'll be away for a day or so. Shall I make contact with you here?'

'Better not,' said Harp-Greavesley. 'Ballard will be in touch. Nothing more natural than a prospective son-in-law meeting a prospective father-in-law, eh? Thank you for coming, Mr Lestrade. Let's hope we can crack this case together. Not a word to anyone at the Yard, I'm afraid. You understand.'

It was Lestrade's turn to nod. Hook walked with him to the sunlight.

'One last thing, Sholto,' he said. 'And I don't know how much faith we can place in it. Nigel doesn't like me discussing this theory. It is possible that our German agent is posing as an officer in the armed forces.'

'Ah, the Artist's Rifles,' suggested Lestrade. It was the biggest collection of cranks and misfits he could think of.

'It may be nearer to home than that, Sholto. A Navy man. One of ourselves.'

'Well, we'll see,' said Lestrade and shook Hook's hand. 'Want me to say hello to anyone at Ports . . . Pompey?'

'No, they'd only say I owed them money,' laughed Hook. 'By the way, did you ever talk to Jamie Snagge?'

'Not since he went to the Baltic, no. When's he due back?'

'Well, that's the funny thing,' said Hook, 'he was taken ill off Jutland. Apparently he's languishing in a Danish hospital somewhere. I'm rather worried about him. Sholto, there's another avenue we have yet to walk down, and, frankly, we need someone totally unknown in Navy and Intelligence circles. If I give you this address,' he tore off a sheet from his notepad, 'I want you to memorise it and destroy it. Visit the lady who lives there and say "Goodbye, Dolly Grey". Understand?'

'Er . . .'

'I can't say more. I'll be in touch. Good luck,' and he disappeared into the bowels of the Admiralty.

Lestrade caught the afternoon train. It was dark before he saw the glittering harbour lights at Pompey and he was relieved to be accosted only once as he paced the Hard in search of a boat. True, he was accosted by a sailor, a man obviously delighted with recent Admiralty directives that the wearing of ladies' apparel in the Navy was no longer punishable by death. But Lestrade had long ago ceased to be surprised by anything human nature threw at him, even when some of it tended to stick. He had missed the daily steam packet to the Isle of Wight by several hours and, it being very much out of season, nobody was anxious to help the pea-jacketed gentleman until he flashed a few coins. Then it was all hands to the pumps and a creaking old brig wallowed its way across in the total dark of a Solent night. There was only one cab at the pier head at Ryde and the growler on board was snoring loudly. Lestrade roused him and was treated to some of the more quaint anachronisms of the Island dialect before he closed the doors over his lap and the cab rattled off into the night. Through the sleeping countryside they sped, the hack keeping a regular pace, but jolting Lestrade at every step.

'Wouldn't it be easier to take the road?' Lestrade shouted.

The driver spat over his right shoulder in reply. 'This *be* the road,' he snarled.

At Hunnyhill, Lestrade had to get out and walk, the traces not being as sound as they might be, and at the prison gates the superintendent was careful to deduct a suitable sum from the growler's tip. The great silent black mass that was Parkhurst Gaol rose before him, dotted here and there with pinpoints of gaslight. Bolts slid, orders were shouted, steelshod boots rattled on dry cobbles. He was conducted through a series of yards flanked by row upon row of windows, like sightless eyes in a blank face. Then he was in, escorted by warders, grim in their blackness, along the wrought-iron landings and spirals of the central block.

At a cell marked '346A' the marching company halted, the grille in the door slid back and Lestrade was shown into a tiny, airless cell.

'Remove that,' he pointed to the bucket in the corner, 'and then yourselves.'

'I'm sorry, sir, we have our orders from the governor,' one of the warders explained.

'And now you have your orders from me,' Lestrade said quietly. There was something in his tone that made the man comply.

'Steinie Morrison,' Lestrade said, looking at the dishevelled heap under the coarse grey blanket in the corner.

The heap stirred, a gaunt yellow face emerged and the fingers clutched at the bedclothes. 'Who are you?'

'Superintendent Lestrade, Scotland Yard.'

'What do you want?'

Lestrade perched on the edge of the low, infested bed, crunching on the roaches as his feet positioned themselves. 'Why do you want to die, Steinie?' he asked.

Morrison, the once dashing, dapper-suited young man about Lavender Hill, turned his face to the wall.

'What's it to you, copper? I don't know you.'

'Yes you do, Steinie. After you were brought in. We had a little chat.'

'That was a long time ago.'

'All right. You know Mr Vensel,' Lestrade gave Wensley his Yiddish name.

Morrison looked at him. 'I know Mr Vensel,' he said, 'he put me here.'

'No, Steinie,' Lestrade shook his head, 'you put yourself here. By killing Leon Beron.'

'As God is my witness . . .' he still had the strength to shout.

'You said at your trial, when the judge put his black cap on, that you didn't believe there was a God.'

Morrison crumpled against the wall. 'I don't know what I believe any more.'

'Is it true you've asked for the death sentence to be carried out?' Lestrade asked.

Morrison nodded. 'Can you blame me, Mr Lestrade?' he

asked, waving an exhausted arm around the narrow, dark cell.

'When did you eat last, Steinie?' Lestrade asked.

Morrison shook his head. 'I don't remember,' he said.

'A ham sandwich, was it?'

'I don't touch that. I'm Jewish.'

'So was Leon Beron. So whose half-eaten sandwich was found near his body?'

Lestrade produced a cigar, lit it and passed it to Prisoner 346A. Morrison hesitated, then took it and puffed gratefully.

'All right,' said Lestrade, 'I'm going to give you a chance the judge didn't. What *really* happened to Leon Beron?'

For a long time Morrison lay silent, staring at the dark green door facing him. Then he said, 'Peter killed him.'

Lestrade stood up, crossing to the tiny window. His heart pounded. 'Peter?' he repeated.

'Peter Piaktow,' said Morrison, 'the Painter.'

Lestrade sat on the chair by Morrison's side. 'Tell me about it,' he said.

'I told Mr Vensel,' he said.

'But he didn't believe you, did he, Steinie? Try me.'

'Oy vey,' sighed the Jew. 'All right. One day, Sol Epstein came to see me. He had a job for me, he said. I said, me, a job, Sol? What for I want a job? I got the laundry. I got a few things going, Mr Lestrade. You know how it is.'

Lestrade knew.

'He said, Steinie, I can make you a few bob.'

'What for?'

'Shadowing Leon Beron. That was all, so help me.'

'Why did this Epstein want you to follow Beron?'

'He didn't say. Not at first. Then I leaned on him.' Morrison chuckled until the cough racked him. 'I used to be good at that, Mr Lestrade, until they put me in here.'

Lestrade looked at the wreck of a man before him. It had taken four constables and Fred Wensley to get him. When they transferred him from Dartmoor, he ran amok at Waterloo

Station and broke an officer's jaw. Looking at him now, Lestrade doubted whether the man could break wind.

'Sol told me Peter had asked him. I said who's Peter? And bit by bit he told me. A group of them had gone to ground with Sol as their front man. The Houndsditch Mob.'

'You knew them?'

Morrison shook his head. 'Only Sol. I'm not an anarchist, Mr Lestrade. All the same, I kept my mouth shut. I didn't know what they was up to, and that's how we all wanted it. I saw that. Only Leon got nosy.'

'What did you do?'

'I was closer to that man than his underwear. He kept asking me, what about the people at Sol's? he'd say. Forget it, I told him. Keep your schnozz out, you schmuck. He wouldn't.'

'And the Common?' Lestrade urged.

Morrison shook his head. 'Look, whatever you think, Mr Lestrade, Leon was a friend of mine. I didn't want to see him dead. I was taking him to a safe place on the Common. I left him near some bushes while I went on to see if it was all right. When I got back, he was lying where the coppers found him, his head bashed in already and the carving on his cheeks.'

'How did you know it was the Painter?'

'He was there. As I bent over Leon, he stuck his gun in my ear.'

'His gun?' Lestrade felt the back of his neck crawl. 'What sort of gun was it, Steinie? Like yours?'

'Like none I've seen before. It had a sort of box thing in front of the trigger.'

'A Broomhandle Mauser,' murmured Lestrade. 'You mentioned carving on Leon's cheeks. I saw that too. What was it?'

'Spic,' said Morrison. '"S" for spiccan – informer, Mr Lestrade. Peter was afraid Leon was going to blow the gaffe. He must have done it with his sailor's knife.'

'His what?'

'He carried a sailor's knife,' Morrison repeated.

'Peter was a Russian Jew?' Lestrade wanted confirmation.

Morrison shook his head. 'He claimed to be. And his Yiddish was good. Too good. If you asked me, Mr Lestrade, I'd say the painter was German – and high born.'

'That's what I'd say as well, Steinie,' said Lestrade. 'Why didn't any of this come out at your trial?'

Morrison raised his scraggy arms towards heaven. 'What was the point? I read the papers, mister,' he said. 'Coppers shot at Houndsditch. Shootin' in Sidney Street. Leon with his brains all over Clapham Common. The Painter did all that. And you still haven't got 'im, have you?'

Lestrade got up, tapping the iron door with his heel. 'That's not all he's done, Steinie,' he tucked his remaining cigars into the crawling lining of the man's jacket, 'but we will get him.'

Morrison stared at him, the dark eyes flashing. 'When you do, Mr Lestrade, give him one for Leon Beron. And for Steinie Morrison.'

The pieces were fitting into place. Slowly, with the air of a man looking for lost jigsaws under the sofa, Lestrade felt his way through the thick pile which was life. The rain lashed the carriage window as he sped north on that first day of December. Early morning saw him breakfastless, tired. Was he down-hearted? Yes.

The piece of paper in the pocket of his pea-jacket came to hand and mind again. He repeated its contents to himself a few times, then threw it from the window. Once in London, he went to the Yard, narrowly missing the waste products recently deposited by Sir Edward Henry's horse and changed into the more apposite though archaic Donegal. Endsleigh Gardens was typical of late-Regency London. He found No. 26 and rang the bell. An elderly lady answered, peering around the art nouveau stained glass they went in for in Bloomsbury.

'Not today, I've got three of them already.'

Lestrade checked his person to see what the old biddy could

possibly mean. He rang the bell again.

'Goodbye, Dolly Grey,' he said, when the old crone reappeared.

'Don't be impertinent, young man,' she said, and fetched him round the head with an umbrella. As he stumbled backwards down the steps, he was grateful she hadn't used the elephant's foot in which the umbrella had been housed. At the bottom of the steps he collided with a young lady of dazzling beauty whom he knocked into the gutter.

'A thousand pardons, madam.' Lestrade helped her up. 'Are you all right?'

'I zink zo,' she said. Lestrade could have cut her accent with an Apache knife. She extended her hand. 'My name is Dolly Grey.'

'Miss Grey.' Lestrade took the hand. 'Oh.' Realization dawned. He tipped his hat. 'Goodbye, Dolly Grey.'

'Goodbye,' she said, and climbed the steps. Lestrade hesitated, unsure in Nigel Harp-Greavesley's odd world of espionage what to do next. In the event, his problem was solved by an anguished cry from the top of the steps. He turned expecting to see Dolly Grey felled by a blow from the old lady. It was all Asquith's fault. Fancy giving them pensions. Whatever became of the workhouse? Miss Grey teetered at the top, clutching her ankle and looking faint. With a superhuman effort, Lestrade caught the young lady for a second time and, balancing himself between the porticoes, rang the bell with what passed for a nose. In a moment of horror, he realised that with the unconscious Miss Grey in his arms, he was now at the mercy of the redoubtable old hag of the umbrella. It came as a relief, then, when another face peered round the door.

'Mrs Mueller,' the doorman said, and fixed Lestrade with a malicious scowl. 'What have you done with her?'

'Caught her just in time,' answered the superintendent. 'Does she live here?'

'Of course. The third door on the right. I have a key.'

'Do you, now?' It was Lestrade's turn for the malicious scowl.

'Of course, I am the landlord. You've already met my wife.'
Lestrade grimaced at the homicidal octogenarian and backed
away.

'Bring her in here.' The landlord led the way into a tastefully
furnished room hung with velvet. A strange mingling of
perfumes hit Lestrade's nostrils as he laid the girl on the sofa. She
moaned and rolled her head from side to side. She was the most
lovely girl Lestrade had seen for a long time, with a wealth of
sable hair that tumbled loose over the Oriental pillows as he
removed her hat.

'I hope that's all you're thinking of removing, young man,'
snapped the landlord's wife.

'Police,' said Lestrade. 'This is an official enquiry. Would you
mind leaving us?'

'Yes, I would—' but Lestrade had pushed the protesting
pensioners through the door and locked it. He laid bowler and
Donegal on a chair and looked around for some brandy.

'Police?' Miss Grey seemed to have made an instant recovery.
Lestrade sat beside her. 'That's what I told them,' he said.
'Actually, Peter sent me.'

'Peter?' She sat up. 'How is he?'

'Well,' Lestrade hedged.

'Who are you?'

'Joseph Lister.' He used his favourite alias.

'You are English,' she said.

Lestrade nodded. 'Peter has many friends. You are . . .?'

'One of zem,' she said.

'No, I mean where are you from?'

Dolly Grey got up and found the brandy for which Lestrade
had been searching. 'I am from Java,' she said. Lestrade
acknowledged, along with the rest of the Yard, that Walter Dew
was the Oriental expert. But he had to admit, this woman had
none of the racial characteristics he would expect. She suddenly
flopped to the ground and flung both arms out to her left, resting
her lovely head on her shoulder. 'I am a dancer at the temple,'
she said.

Lestrade was unaware they had dancers at Courts of Law these days, but it was true he spent most of his time at the Bailey.

'So, you weren't hurt?' he asked her.

She laughed, handing Lestrade his brandy. 'Of course not. Zat was just a ruse to get you inside.' Their hands touched briefly. 'Zo,' she chinked her glass against his, 'we shall be working togezzer,' she said. 'We had better get to know one annuzzer. What were Peter's instructions?'

Lestrade was beginning to wonder what Ballard Hook had landed him with. 'I was to take orders from you,' he bluffed.

'Wait here,' and she glanced back coyly before vanishing behind the bead curtains.

For a long time Lestrade waited. When it seemed the coast was clear, he rummaged in the lady's drawers. Perfume, handkerchiefs. Nothing incriminating. No letters. Nothing to link her with the Painter. He checked the fringed mantelpiece, the Oriental dogs, the crystal chandelier lamps, the mirror.

'The gramophone,' she called from the next room.

'Thank you.' It was as though she had suggested where Lestrade might look next. He glanced up in surprise to make sure she hadn't noticed.

'Put it on,' she murmured.

He wound up the machine and placed the needle on the record. It scratched into life, not 'The Wings of a Dove' which he had expected, but some resonant, mystic hum that was totally alien to him. The bead curtain shimmered aside and Miss Grey glided into the room. Lestrade found himself sitting down involuntarily. Gone was the prim bodice and pelisse and the layers of petticoats. In their place was a lithe, dark body, and around hips and breasts tight, crusted leather garments barely concealed Miss Grey's all. She slithered along one wall, jerked her head from side to side as though to check whether her neck was broken and generally behaved like a demented marionette. Even so, despite himself, Lestrade's loins began to appreciate the gyrations of Miss Grey's hips, and the way she swivelled them, circling his nose with her navel, certainly made his eyes water.

He felt rather like a mongoose swaying before a cobra in the stereoscopes he used to enjoy as a child. She sprawled across him, one hand stroking his hair, the other expertly unbuttoning his trousers.

'Miss Grey . . .' he began, but his words were choked by her lips, followed swiftly by the cobra's darting tongue.

'Dolly . . .' he tried again.

'Call me Mata,' she sighed, her whisper in his ear sending shivers up his spine.

'Mata,' he obeyed her. 'About Peter . . .'

'Forget him, he's gone.' She had found the secret of his combinations. 'My, my, they're improving in their selection of agents all the time,' she murmured. Her head lowered to his lap when he heard a whirring sound behind him. He pushed her off and quickly buttoned himself up. Nothing. No one. She renewed the attack standing up, sliding a delicious thigh between his.

'I know he's gone,' Lestrade persisted, desperately fending her off. 'But what of the Cause?'

'To hell with the Cause,' she moaned. 'Take me, take me.'

Again Lestrade held her at arm's length. Wait till he saw Ballard Hook again. No wonder he hadn't done this himself. The woman was a man-eater. 'Madam,' he shouted, realising the ridiculousness of the situation.

'Mata,' she corrected him, flashing messages from her eyes. 'Let's make love.'

'That's very flattering,' he croaked, trying to loosen her stranglehold, 'at my age particularly. And no doubt at some other juncture I shall be delighted, but now we have much to discuss.'

At last she gave up the struggle and squeezed her breasts back into place. 'Very well,' she said. 'But first, annuzzer drink. I always zink zere is nothing worse than anarchy when you're stone cold sober.'

She poured them both a glass while Lestrade finished adjusting his dress. The gramophone was still playing its odd temple music as he accepted and quaffed the brandy.

'Now,' Mata sat beside him on the sofa, 'your instructions are as follows. The instructions given to me in his absence by der Haken . . .'

She sat smiling at him as his eyes crossed and he pitched forward into the pillows, his nose landing in her lap. 'Tut, tut!' She tapped him playfully around the head. 'You naughty policeman. Charlie,' she called to the wall behind her, 'he's all yours.'

'Mr Lestrade, sir.' A coarse voice he vaguely recognised woke the superintendent up. 'Oh dear, oh dear. Celebrating Christmas a little early, are we?'

Lestrade focused with difficulty on the helmet and the cape. That displeased him enough, but to find what grinned between the two was even more depressing. Constable Reginald Blevvins, Metropolitan Police. What depressed Lestrade even more was the cold, dead sensation all around him, and he realised he was slumped in a Metropolitan Horse Trough, the Donegal clinging to his numb body like a shroud. Blevvins helped him out and, as Lestrade's feet and legs had lost all feeling, had to continue to help him down the street.

'I won't say a word, sir, of course,' Blevvins reassured him. 'We all have our little peccadilloes.'

'You speak for yourself,' Lestrade managed through clenched teeth, remembering with a little pride that Miss Grey had thought his rather large. 'Get me to the Yard, Blevvins. What day is it?'

Blevvins gave Lestrade an odd look. Obviously his guv'nor was worse than he'd thought. 'Friday, sir.'

'Friday!' Lestrade stopped him. 'My God, I've lost two days of my life. It was the brandy.'

'Yes, sir, that would be it. It's a killer, brandy. Guaranteed to lay you flatter than a hedgehog under a drayhorse, brandy is. I remember the time—'

'Thank you, Blevvins. I have no wish to relive drinking bouts with you. Get a cab, for God's sake.'

Blevvins propped the shivering Sholto up against a lamp-post while he carried out his orders. As luck would have it, it was Alfred Bowes' hansom that creaked to a halt.

'Drunk, is he?' Bowes asked.

Blevvins nodded discreetly, but Lestrade whispered adamantly, 'No.'

Blevvins helped the ailing superintendent towards the vehicle.

''Ere,' squawked Bowes. 'He's soaking bloody wet. He's not getting in there like that. He's stinking.'

'It's the horse trough,' Lestrade explained, and for a moment the man's face seemed familiar. But since his vision was jigging up and down in time with the staccato snapping of his jaws it wasn't easy to focus and he thought no more of it.

'In my capacity as a constable of the Metropolitan Police,' Blevvins was pompous, 'I order you to take this man in your cab.'

'Or what?' Bowes, up on his perch, was still six feet or so taller than Blevvins.

The constable reached up to him. 'Or I'll kick your horse,' he whispered.

For a moment Bowes contemplated the pistol under his blanket. Blevvins saved his own life and perhaps Lestrade's too by what he said next. 'Take this man to Scotland Yard.'

'Delighted,' Bowes beamed, and steadied the hack, while Blevvins bundled the dripping detective into the cab.

'Have you got a bob, Blevvins?' Lestrade murmured. 'I appear to be financially embarrassed. Temporarily, of course.'

'Of course,' smiled Blevvins, and handed the coin to Bowes, who cracked the horse into motion.

Several people commented later that day how oddly that large policeman was behaving. The one who kept skipping down his beat, giggling to himself.

Lestrade dripped on Henry's carpet. He sprinkled water on Henry's cat. He had at least avoided the droppings of Henry's horse. But that was probably because the animal wasn't there. The place was like a morgue. Sergeant Peabody had saluted him uneasily at the desk. He'd got no more than an enquiring look from John Kane. And Frank Froest had patted his shoulder and turned away. All right, so he'd missed two days' duty and for that he was a leper? It didn't make sense. Not, that is, until he saw what lay on the assistant commissioner's desk.

'I've been back a week from Delhi,' Henry articulated through clenched teeth, 'I've seen it all. I've served most of my adult life in India. I've hunted jackals and played polo and I've been shot at by Boers on the veldt. But I've never, *never* heard of such disgusting behaviour by a senior police officer.'

Lestrade examined the photographs splayed on the desk. They showed Miss Dolly Grey, alias Mata, alias Mrs Mueller in compromising and seemingly impossible positions with a very senior police officer to whom Sir Edward was referring.

'That's not me,' said Lestrade.

'Not you?' Henry glowed purple under his Delhi tan. 'Of course it's you, Lestrade. Look!' He jabbed his finger down on the photographs.

'Oh, it's my face all right, probably me from the waist up, but below the waist, never.'

'You mean this . . . your . . . how do you know?' Henry scrutinised his lieutenant carefully.

'I am fifty-eight years old, sir,' said Lestrade, 'various parts of my anatomy have been with me for as long as I can remember. That is not me.'

'Are you telling me your . . . ?' Henry stood up.

Lestrade leaned forward and whispered in his ear, turning his hands in a variety of ways like an angler telling a story of one that got away.

'You're not just boasting, Lestrade?' Henry asked him. 'If there's one thing I can't abide more than a degenerate, perverted policeman, it's a boastful one.'

'You have my word, sir.'

Henry paced the floor. 'By now,' he said, 'the whole of the Yard will know about these. I shouldn't be surprised if they aren't in the *News of the World* the day after tomorrow. I shall need more than your word.'

'You mean . . .?'

Henry looked his man straight in the eye. 'I shall need evidence, Lestrade.'

Silence hung in the air while Lestrade steamed, what with the water and the humiliation.

'Evidence,' he repeated.

'Of two types, I should have thought.' The man who had created the Fingerprint Department was ever the scientific policeman. 'One: the laboratory will try to establish whether these photographs are fakes, been pasted together somehow. And two: er . . . it will be necessary to . . .'

'Would you accept the word of the Metropolitan Police doctor?' Lestrade clutched at the only remaining straw.

'Doctor Straw? Certainly.'

Lestrade sighed silently in relief. At least his manhood wasn't going to end up as exhibit B in the cross-examining clutches of a King's counsel.

'Now, Lestrade, who is she?' Henry returned to the photographs. 'Powerful young filly, by the look of her.'

'I am not at liberty to say, sir,' Lestrade replied.

Henry looked up, eyes watering. 'Dammit, Lestrade. You may be able to wriggle out of this by the skin of your . . . um . . . but that's a technicality. You admit the upper portion of the body in these photographs is you. That means you must have had *some* physical liaison with her.' He snatched up the photographs. '*And* you're enjoying it, man! Look, your eyes are closed.'

'That's because I was unconscious, sir,' Lestrade explained calmly.

Henry hovered over his desk, waving the photographs under Lestrade's bedraggled moustache. 'Who is she, Lestrade?' he asked again.

'I'm sorry, sir.' Lestrade stared straight ahead, 'I really cannot tell you.'

'You're facing suspension,' Henry wheedled. 'You realise that?'

Lestrade realised. Edward Henry circled the steaming superintendent a few times. He tried the gentle touch. Softly, softly.

'Well, we'll talk later. Let's get you out of these wet things, Sholto. Come home with me now. You can borrow some things of mine. A hot bath and a good meal will do you good. Lady Henry has wheatears.'

For the life of him Lestrade couldn't imagine why Sir Edward should be so rude about his wife, but the dry clothing sounded good. He was also grateful that the assistant commissioner ordered round car and chauffeur to take them both home. He hadn't fancied the six-mile walk even if he didn't have to hang on to the polo player's stirrup irons. He was grateful, too, when he saw Henry lock the offending material away in his office safe.

They drew up outside Camden House Court and Henry waved to little Hermione, who beamed at him from her bedroom window. Lestrade's Donegal had assumed the wrinkled look of a very old sheet and his body felt much the same. No one noticed the hansom parked unobtrusively under the planes across the road. No one noticed the cabman climb down and remove something from under the blanket.

'That's all for tonight, English,' Henry said to his chauffeur, 'Superintendent Lestrade will be able to find his own way home.'

The cabman walked up to Henry. 'Excuse me,' he said in his

belligerent Acton tones, 'I want a word with you.'

'Not now,' the commissioner answered, 'I'm busy. I suggest you telephone my office.'

Even as he finished, Alfred Bowes drew his pistol. Lestrade reacted first and leapt at him but not before the gun had fired once, the bullet smashing into Henry's chest. Lestrade struggled with Bowes, grappling for the gun as shots rang out in the quiet evening mews. Lestrade's knee came up into Bowes' groin and the growler jack-knifed as he went down. By the time the chauffeur had got out of the car it was all over. Henry was hanging on his front door, his hysterical daughters clambering all over him.

'Let me go!' Bowes shouted as the chauffeur took Lestrade's place on the cabman's chest. 'This man has done me a great wrong. Let me go!'

'Lestrade?' Henry lolled back in a chair in the hall, blood drenching his shirt and waistcoat. 'Is that you?'

The superintendent held the commissioner's hand. 'I'm here, sir.'

'I don't think I'll have the wheatears tonight,' and he rolled gracefully onto the floor.

Victory

Assistant commissioners through the ages had tried to root out the infestation that was the sergeants' stews in the basement of Scotland Yard. To a man, they had failed. And so it was that Sergeants Peabody and Jones faced each other over a cup of cocoa and a game of dominoes that Christmas Eve.

'You mean he just went like that?' Jones asked.

'Like that.' Peabody snapped his fingers. 'One minute he was standing outside his front door; the next, poof, he was gone.'

'Well, I'm blowed.'

'Yes, when that Great Commissioner in the sky calls, there's no time to put on your helmet.'

'How's his family taking it?' Jones asked.

'I suppose in their shoes they learn to expect such things.'

'Is it right Lestrade was with him at the end?'

Peabody nodded. 'Died in the guv'nor's arms, he did.'

'My God.' Jones gazed wistfully into the middle distance. 'And he was no age.'

'Eighty-five next March.'

'Never,' asserted Jones.

'As I live and breathe.' Peabody was adamant.

'Well, they don't make coppers like George Dixon any more.' Jones grew philosophical.

'But hold on. You couldn't have known him. He retired years ago.'

'You forget my old man was on the Force. Dixon was in the

Bluebottles before he got the front desk job.'

'Oh yes. Talking of coppers they don't make any more,' said Peabody, 'how's Lord Love Us?'

'Right as rain, last I heard. I don't know what the Great British Murderer is coming to, Buildings. That growler shot him at point blank range and all he got was a scratch.'

Peabody tutted and shook his head. 'You know,' he said, 'I've got a theory about dominoes . . .'

Jones nudged his elbow and all of them crashed to the floor.

'Never mind, Buildings. It's a minute to midnight.' He poured some Scotch from a hip flask into their cocoa. 'Merry Christmas, Tom.' He raised his cup. 'Here's to crime.'

'To crime,' echoed Peabody, and they drank deep.

'Merry Christmas, my love.' George Wilkins reached over, holding the mistletoe above his head, and kissed his new bride.

'And to you, my sweetheart.' Freda stroked the gaunt cheek, the thick, bristling moustache. She giggled as he ran his fingers over her breasts. 'Ooh, no,' she scolded him. 'Not now, dear one. It's Christmas.'

'Well then, Santa won't be the only one who's coming,' he beamed.

She sat bolt upright on the sofa before collapsing into fits of laughter. 'You're dreadful, George Wilkins,' she upbraided him gently.

'Let's retire early,' suggested Wilkins, now rich enough to do so. 'I've boiled the water for your bath.'

'Oh, how kind, my love,' she cooed.

He unhooked her bodice and helped her out of her layers of petticoats. She swayed and giggled. 'George,' she said, 'I do believe I'm tight as a tick.'

'Well, dearest sweet,' he ran his fingers tantalisingly over her bare shoulders, 'we'll soon put that to rights, won't we?'

She folded over, giggling helplessly. He caught her deftly and swung her up into his arms, carrying her up the twisting snake of the stairs. She rocked backwards and forwards on the landing, while he stripped away her chemise. 'Ooh, it's cold.' She shivered.

'The bath will warm you, dearest,' he said and he helped her in.

She stretched out so that her breasts bobbed on the water's surface. They reminded her husband momentarily of fried eggs in a pan.

'By the way,' he said, 'Freda, heart, did you make the necessary arrangements at the Post Office today?'

'I thought I'd told you.' She luxuriated in the steamy water while he rolled up his shirt sleeves. 'All I have to do is go along on Boxing Day and sign for the money . . .'

'No, dearest.' His tone was suddenly harsh, then sweeter: 'Don't you remember? I asked you to let *me* take the money out for you. I didn't want you to have to be bothered with it further.'

'Oh, yes,' she chuckled. 'They said that would be all right. Only I couldn't remember why you wanted it in the name of Smith, dearest love.'

'I explained to you, my sweet.' He soaped his hands carefully. 'That's how things work in the City. When you have as many investments as I, people become jealous. What with the shipping lines, the silver mine . . . It doesn't do to use your own name.'

'Ah, I see,' she hiccoughed.

'Do you, darling?' He placed his hands under her knees. 'Well, I'm glad, because, you see, that isn't something you'll need to do again.'

And he jerked her legs up and out of the bath so that her head and body dipped under the water. He stood up, locking his arms tightly around her thighs, avoiding the madly kicking feet and jamming his own foot into the bath so that it rested firmly on her throat. She thrashed wildly, spraying foam and water over the carpet, causing the fire to spit and flare. Once, twice, her hands came up at him, clawing the air in her frenzy. Then the bubbles stopped and he felt her legs fall slack. He stepped out of the bath, shaking one soggy shoe, and dropped her feet so that they flopped grotesquely over the edge. He watched for a moment as her face floated up, eyes staring and glazed, hair plastered to her head. He took the glass of brandy from the sideboard and raised it to the corpse of the recently departed.

'Merry Christmas, my love,' he said. 'Here's to crime.'

The shooting of Sir Edward Henry was an open and shut case. The victim himself, not to mention Superintendent Lestrade; English, the chauffeur; Henry's two daughters and other potential passers-by, could all bear witness to what had happened. At first the truculent Alfred Bowes tried to imply that all the above had suffered the same mass hallucination. When that failed he fell back on his usual ploy about conspiracies. After all, Sir Edward Henry, for reasons of his own, was denying Bowes the right to drive a motor taxi. Would such a man stop short of accusing the said Bowes of murder too? And when the range of eye witnesses was pointed out to Bowes, it surprised him not one jot. They were, after all, Henry's family and cronies. *They were all in it together.*

After precisely six minutes in the Charge Room with Superintendent Lestrade, Bowes had changed his plea to guilty. For most people there was no more to be said, but busy as he was Lestrade was a thorough policeman. And so he returned the next day to Camden House Court, where a much less distraught Henry family were enjoying the last of Christmas.

'But what I can't understand . . .' Henry's eldest daughter Helen was saying.

'Now, Helen,' her mother scolded her, 'the superintendent is a busy man. He's already saved dear Papa's life and you must take up no more of his valuable time.'

'It's all right, Lady Henry,' he said, knowing the ways of policemen's daughters himself. 'What is it, Miss Helen?'

'What was that other man doing?'

'Other man?' Lestrade's smile began to fade.

'The man Hermione saw,' she said. 'The other man with a gun.'

Lestrade spun round to little Hermione, who clutched her new teddy bear as though her life depended on it. He knelt beside her. 'Miss Hermione,' he said, 'I want you to think very carefully. The night your Papa was hurt, did you see another man?'

Hermione nodded.

'Where was he?' Lestrade asked. 'Show me.' He held out his hand and the family toddled off down the hall to the front steps.

'Over there,' Hermione pointed to a clump of planes, near which Bowes had parked his hansom.

'This man,' Lestrade tried to remain calm. 'Can you remember what he looked like?'

Hermione wavered, looking at the fierce burning eyes of the superintendent. She looked at her mother and her sister. Back to Lestrade again. But she saw there, beyond the yellowed, scarred face and the heavy moustache, a kindly twinkle with which she felt somehow safe.

'He had a beard,' she said. 'He was a tall man.'

Lestrade stood up. To somebody of Hermione's age and height anybody but a midget would have been tall. Unless, of course, the midget had been a master of disguise.

'What did he do, Miss Hermione?' Lestrade crouched beside her again.

'As that man came towards Papa—' she started.

'Mr Bowes?' Lestrade checked.

'Yes. As he came forward I saw this other man come out from behind the trees. He pointed a gun. Then I heard a bang and saw you fighting with the man on *this* side of the street.'

'What did the other man do?' he asked.

'I don't know. When I saw that Papa was hurt, I ran down to help him.'

Lestrade squeezed her hand. 'You're a brave little girl,' he

said. 'Miss Helen, Lady Henry, did either of you see this man?'
They shook their heads. Lestrade bent down again to Hermione.
'I want you to shut your eyes tight,' he said to her, 'and think as
hard as you can.'

Little Hermione did as she was told.

'The other man's gun,' he said. 'Did it have a sort of box in
front of the trigger, where his hand would be?'

'Yes,' said Hermione. 'It was a Broomhandle Mauser all
right.'

Lestrade stood up with astonishment.

Lady Henry chuckled. 'It's not so surprising, Superintendent,'
she said, 'Edward has a whole case of guns in his study. He
bought the Mauser only recently. I've told him it's not healthy
for girls to be interested in such things.'

'How recently, ma'am?' Lestrade asked, 'did your husband
buy his Mauser?'

'Last month, I believe.' She took Lestrade aside. 'Superintendent, like most policemen Edward is very cagey about his work.
But, like most policemen's wives, I do manage to wheedle a little
out of him. I know you are looking for a killer with a Mauser.
Do you imagine my husband is capable of being on two sides of
the street simultaneously and arranging his own attempted
murder?'

Lestrade placed the bowler on his head and patted it into place.

'No, ma'am,' he said. 'I think Sir Edward is capable of many
things, but not that.'

'Then what is the significance of the other man? Did Bowes
have an accomplice?'

'I don't think so, Lady Henry.' Lestrade shook his head. 'I
believe Alfred Bowes was strictly a unique experience.' He
looked into the woman's worried eyes. 'No cause for alarm,' he
assured her. 'The other man was not after your husband,
ma'am. He was after me.'

Lestrade checked the Sunday papers for the next three weeks, just in case his face and somebody else's anatomy should indeed appear. He needn't have worried. The photographic evidence of his encounter with Dolly Grey remained locked in Sir Edward Henry's safe. The superintendent offered up a silent prayer of thanks to the belligerent little Acton growler. After all, Lord Love Us was too busy nursing his chest to worry about suspending Lestrade or even to pursue the little matter of how Lestrade came to be in the presence of the photogenic lady in the first place. He went back to Endsleigh Gardens, flashed his credentials at the elderly couple in the foyer and insisted they show him to her rooms. The lady they knew as Mrs Mueller had suddenly vacated her premises the day after the gentleman had called. She had been called away to visit a sick relative and there was little chance of her returning. She had paid them a month's rent and had vanished as suddenly as she had arrived. The elderly couple were a little surprised as Lestrade checked each room systematically, tapping mantelpieces, looking up chimneys, peering into recesses. As he wiped his face to remove the soot, he suddenly lay on the floor in the position of the settee and turned to note the position of the wall behind him. They looked at each other, first in astonishment, then in fear, as the Yard man began tapping his way along the wood-panelled walls. They clutched each other convulsively as he reached one section and the wall swung aside. They all three peered into a small room hung with black.

'It's a photographic studio,' said Lestrade. 'Mrs Mueller's other hobby. Did the lady have any gentlemen callers?'

'There was you,' the old landlady sneered at him.

'*Apart* from me, madam.' Lestrade was the epitome of patience.

'There was that bearded gentleman,' the old landlord reminded her.

'Oh, yes, he reminded me of the King. Such a nice boy. And doesn't he do a good job of running the country?'

Lestrade hoped his basilisk stare would do the trick. It didn't.

The old woman stayed on her feet, marginally mobile.

'Did this bearded caller have a name?' he asked.

'He was a tradesman. He came to decorate a couple of times. Mrs Mueller didn't know him,' the landlord volunteered, as though to correct his demented wife's testimony.

'Decorate?' Lestrade checked the walls blackened with oil-lamp smoke. 'No one's decorated in here for years.'

'I've got his card here somewhere,' said the landlord, and he disappeared to fetch it. Lestrade gave the landlady a wide berth in case she resorted to her former tactics with the umbrella.

The old boy returned. 'Here it is,' he said.

'"Mr Rock",' Lestrade read out loud. '"Interior Decorator". How's your New Testament?'

'Eh?' the couple chorused.

Lestrade spoke louder. 'The New Testament,' he said. 'Who is called the Rock?'

'Peter,' they said in unison, products of the Methodist Revival as they were.

'Exactly,' mused Lestrade, 'Peter the Painter. Good day.'

'Sholto, I'm sorry,' Ballard Hook chuckled, 'I was wrong to send you to Bloomsbury. I should have used one of our chaps. The trouble is it's difficult to know whom to trust these days. McPherson's sure there's a Mudewarp in the Navy.'

Lestrade accepted the captain's outstretched drink. 'You know, Ballard, I always think we'd fare better if we all spoke the same language.'

Hook laughed. 'I'm sorry, Sholto. McPherson is my opposite number on Nigel's team. A mudiewarp is a mole, our code for an inside man, an informer.'

'Spiccan,' said Lestrade.

'What?'

'Our code for an inside man.' Lestrade smiled. 'That woman had a damn good shot at ruining my career,' he said. 'Tell me about her.'

'Mata Hari?' said Hook. 'There's not a lot we know. She's Dutch, sometime wife of a man called Mueller. She's a temple dancer from Java and she's in the pay of Germany, we think.'

'She certainly knows the Painter,' Lestrade said. 'Would you like his card?'

'His card?' Hook was incredulous. 'Are you serious?'

Lestrade handed it to him.

'I've checked it for fingerprints, of course. Put our man Collins through his paces.'

'And?' Hook leaned forward.

Lestrade shook his head. 'Clean as a bos'n's whistle,' he said.

'Well, there it is. I've got a feeling we've missed our man, Sholto. I think the Painter's gone.'

'I'm not so sure,' said Lestrade.

'Oh? Why's that?'

'Well, for one thing, he missed William Stead. If I read the Painter right, he's a professional. Everything is planned, careful, meticulous even. I also think he's too good to waste on small-fry like the Peace Movement. I think they were just practice for the big one.'

'Ah, a sort of hors d'oeuvre, you mean?'

'That's easy for you to say.' Lestrade quaffed his drink, hoping he had responded correctly.

'Who's your big one?' Hook asked.

Lestrade stared into the fire. ' "Last year",' he quoted, ' "in Marienbad".'

'What?'

'Nothing.' He stood up. 'Ballard, you'll have to bear with me. I think I know what the Painter has in mind, but I need to be able to prove it. It would be easier if I could use the Yard's resources.'

'Sorry, Sholto, we just can't risk it. There's too much at stake.'

Lestrade nodded and slapped the captain's arm. 'By the way, how's that daughter of mine? When do you intend to make an honest woman of her?'

'It's a leap year,' beamed Hook.

'I don't follow.'

'Traditionally, ladies propose to gentlemen in leap years, Sholto.'

Lestrade laughed. 'I see. So the ball's in her court?'

'I don't know about that. She's a fair hand with her diabolo set, though,' and Lestrade braved the bitter night.

Morning found him in the Round Tower at Windsor, head bowed before his King.

'Mr Lestrade, is it?'

'Your Majesty. Thank you for this audience, sir.'

'Well, I can't give you long.' The King fumbled in his pockets. 'Got a cigarette?'

'No sir, I only smoke cigars.'

'Ah well, break the habit of a lifetime.' He held out his hand while Lestrade lit a match. 'Oh, have one yourself, dear fellow. But . . . er' – he became confidential – 'if you should happen to see my wife, don't mention this, will you?' He threw his head back. 'Queens, eh?' and tutted. 'Now, to the point.'

'It concerns your late father, sir,' said Lestrade.

'Ah, yes. Most things do, I've noticed. Terrible being a new boy, isn't it?' He noticed the grey hair, the lined face. 'Not that you'd know, of course.'

'Shortly after His late Majesty's death, I received a letter from him.'

'No, I'm sorry, Lestrade. I've never shared Grandmamma's belief in the hereafter. He must have written it before he died.'

'Quite so, sir,' Lestrade humoured him. After all, he was new to the job. 'He mentioned Marienbad. He said, or rather implied, that something had happened there. Something that frightened him. This would have been three years ago now.'

The King paced about, flicking ash expertly into pot-pourris with the air of a practised neurotic.

'Yes,' he said. 'I remember Papa was at pains to keep that quiet. The press did their best of course to get their less-than-perfect teeth into it. I expect they'll be publishing his private correspondence one day—' He suddenly broke off to yell out of the window, bitter day though it was: 'David, who's that with you?' he called to the orchard below.

Lestrade heard a muffled voice answer.

'Wallis who?' the King asked.

Another muffled answer.

The King shut the window, then threw back his head. 'Princes of Wales, eh?' and tutted. 'I'll be glad when he's gone up to Oxford. Now, where were we?'

'Marienbad, sir. Nineteen-o-nine.'

'Ah, yes,' the King sat down, puffing on the cheroot like a man facing a firing squad, 'there was an attempt on Papa's life. Oh, it wasn't the first, I'll grant you. He normally bounced back from them. But this one came close, damn close. No one was ever caught, of course. But rumour had it the assassin was a German naval officer. Close to the top brass.'

'And he used a Broomhandle Mauser,' said Lestrade.

'Good God,' said the King, 'so we didn't play it down all that well, then?'

'Yes, sir, you did. I am merely putting two and two together.'

'I see. Well, Papa had it out with Willie, of course. There was a terrible scene.' He threw his head back. 'Kaisers, eh?' and tutted.

The door burst open and another bearded man entered, shinier, better groomed, in the undress frock coat of the Guards.

'Oh, Nicky.' The King leapt up. 'Not now. I'm rather busy.'

Nicky made to go, but Lestrade stopped them both with a rather curt 'No. Wait.'

'Lestrade,' said the King, 'I am King of England. This, since the cat is rather out of the bag, is His Majesty, Nicholas, Tsar of All the Russias. Has no one ever told you it is not the done thing

to give orders to Emperors?' He turned to Nicky. 'Superintendents, eh?' and tutted, forgetting, in his annoyance, to throw
back his head.

'Forgive me, Your Majesties, but I believe this to be a matter
of life and death. May I ask, sir,' he addressed Nicky; 'is it
common knowledge that you are in the country?'

'Have you got a cigarette?' Nicky asked in impeccable
English. 'I'm gasping for a smoke.'

Lestrade wearily produced his box of cigars.

'Havana?' Nicky asked.

'Yes, sir.'

'No thanks, I only smoke Turkish. In answer to your question
... er ... Superintendent ... no, I am here by personal invitation of my cousin here. No need to involve you fellows of
the Okhrana, eh?'

'With respect, Your Majesties, these are dangerous times. We
must—'

'No, Lestrade,' the King remained adamant, 'Nicky and I
haven't seen each other in months. This is not a State occasion,
with pomp and circumstance. It's a holiday. Nicky is incognito.
At the moment he's posing as an extra ADC from the Guards.
That uniform is quite fetching, old boy.' The King poured a
brandy for the Tsar. 'At the review, he'll pose as my Naval
Attaché.'

'Review?' Lestrade echoed.

'Tomorrow. At Portsmouth. No fuss, Lestrade. Distinguished
as Nicky is, I'm afraid he's not widely known in this country.
And in uniform his own mother wouldn't know him.' He threw
back his head. 'Dowager Empresses, eh?' and tutted.

'Sir.' Lestrade closed in on the King. 'I have reason to believe
that the Tsar's life certainly, yours probably, is in the gravest
danger.'

'Come, come, Lestrade. You mustn't let Marienbad colour
your judgement. This is England.'

'Yes, Your Majesty. The same England that has seen the

deaths of many a good man – and one good woman – in the last two years. A good many quiet corners of your Kingdom, sir, have been witness to violent deaths of late. London, Virginia Water, Bognor—'

'Oh, bugger Bognor, Lestrade. What is your point?'

Lestrade closed even further on the King. 'The point, sir, is that the German naval officer who tried to kill your father is now in England. He has killed already, several times, systematically removing people he sees as a threat to worldwide aggression.'

'Here in England?'

Lestrade nodded. 'And he's waiting for his chance, sir. We have reason to believe that the man is an assassin working for the German government. His job is to destroy all that remains of Anglo-German friendship. Just imagine what an opportunity you've given him. Two crowned heads of Europe, neither exactly enchanted with the state of affairs in Berlin. It's heaven-sent.'

'But no one knows Nicky's here,' the King objected.

'Peter the Painter knows,' said Lestrade. 'Don't ask me how, but he knows.'

'Peter the Painter?' the King repeated. 'That anarchist chappie in the East End? I thought he was one of yours, Nicky?'

'No, you're thinking of Joseph Stalin – he's one of mine.' Nicky had found a loose cigarette in a drawer and was savouring it.

'He has many aliases,' said Lestrade. 'He befriends retired magistrates on walks by the sea, he stops to help lady motorists who have broken down . . .'

'Lady motorists, eh?' The King and the Tsar *both* threw back their heads and tutted.

Lestrade slammed his hand down on the nearest table. 'Gentlemen,' he growled. 'I'm trying to save your lives and perhaps stop a war. I—'

'You're impertinent, Lestrade.' The King stopped him. 'One

word from me and I could have you pounding your beat again.'

'I am aware of that, sir,' Lestrade was calmer, 'but I must beg you to cancel all your public engagements and I humbly request that His Majesty the Tsar goes home by the next Continental boat.'

The King took Lestrade's arm. 'Superintendent,' he said, 'I don't want you to think me ungrateful. Believe me, I can rest easy in my bed knowing such men have our welfare at heart. But if people like us – Kings and so on – start hiding under our beds every time some maniac—'

'The Painter is not a maniac, sir. He is a ruthless, calculating assassin. We don't get too many of those in this country.'

'My point exactly,' the King beamed, leading Lestrade to the door. He whispered, 'Now, Nicky *does* have problems. They got his Prime Minister the other day, you know. Ruskies, eh?' and he threw back his head.

'Sir,' Lestrade fired his last salvo, 'the Painter missed your father in Marienbad. He's had a lot of practice since then. I can't guarantee he'll miss you.'

The King patted the Donegalled shoulder. 'Don't worry, dear fellow. We'll just get the Naval Review over tomorrow and I'll send Nicky home. Everything will pass off smoothly, you'll see.'

Lestrade cranked the Lanchester into life and screamed along the Royal Mile before driving through the foggy quiet of Virginia Water.

'Sholto!' A voice hailed him from the roadside.

He snatched at the handbrake. 'Fanny.' His grim face broke into a smile. 'How are you?'

'How am *I*?' She reached up and held his hand. 'I read about that lunatic who shot Edward Henry. He could have killed you too.'

He noticed the anxiety stamped on her quiet face. He lifted her chin. 'But he didn't. Can I drive you somewhere?'

She climbed up beside him, nuzzling into his shoulder and

tucking her hands into her muff.

'Where were you going?' he asked.

'Just walking,' she said. 'It was a nice morning before the fog came down. I passed that cottage again. You know – Philomena Marchment's. It's even sadder now than when we saw it last. What are you doing here?'

'Trying to give an idiot some advice.' He threw back his head and tutted. 'Battenbergs, eh?' he said.

'By the way, I bumped into that shy young man the other day,' she said.

'Young man?' he asked, slowing for the sheep to cross the road.

'Yes, that naval chappie who was looking at Philomena's cottage. Jamie Snagge, wasn't it? He's grown a beard. Very fetching.'

Lestrade let the engine idle. 'When did you see him, Fanny?'

'Let me see. Today's Wednesday ... Monday afternoon. Up in town.'

'What was he doing?'

'I've no idea. He was in mufti and didn't seem to want to talk. He raised his hat but hurried away. I think women frighten him.'

Lestrade drove into the forecourt of Tom Berkeley's country house.

'You're coming inside?' she asked him.

There was nothing he would have liked more. Fanny Berkeley, warm, soft, and a cosy fire. He wrenched himself away. 'I can't,' he said, and urged the Lanchester into gear. 'By the way, I'd ask my daughter this if she were here. See if Monsieur Le Petomaine's Academy for Young Ladies is worth all the money Harry Bandicoot and I have poured into it over the years. How's your German?'

'My German?' Fanny laughed. 'Rather idiomatic, I'm afraid.'

Lestrade didn't believe that. He knew Fanny Berkeley well enough to know she was far from being an idiot.

'At least,' he said, 'I *think* it's German. Something a rather persuasive young lady said to me recently . . .'

Fanny arched an eyebrow. 'Do you think I should be listening to this, Sholto?'

'What does the word "Haken" mean?' he asked.

'Haken?' she repeated. 'Well, if my memory serves me correctly, it means a problem.'

'A problem?' Lestrade was none the wiser.

'Yes, you know, a hitch, a snag.'

Lestrade's eyes widened in realisation. He reached down and kissed her, the Lanchester's engine screaming as he drove like a madman for the gate. Luckily he missed it and went straight through.

'I love you, Sholto Lestrade,' whispered Fanny to herself. 'Mind how you go.'

The sun danced and sparkled on the waters of the Solent. It was barely dawn and Lestrade had been up all night. There hadn't been time to enlist the services of his sergeants, nor indeed to inform the Yard of his whereabouts. He trusted to luck and to the Apache knife in his pocket, as he stood like a gargoyle on top of the Round Tower.

'Placed here by King Henry V,' he heard an old sailor tell a party of sightseers that had gathered, 'so that the safety of the King's ships might be assured.'

'Amen,' murmured Lestrade. From this vantage point he could see the dreadnoughts riding at anchor, the flags fluttering from their mastheads, and he heard the whistles and shouting of marines, boots crashing on the courtyards of the Garrison Church.

'Which way will the King come?' he asked the old sailor, who seemed to be in the know. 'And how?'

''E's usually in a launch, sir,' answered the old man; 'and if 'e follers his dad's 'abit – it's a filthy one, mind – 'e'll come across that way from Portchester direction.'

Lestrade followed the pointed finger to the low Norman keep of Portchester Castle, a mellow pile in the early sun.

'It'll be an open launch, then?' Lestrade asked the sailor.

'Don't worry, you'll see 'Is Majesty,' he said. 'And this mist'll clear before long. 'E'll pass right below us 'ere and out to the Motherbank before turning back.'

'Where can I get the best view?' Lestrade asked.

'From 'ere.' The sailor lit his pipe.

Lestrade stepped aside as the crowd behind began to jostle. Children scampered by waving little Union Jacks. For all the chill wind, the crowds were flocking to the sea to shout for their king.

'No, no,' said Lestrade. 'I mean the best *private* view. Somewhere where I won't be disturbed.'

The old sailor looked at him oddly. 'Well, that be the *Victory*, then. But you'll need a pass to get on 'er. She be the flagship, y'see.'

Lestrade scanned the dreadnoughts again. 'Which one is the *Victory*?' he asked.

The old sailor spluttered on his pipe. 'Landlubber.' He spat copiously and pointed to the larboard of the battleships to the tall, black masts and spars of Nelson's flagship. Something about the way she rose and fell with the swell of the sea caused the hairs on Lestrade's neck to tickle. He fought his way through the crowds and down to the ground, running along the quay with its brightly painted taverns and houses, bedecked now with flags for the Review. Sightseers and street traders cursed and growled as he dashed among them. Chestnut sellers, flag purveyors, fishermen: all joined together in their collective grumblings about the idiot in the shabby Donegal causing pandemonium on the Hard. The old sailor watched him cut a swathe through them and wondered where the lunatic had escaped from.

At the Queen Anne Gate that marked the entrance to His Majesty's Dockyard, an armed sailor stopped Lestrade. He flicked out his superintendent's card and hurtled over the cobbles, crossing the wide-open spaces. There were no crowds here, just the deserted red brick buildings of the Royal Navy. He heard the flags snapping at masthead and pole as he rounded the corner. The murmur of the crowds was very distant and the sea roared and crashed to his left.

The *Victory* towered over him, black and imposing. For a moment he stared up at the ornate prow, festooned with ropes and rigging.

'You!' A voice hailed him. 'Members of the public aren't allowed in this area. What do you want?'

'Who's on board?' He replied with a question.

'Nobody. The *Victory*'s an accommodation ship now. The Commander-in-Chief Portsmouth uses it when he's in port. Who are you?'

'Superintendent Lestrade, Scotland Yard. Who are you?'

'Petty Officer Tingle. Something up?'

'Could be. Do you know what time the King is due past the point?'

'Better ask the Officer of the Watch. Ha, ha. Get it?'

'I'm not in the mood for attempted humour, Petty Officer.'

'Sorry. In about half an hour. Eight bells to you.'

'And to you. Can you get me some men? I have reason to believe there is going to be an attempt on the King's life.'

'Men? Come off it. All the men in Portsmouth are either on those ships,' he pointed to the dreadnoughts, 'or on the Hard. This area's out of bounds.'

'You expect the murderer to obey your signs, do you?'

'Well, where do you think he is, then? If an ant moved on this quad, I'd see it.'

'What about up there?' Lestrade pointed to the *Victory*.

'That's empty. I checked her stem to stern earlier this morning.'

'At least come with me and check her again,' Lestrade urged.

'More than my job's worth, mate,' the Petty Officer about-faced and began marching.

'Mind if I do, then?' Lestrade called after him.

'Well, seeing as you're a copper and all,' shouted the Petty

Officer, 'but I haven't seen you, all right?'

It was far from all right. But Lestrade had half an hour. No doubt if Sergeant Dickens or Jones were with him, they would be able to give him a shot by shot account of the noble pile up whose sides he now scrambled by rope ladder. He reached the deck, the drop below him horrendous, and the grey sea swelled and wallowed as he gazed down. Above him, the gulls screamed and wheeled and each one seemed to call his name. Only one hit him, though: a crack shot in the centre of his bowler.

He checked the main deck. All seemed ship-shape, he thought. But then Lestrade wasn't sure which end he was at. He constantly checked the dockyard walls to get his bearings. Ahead of him, a band struck up. 'God Save the King'. He strained his eyes to make out the little flotilla of boats bobbing before Portchester. The royal launch carrying the King and the Tsar. The next thing he saw was the tar-covered deck of the *Victory*, having tripped over something and fetched his full length. The brass plate jutting above the timbers read 'Here Nelson Fell'. It somehow gave Lestrade a crumb of comfort to learn that England's greatest sailor was as clumsy as he was.

A click ahead brought his eyes up level with a hatch. He saw a pair of uniform boots scuttling across the deck in front of him. In an instant he was on his feet and running. Nothing. The mizzen mast loomed up ahead, wrapped in tarred ropes. Another click. Behind, this time. He turned to see the hatch go down. Whoever it was had gone below and Lestrade did likewise. In his eagerness he completely underestimated the size and agility of Nelson's sailors. Not only did his feet fail to grip the polished brass of the stair treads, he also dented his bowler on the beams above and somersaulted onto the orlop deck where Nelson had been carried after his fatal wound. He sat upright, allowing his eyes to become accustomed to the gloom. Before him ran a gallery, the whole length of the *Victory's* underdeck, hung with tables and hammocks; blocked here and there by cannon, jutting defiantly through open portholes. The watery sun of the January morning sent its shafts of light, dappling the creaking boards. Lestrade crept as quietly as his aching hip would allow, past the housing of the mizzen, easing the hanging tables aside. There was a squeaking sound ahead. A wharf-rat? A drunken sailor? What would Lestrade do with him? But he had seen the boots on the maindeck. And the Petty Officer had assured him the vessel was empty.

He crept forward until another deck emerged in the half light, on a level with his head. He glanced up and saw the feet again. As he climbed up the rope stairs, swaying precariously beneath him, he saw the outline of a naval officer framed by an open porthole, gazing out to sea in the direction of the King's launch.

'Stay where you are, Mr Snagge,' Lestrade said, pointing his finger in the pocket of the Donegal as though it were a gun. 'Move and I'll shoot.'

The figure at the porthole stiffened.

'Put your hands on the timbers on each side of you.'

The sailor did as he was told. 'H-how did you know it w-w-was me?' he asked.

Lestrade moved forward. He couldn't carry out the bluff for long. After all, he was fifty-eight years old. His finger didn't have the range it once had.

'As the late great Sherlock Holmes apparently never said, "It was elementary" really.'

'H-humour me,' said Snagge.

'Very well.' Lestrade edged closer, trying to find the Mauser. 'You're a crack shot. As a naval officer you have access to aircraft – hence the murders of Percy Hinchcliffe and John Watson. Your parents are Austrian. I checked the map. That's next to Germany, isn't it? An easy matter to gain employment in Berlin.'

'Th-that would n-never stand up in a c-court of law,' Snagge sneered.

'You have lived in Africa and South America,' Lestrade moved to his left. 'That gave you knowledge of the kind of knot you used to kill Thomas Portnoy at Clement Danes. And the blow pipe and curare to despatch Arnold Tasker at the Bioscope.'

'C-c-circumstantial,' stammered Snagge.

'Then there were your numerous sailings, were there not?' Lestrade was going to have to grab the man any minute. 'Your convenient tours of duty in the Mediterranean and the Baltic. That nonsense of your illness off Jutland. You weren't ill at all, were you? You jumped ship, in effect, in order to double back to England. Except that you were seen.'

'Oh? B–by whom?'

'Miss Berkeley. That's the thing about policemen's children, Lieutenant, like their dads, they never forget faces. She'd met you hanging unconvincingly around Philomena Marchment's house at Virginia Water. And that was the most despicable crime of all in my book. You pretended to be in love with that woman in order to get close to her and kill her. You were the "J" of her letters, weren't you?'

'And if I w–was?'

'In fact it was Miss Berkeley who finally put me on to you. She and your confidante, Mata Hari. In a weak moment, your exotic accomplice mentioned your code name, "der Haken". Miss Berkeley told me what it meant – a hitch or a snag. The rest was easy.'

'H–how did you know w–where to f–find me?'

'Let's call that a leap of imagination, shall we? I reasoned that der Haken, alias Peter the Painter, alias Jamie Snagge would not be content with the small-fry, the unknowns of the Peace League. There had to be a bigger target. I thought naturally of the King, but the presence of the Tsar, unannounced, incognito, was a bonus I knew you couldn't pass up. The Naval Review was a perfect chance. Who but a naval man could pass unnoticed among naval men? And now, Mr Snagge, I think we've talked for long enough. Turn around, slowly now and no tricks.'

'Daddy!' His daughter's voice behind him made him lose

concentration for that fatal second. Lestrade turned to see not only Emma, but Jamie Snagge. Before he had a chance to turn back, there was a roar of gunfire behind him and Snagge crashed back against the *Victory*'s hull, blood spurting from his throat. Lestrade was knocked sideways by the wooden rifle stock of the Mauser and when he surfaced he saw his daughter gripped in the powerful lace-encrusted arm of Ballard Hook.

'Stay down, Lestrade,' he snarled, 'or she dies.' He clicked back the hammer and nuzzled the muzzle behind her ear.

'Ballard . . .' she began to sob.

'Quiet,' he snapped, 'your father and I have some unfinished business.' He glanced out of the porthole. 'I estimate about ten minutes before the royal launch comes alongside. That gives me just enough time to put you right, Sholto, in your pathetic little attempts at deduction.'

'Why did you pretend to be Jamie Snagge?' Lestrade asked, moving across to his body.

'I said stay down,' Hook snarled, forcing Emma's head sideways with the gun. 'It amused me,' he answered more calmly, 'just as it amused me to pretend to Thomas Portnoy that I wanted a lesson in bell ringing. I met him quite by chance, of course,' he grinned, 'and he was delighted to show me. Bumptious buffoon. He ended up hoist with his own petard, of course.'

Lestrade hadn't realised Hook had used a petard as well.

'Just as it amused me to impersonate Haverstock Irons,' he went on. 'In your fuddled state you didn't notice the change of voice in the Greek Street den, did you, Sholto? Mind you, I thought the handshake might give it away.'

'The gold fob in the Bioscope,' said Lestrade. 'The one Miss Fitzgibbon the organist saw . . .'

'Yes, bit of a rush job, that. I had to get rid of Tasker quickly, so I was still in uniform under my greatcoat. What your hawk-eyed old biddy saw was the lace on my cuff. You, of course, with your unerring nose missed that entirely.'

'And Percy Hinchcliffe?'

'Mildly eccentric people can be relied upon to do stupid things. He had this half-baked ambition to swim the Channel. I assured him I could keep him supplied with food and water from the Voisin. I supplied him with a bullet.'

He twisted Emma round by the hair so that she was closer to him.

'Stand up, Lestrade, and empty your pockets. One hand at a time.'

'Andrew McAbendroth?' Lestrade did as he was told. The string, the bus ticket, the Apache knife.

'I thought so,' mused Hook when he saw them. 'No gun. It's not your style, is it, Sholto? McAbendroth took regular constitutionals across the cliffs. I merely invited him for a sail around the headland. We discussed the delicate situation in Europe. Until I shot him, and then he had very little to say.'

'You callous b—'

'Ah, ah!' Hook retreated, yanking Emma aside so that she squealed.

'Daddy!'

Lestrade checked himself.

'And what about Snagge?' He tapped the lifeless body with his foot.

'I set him up perfectly. You see, McPherson was right about the Mudiewarp. Me. I was the inside man. Fisher and Harp-Greavesley fed me information one way. You and Emma another. That's why I wanted you and not Quinn as our Yard man. I couldn't monitor his doings. I could, through Emma, monitor yours.'

'So *you* are the son of the Austrian Ambassador, with knowledge of African knots and South American poisons?'

'Knots and poisons, yes. Son of the Austrian Ambassador, no. But near enough. Let's just say, as admirals go, I feel closer to von Turpitz than to Fisher,' and he clicked his heels, Prussian-style.

'What about Philomena Marchment?' Lestrade asked.

'I knew Snagge had had a relationship with her. Poor,

hopeless Jamie. Oh, he did jump ship off Jutland all right. The Navy was about to cashier him. He went to pieces after Phil's death. I merely cut her fuel pipe so that she ran out of petrol, and offered my services by the roadside. Emma here had given me her cherished diabolo set as a keepsake. I merely substituted a steel peg for the wooden one. I fancied a change from the Mauser. It was surprisingly effective.'

'You used me,' Emma hissed, unable to move her head because of the tightness of Hook's grip.

'He used us all. Jamie Snagge, Fisher, Harp-Greavesley.'

'And that's not the half of it. You're forgetting Houndsditch and Sidney Street.'

'You killed Leon Beron,' said Lestrade, 'and let Steinie Morrison go down for it.'

Hook nodded. 'And when I left you and Wensley in the alley that day and disappeared, as you thought for good, behind the smoke, I got my friends out. You see, I'm not all bad, Sholto. They'd done me a good turn; drew the attention of every London policeman, save your tenacious self of course, away from me.'

'What about Mata Hari?' Lestrade asked, watching each move, waiting for his chance.

'Yes, she's not bad. A bit more practice and I think she'll make quite a respectable agent. Shame about the der Haken slip. I didn't know about that. I must have words with our Mata. Still, it's just as well Miss Berkeley's German is rather slipshod, isn't it?'

'What is your real name?' Lestrade played for time as he heard the launch's engines drone nearer.

'That hardly matters, does it? Peter the Painter, Ballard Hook, take your pick. Which of us doesn't have several names, several faces, Mr Lister?' Then serious: 'I gave you your chance, Lestrade. I gave you the scent of Jamie Snagge, feeding you false and contradictory clues. I gave you to Mata Hari, hoping the photographs would discredit you. When all that failed, I realised you would have to die. So I waited while you went to Sir Edward Henry's. That maniac cabbie saved your life.'

'And now?'

Hook nodded. 'Shrewd of you to guess the Tsar. The last of the Romanovs. Has quite a romantic ring, don't you think, Emma?'

She squealed again, tears running down her cheeks.

'Shrewd of you, too, to guess the *Victory*. Once aboard, I made it devilish easy for you. Letting you see me here. Standing with my back turned while you crept up with all the finesse of an enraged elephant. That was nicely done, Lestrade. Of course what all of you missed, except dear little Emma here, was good old Prof. Holliday.'

'Holliday?' the Lestrades chorused.

'Yes, of course,' beamed Hook, 'that was the messiest of all. My first and I nearly bungled it. I'd known Holliday of course at Eton. Sanctimonious old pacifist. Another member of your League. You hadn't checked that, had you? And he was a Germanophobe too.'

Lestrade hadn't known about the blood disorder.

'When I grabbed him on Hobsbaum's yacht I thought it would be plain sailing, but Rupert saw me.'

'You . . . you killed my brother,' Emma snarled.

'Hardly your brother, Emma dear. Luckily for me, Holliday couldn't swim and I was able to silence both Bandicoots by dragging them over the side. Messy, though. I've improved since. A stroke of luck Ivo's memory going. At first I toyed with finishing him off. That's why I was at Bandicoot Hall, Sholto, the day we met. When I saw Ivo I realised there was no danger. You, of course, flat-footed landlubber that you are, missed the salient point. Ivo's head was battered. What was it the doctor said – "by the rocks"? What rocks, Sholto? The coast there is smooth sand. Mud flats in fact as you both found out later. I put those dents in Ivo's skull and Rupert's, too. The crabs must have finished him.'

Hook glanced behind him again.

'Well, it's been fun,' he said, 'but the game is nearly over and I must get back to work. Goodbye, Lestrade.'

The superintendent stared ahead. He couldn't move to left or right and the Broomhandle Mauser was pointing straight at him. The gun crashed once, but the bullet went wide. Lestrade blinked in disbelief as he realised that Emma had brought her heel back sharply into Hook's shins and as he buckled she spun free of him and wrestled with the gun. He slapped her around the head and she went down. Lestrade launched himself on the captain and they struggled against the cannon, Lestrade desperately trying to wrest the Mauser from Hook's superior grip.

Lestrade's knee came up and the gun hurtled across the deck. Seeing his path blocked, Hook jabbed Lestrade in the stomach and leapt back, clawing free his sword as he did so. Lestrade lunged for the gun, but Hook was faster, slicing off the tip of Lestrade's finger as he did so. The superintendent grabbed the Apache knife lying on the table and the blade flicked out.

'My, my,' said Hook, crouching with the ease of a trained swordsman, 'four inches against three feet, eh? Isn't that how it's been throughout all this?'

'Boasting again, Ballard?' gasped Lestrade and lunged at his man. Steel clashed with steel, ringing in echoes around the *Victory*. Hook glanced again out of the porthole. He would have to hurry now. The launch was almost alongside. He advanced one step, two. Lestrade saw the launch too. The King and the Tsar laughing on the bridge. He felt the body of Jamie Snagge behind him and the air whistled past him as Hook's blade hacked off first one wing of his collar, then the other. He felt blood trickling on both cheeks. Another sweep of the blade and Lestrade felt his cheekbone crack.

'Duelling scars,' said Hook. 'Very fashionable in my country. You know, I once saw a man decapitated in a duel, Sholto. Of course, that was with a sword made in Germany. I'm not sure your inferior British weapons are up to it. Let's find out, shall we?'

Like a rabbit dazzled in the lights of his own Lanchester, Lestrade raised his arms to fend off the blow, totally unable to predict the angle from which it would come. The Apache knife was as much use in this situation as a straw.

'Ballard!' It was Emma's voice ringing loud and clear.

Both men looked at her. She stood, crouched over a swinging table, both hands clutching the Mauser. She fired once and Hook stumbled sideways, blood trickling over the shoulder boards of his rank.

'Emma,' he called to her. 'Don't . . .'

She fired again and he went down, the sword clattering harmlessly to the ground. She fired again and again until the jumping corpse relaxed and she let the gun fall.

In the silence and the smoke the royal launch swept past.

'What's that noise?' Nicholas Romanov asked George Battenberg.

'Fireworks, I expect,' said the King. 'Left over from November the Fifth. You see, Nicky, I told Lestrade this was England. We're safe as houses. Scaremongers, eh?' and he threw back his head and tutted before taking the salute from the dreadnoughts.

Lestrade held his daughter to him. She shivered and sobbed in his arms.

'Oh, Daddy.'

'I know, I know.' He hugged her. 'What are you doing here?' He pushed her to arm's length. 'How did you find me?'

'It was Jamie,' she said. 'He came to see me. He'd suspected something was wrong for months. Your asking him about Professor Holliday did it, I suppose, although he didn't mention that to me. It was little things that Ballard said and did. He told me of his suspicions.'

'What did you do?'

She shook her head. 'I remembered the robbery at Ballard's house. The missing silver, the stolen family tree. When I went there his parents were away. Thinking about it now, it was all rather vague. Ballard had no past. But I didn't believe Jamie.' She sighed. 'He said he would prove it to me. We went to the

Admiralty and talked to Commodore Harp-Greavesley. He denied all knowledge of Ballard, but while Jamie was talking to him I read the roster sheet. Ballard was on duty in Portsmouth. On the accommodation ship of the Commander-in-Chief. And here we are. I came, I suppose, to prove Jamie wrong. And of course, to see Ballard. He . . . he'd named the day, you know.'

Lestrade led his sobbing daughter over the bodies of Hook and Snagge to the staircase down which he had recently tumbled. His left eye began to close with the swelling and his hand throbbed uncontrollably.

'What did he mean?' he asked her, 'when he said Fanny Berkeley's German was slipshod?'

'Der Haken,' she answered. 'It means a hook. Oh, Daddy, I loved him so,' and she buried her face in his bloody Donegal.

He stroked her soft, golden hair and looked down at the captain's body. He counted four bullet holes. 'One for Leon Beron,' he said to himself, 'one for Steinie Morrison, one for John Watson and one for Rupert Bandicoot.' He stooped with difficulty and picked up the Mauser, wiping it clean of prints.

'Don't want to make life too confusing for Inspector Collins, do we?' and he twirled the gun slowly in his hand, making sure his prints were everywhere. He turned to his daughter again. 'Emma,' he said, 'this didn't happen. You were never here, understand?'

She blinked uncomprehendingly. 'Daddy, that's—'

'Dishonest? Yes, I know. It's a dishonest world, my lovely.' He held her to him. 'And you've got enough to live with, I think.'

They screeched to a halt inches from each other, the battered little Lanchester and the immaculate Silver Ghost.

'Sholto, Emma.' Harry Bandicoot, buried in his driving furs, leapt from his seat to greet them. 'He's remembered. Ivo's remembered.'

Ivo jumped down the other side. 'I had a blow to the head in the scrum the other day,' he said. 'It all came flooding back. It wasn't an accident after all. It was . . .' He stopped, taking in the bandaged Lestrade and the pale, shocked Emma. 'Oh, Emma,' and he hugged her.

Harry looked bewildered, his usual pose.

'It's all right, Harry,' Sholto took his arm and led him towards Bandicoot Hall, 'Emma and I have got something to tell you.'

Bon Voyage

George and Bessie Williams walked the dock at Southampton that day in April, arm in arm. She had forgiven the past; his leaving her eighteen months before. After all, he had been searching for her high and low and had merely forgotten her address and the names and addresses of all her relatives. But that was then, and now they sauntered on that spring morning to watch the new ship, decked out in her ribbons.

'I do think we should both make wills, dearest heart,' he was saying. 'After all, if something should happen to me . . .'

'Nonsense, darling,' she smiled at him adoringly, 'nothing ever will. You and your worries! But, dearest, as long as you have me and I have you, nothing can harm either of us, can it?'

He patted her hand lovingly.

'And as long as you've got the sea to gaze at.'

'It's not so much the sea, heart's-ease,' he explained, 'it's water. Any water will do,' and he tipped his top hat to the bevy of ladies and gentlemen coming towards them.

'I know that fellow from somewhere,' said Lestrade, 'though I can't place the woman.'

'You need this holiday, Sholto Lestrade.' Fanny Berkeley squeezed his arm. 'You've been looking at too many criminal photographs.'

Lestrade breathed a sigh of relief when he remembered that he had seen his own criminal photographs burning in the bin in Sir Edward Henry's office. The nut-brown nizam had considered the case closed, though he retained his doubts. Only the fact that Lestrade had followed him on his secret mission of mercy to Alfred Bowes' widowed mother in Acton, and had seen with his own ferret eyes the bundle of notes he had passed her, had forced the assistant commissioner to comply with Lestrade's request that the photographs be burned. If those photographs had been published, or it was discovered that Edward Henry had a heart of gold after all, the careers of two of the Yard's finest would come to a rapid end.

He had said his goodbyes already to Letitia and Harry. Now it was a last hug and a final handshake, though Harry was a little surprised to receive the former. He held Emma to him for a long time. She had grown up beyond her years in the last few months. She was over the worst, but the hurt in her heart would show in her eyes for ever.

'Daddy,' she whispered. 'Enjoy yourself. Write, won't you?'

'If you do.' He kissed her. 'Look after Harry and Letitia for me.'

She nodded. 'It's hard to lose three men you love so quickly.'

'Now, now.' He held up her chin. 'You're not losing me. It's a little holiday, that's all. I'll be back.'

He kissed her forehead and turned to Fanny. 'Well,' he said.

'Well,' she repeated.

'Thank you, Fanny Berkeley,' he said.

'What for?' She was trying to hold back the tears.

'For being there,' he said. 'Just for being there.'

He kissed her full on the lips. She looked at the sallow, care-worn face, scarred and bruised, under the ubiquitous bowler.

'Walter,' he called.

Chief Inspector Dew came forward. The experienced sailor, he had made this trip before. 'Sir?'

'A little job for you—'

'Sir? May I butt in, sir?' A plainclothes man pushed his way forward.

'Why break the habit of a lifetime, Blevvins?' Lestrade answered.

'I realise I'm being forward, sir, and I'm very grateful to you already. But . . .'

'But, Blevvins?'

He led the superintendent a few feet away. 'Well, sir, to be frank and candid, anything Dew can do, I can do better. I can do anything better than Dew.'

'No you can't', said Lestrade.

'Yes I can.'

'No you can't!' Lestrade was adamant. 'Blevvins, I got Mr Stead to drop the charges against you. I got you out of horse troughs—'

'No, sir, I got *you* out of horse troughs.'

Lestrade eviscerated his man with a glance.

'And I've got you back into plainclothes at the Yard. Don't ask me why I've done all this for you, Blevvins. I can't answer that one myself. But when I ask to speak to my chief inspector it's because I want a man of intelligence, dedication, intellect. Not some maniac who enjoys beating people up! Am I clear?'

'As a bell, sir.' Blevvins saluted and stood back.

'Now, Walter, this little job. I want you to give anything major that comes along to John Kane. Failing that, Alfred Ward. All right?'

'Er . . . What about me, Mr Lestrade?' Dew was a little crestfallen.

'I know how busy you are on your book, Walter.' Lestrade patted the man's arm. 'Wouldn't want to let a little thing like police work cramp your style.'

He turned again to Fanny Berkeley.

'It's a leap year, Sholto,' she said.

'Is it?' he said.

'You know what we women can do in a leap year, don't you?'

'Er . . . vote?' he asked.

She kicked him on the shin. 'No, you superintendent, you. We can ask you men to marry us.'

Lestrade's astonishment broke into a smile. 'Well, well.' He shook his head. 'It's not the most romantic proposal I've heard. I shall have to think it over.'

He kissed them all again, drawing the line at Dew and Blevvins and leaving Harry looking even more bemused, and made for the gangway. Halfway up, he turned and called, 'Fanny, I've thought it over. The answer is . . .' and the ship's siren drowned the word.

'What?' she shouted above the din.

'I said,' he cupped his hands, 'the answer is . . .' and the siren sounded again.

Only Fanny Berkeley heard. Heart pounding, lips smiling, tears running. It was enough.

On the deck, Lestrade met William Stead.

'What do your family think of this?' the journalist asked him.

'The Peace Conference?' asked Lestrade. 'They don't know. They all think I'm having a holiday. So does the Yard.'

'A holiday in America?' Stead was incredulous. 'Unheard of.'

'You think there's going to be trouble?' Lestrade asked him.

'Do you suppose Captain Hook was the end of it?' Stead asked. 'He was one of many. And one day, unless we stop it, there'll be another Ballard Hook. And he won't miss. It might be Paris, Vienna, New York, Sarajevo, who knows? Somebody, some crowned head or politician, will be brought down, and millions – millions, Lestrade – will pay for it with their lives.'

'Is that why you do it? You Peacemakers?'

'"Blessed are the Peacemakers,"' said Stead, '"for they are the Children of God."'

'"Stand to your work and be wise,"' said Lestrade, '"Certain of sword and pen, Who are neither Children nor Gods, but men in a world of men."'

'Why, Mr Lestrade,' smiled Stead, 'I had no idea you had a literary bent.'

'Just something a friend of mine wrote,' said Lestrade.

'And is that England's answer?' the journalist asked him.

'It always has been, Mr Stead,' he said. 'It always has been.'

The band struck up and the ropes fell away. Lestrade leaned over the side to wave to the knot of watchers on the quay below, loved faces in a sea of faces.

The White Star Liner *Titanic* began her maiden voyage.

Lestrade and the Deadly Game

Volume V in the Sholto Lestrade
Mystery Series

M.J. Trow

A Gateway Mystery

REGNERY
PUBLISHING, INC.
Since 1947 • An Eagle Publishing Company

As flies to wanton boys, are we to the Gods;
They kill us for their sport.

King Lear Act IV Scene i

Chapter One

1

One To Get Ready . . .

The Greeks had a word for it. It was a short one and it translated rather well into Anglo-Saxon. Someone had pinched their Games.

But in other ways, the year was set fair. The Congo was annexed by Belgium. Bosnia and Herzegovina, the terrible twins of those tiresome Balkan States, were annexed by Austria. There was even a new annexe at Scotland Yard. The British Army of course excelled itself by devising a new pattern sword with a pistol grip hilt of gutta-percha. To the Yeomanry who had served so well on Veldt and Nek, it declined to give any swords at all. And weary gentlemen, then abed, shook their heads and muttered as they read their morning papers. That buffoon Haldane had introduced a new part-time soldier he called a 'terrier'. The country was of course going to the dogs.

Mr Edward Henry crossed again to his window, the only one that permitted a decent view of the river, sparkling now in the morning sun. He looked at the grandmother on the wall.

'Yes.' He heard the monotone behind him. 'Half-past. It's certainly getting on.'

He turned to Inspector Gregory and gave him the old Pukka Sahib's look which had decimated the natives of Ceylon. But Gregory was too white-skinned to notice.

'You'd think they'd be here by now,' he said, trying to fix an air of even average intellect on to his bovine face.

'Indeed.' Henry's temper, no longer than he was, was within an ace of snapping. He flicked open the silver box and cut himself into a new Havana.

'Ah,' said Gregory, with the air of a man about to be offered a smoke. 'Ahhmmm,' and he had the grace to turn disappointment into a cough as he fidgeted on his chair. 'Did I ever tell you about that case in Piddletrenthide, Chief?' he asked hopefully.

'Yes,' said Henry.

'The old pedlar with the monkey?'

'Yes.'

'The one with the missing third finger, left hand?'

'Yes.'

'Well, it was back in '96. Or was it '97 . . .?'

Mercifully, Henry was not to find out, for the knock at the door heralded the arrival of Inspector Mungo Hyde of the River Police.

'Sorry, Mr Henry,' he blustered, struggling with his forage cap. 'Lighter broke loose at the East India. My boys and I have been out since dawn.'

'Thank you, Inspector. Take a seat.'

In the event, Hyde took two. It had to be said that the bacon buns of Mrs Squatt of Rotherhithe had done immeasurable harm to the good man's waistline. It was rumoured in the River Police that he had to take soundings to make sure his feet were still there, for even in a strong nor'westerly, he'd lost sight of them years ago.

'Did I ever tell you, Mungo, about that case in Yorkshire last year?'

'Yes, Tom,' the River Policeman answered.

'Right in the centre of Arndale, it happened.'

'Yes.'

'You'd have thought he'd have been past it, wouldn't you, a man of his age?'

'Yes.'

'But not a bit of it. He . . .'

The door crashed back and a tall, square policeman stood there, a bridle draped over his shoulder.

'Sorry I'm late, Assistant Commissioner,' he said in a bluff accent from somewhere north of Watford. 'Dray horses bolted along Fleet Street. Must have got a whiff of a mare, I suppose. At least those lazy bastards of reporters had a jammy time. All they had to do was to lean out of the window for a story.'

'Gentlemen,' said Henry, 'I don't believe you know Inspector

Edgar-Smith of the Mounted Division. Inspector Hyde of the River Police and Inspector Gregory of . . .'

'L Division, sir.' Gregory rose and shook the man's hand. 'I used to ride a horse, you know . . .'

'Really,' grunted Edgar-Smith, a little less than captivated by the admission. 'Well, I never.'

'Oh, but surely.' Gregory was surprised. 'You being in the Mounted Division, and all . . .'

He met six hostile eyes in his usual blank manner, but they were quickly joined by two more.

'Ah, Abberline.' Henry gestured the newest arrival to a chair. 'Gentlemen, I believe you all know Chief Superintendent Abberline.'

There were nods and rumbles all round. Then Abberline realized that Henry was looking at him for an explanation.

'Ah,' he said, adjusting the gardenia in his buttonhole. 'Minor derailment at Penge.'

'But you live in Norwood, Mr Abberline,' Gregory said innocently.

Abberline withered him and noticed that Mungo Hyde's left eye was flickering with a life of its own. His head began to dip towards his shoulder. When he realized everyone was looking at him, he began to tug at his collar. 'Damned thing,' he said. 'This patrol jacket seems to have shrunk in the wash.' He could help Abberline no further.

Henry was altogether less concerned. 'You appear to have a lipstick smudge on your cheek, Chief Superintendent,' he said blandly, sitting back behind his desk.

Abberline rose sharply, glancing behind him. Quickly realizing all was well, he produced a monogrammed lace handkerchief and dabbed his face. 'Mrs Abberline,' he grinned sheepishly. 'You know what women are.'

As he dabbed, the lacy scrap floated to his feet. He bent to retrieve it – and what he could of his dignity – and his eyes met a pair of less than reputable boots. He followed up the matching trousers and was within a whisker of snatching the handkerchief when the owner of the boots did it for him.

'M,' said the owner, reading the ornately embroidered initial. 'That must stand for Mrs Abberline. How is Ermintrude?'

'Lestrade . . .' Abberline began, but the Assistant Commissioner cut him off.

9

'We're already forty minutes late, Lestrade. Mr Gregory has been here since ten.'

Lestrade crossed the room and shook Henry's hands warmly. 'How can I ever forgive myself?' he asked solemnly. He looked deeply into Henry's eyes. He knew what those forty minutes had cost him.

'May we please begin?'

All eyes settled on Henry as he leaned forward in his leather chair. Simultaneously, all legs except Hyde's crossed at the knee.

'Gentlemen,' said Henry, his eyes dark and serious through the smoke of his cigar, 'we all know that the Congo has been annexed by the Belgians. Rumour has it that Bosnia and Herzegovina will, after all, be annexed by Austria. It is not of course for us to question the machinations of the Government in creating the Territorial Army. By the way, Edgar-Smith, have your chaps had a crack at this new pattern sword yet?'

'Sword be buggered!' snapped the man from the Mounted Division, slapping his shoulder anew with the bridle. 'Give my boys six inches more on their hardwood truncheons, that's all I ask. We'll crack these suffragists' skulls . . .'

'Yes, thank you Inspector,' Henry interrupted. 'Gentlemen, you've seen my memoranda to your various departments. All leave is cancelled forthwith. Rest days will be suspended until the matter in hand is passed.'

'The . . . matter in hand, sir . . .' Lestrade twitched his moustache. As usual, he had seen no memorandum at all.

'Haven't you seen my memoranda?' Henry quizzed him.

'No, sir, I confess not,' said Lestrade.

'Imbert!' roared Henry. 'Get in here.'

A curly-haired constable stuck his head round the glass-panelled door. 'Sir?'

'Did you or did you not place my recent memoranda on Mr Lestrade's desk?'

'Yes, sir,' the constable replied. 'In his In tray.'

Henry turned to Lestrade again. 'Do you remember an In memoranda?'

'No, sir, I'm afraid not,' Lestrade admitted.

'Tsk, the Olympic Games, man,' Henry snarled. 'Imbert, get out!'

'Yessir,' and he was gone.

10

'Within the fortnight, thousands of foreigners will descend on London like bees to the hive. Superintendent Quinn of the Special Branch is not with us this morning because even now he is combing his files on Undesirable Aliens. He tells me they are bulging. We shall have the scum of Europe on our doorstep, gentlemen, as surely as if there were a tunnel under the Channel itself.'

'Heaven forbid!' gasped Mungo Hyde, who perhaps saw his trade dropping off.

'I'm sure the athletes aren't that bad, sir,' Gregory proffered.

Henry scowled. The morning was not going well. 'I was not referring to them,' he still had the patience to explain. 'Their presence will attract thieves, vagabonds, swindlers and confidence tricksters by the yard. Our job is to be ever vigilant. I need hardly remind you that the Entente is, at the moment, a little less than Cordiale. Then of course, there are the Germans . . .'

'Why *are* the Americans coming, exactly?' Abberline asked.

There was a silence. Clearly, there was no answer to that.

It was luncheon, that day or the next. Chief Inspector Walter Dew, Criminal Investigation Department at Scotland Yard, was looking into the matter of the misappropriation of a number of old-age pensions. To be more precise, he was looking into the bowels of the upright Remington which had worn a permanent groove into his desk. The capital L was playing up again. It was the one he used most, by virtue of his guv'nor's name, and the thing had clashed with the exclamation mark and a number of other careless keys to grind right through the headed notepaper with the unusual watermark and into the impossible-to-reach little void behind.

'Rosie Lee, guv?' a cheery voice called.

Dew cursed anew. 'I should have been at the Collar by now, Hollingsworth. The last thing I want is a cup of gnat's pee I've got to blow on for half an hour. Know anything about typewriters?'

'I've had a few in my time, Insp.' The constable winked.

Dew turned to face him.

'Ah, you mean *machines*?' Hollingsworth said with a broad grin. 'Nah. I always use me old Dirty Den.'

11

Dew had been more years on the Force than he cared to remember. Twenty if it was a day. And all of it more or less within tinkling distance of Bow Bells. But this man's professional Cockneyism got right up his doublet and hose. 'Dirty Den?' he repeated with all the patience at his disposal.

'Pen, Insp,' Hollingsworth smirked. 'Well, never mind. I'll drink it, then. 'Ere, do you know, I do believe . . . yes . . . yes, there it is.' He put the cup down quickly, staring intently at the top of Dew's head.

'What's the matter?' Dew instinctively felt his parting.

'Grey, Insp,' Hollingsworth whispered in his ear. 'The old grey hair's a-lying in the meadow. First of many, of course.'

'In my day, Hollingsworth,' Dew fumed, 'young constables were expected to be seen and not heard. Now get out. I'm busy.'

'Very good, Mr Dew sir.' Hollingsworth tucked the cup in the crook of his arm and made for the door. 'Oh, by the way.' He paused. 'There's a bloke out 'ere. To see Mr Lestrade.'

'Who is he?' Dew asked.

'I dunno. He gave me his card somewhere.' Hollingsworth fumbled in his waistcoat pocket. ''Ere. The Marquess of Bolsover. Funny 'andle, ain't it?'

Dew sprang to his feet. 'You blithering idiot! Don't you read the papers? The Marquess of Bolsover is a nob of the first water. How long has he been waiting?'

'A few minutes.' Hollingsworth shrugged.

'A few . . .' Dew was speechless.

'Do you know,' Hollingsworth grinned, 'when you're annoyed, a little lump comes and goes in your neck.'

'When I'm *really* annoyed, Hollingsworth, there'll be lots of lumps coming up in your neck because it'll have my fingers round it. Show the Marquess in – and put your jacket on, man. This is Scotland Yard.'

'Right, Insp.' Hollingsworth sensed the urgency. 'But don't worry. I gave him a cup of Rosie.' Dew waved him out. He pulled on his best serge and adjusted his tie in the foxed grime of the mirror. With one last desperate swipe he dislodged the typewriter keys and flicked the dust off the depositions neck-high in the corner.

'His Excellency the Marquess of Bolsover,' Hollingsworth announced as though at the Lord Mayor's Show.

12

A stumpy little man in tweeds brushed past him. 'Lestrade.' He thrust out a martial hand.

'Er . . . no, sir. Chief Inspector Dew, sir.'

'Eh? Well, where's Lestrade?'

'Er . . . at luncheon, sir.'

'Luncheon? Good God. Police force. Going to dogs; country. You.' He rounded on the beaming Hollingsworth. 'Smirking.' He cuffed the lad around the ear. 'There. Something to smirk about. Lestrade; where d's he eat?'

'Er . . . the Collar, sir.' Hollingsworth's cheek smarted.

'Collar?'

'The Horse and Collar, sir,' Dew explained. 'It's a public house in . . .'

'Damn and blast it. Fetch him. Send your chappie here.' Hollingsworth looked at Dew who looked in turn at the Marquess. 'Now!' Bolsover roared and Hollingsworth scarcely had time to grab his bowler before he was hurtling along the corridor as though his tail was on fire.

'Please your Grace,' Dew bobbed, 'won't you have a seat?'

'Got one,' snorted Bolsover. 'Berkshire. D'you know it?'

'Well, I . . . er . . . don't leave London much, I'm afraid.'

Bolsover sat heavily on Lestrade's new swivel, the one he'd managed to misdirect by a bit of nifty paperwork before it reached Abberline's office.

'Should. Spot of rough shooting. Nothing like it. Soon be the Twelfth.'

Dew looked at Lestrade's calendar. It was June the fourteenth. The old boy must be a little confused.

'Rank?' Bolsover snapped.

'Er . . . Chief Inspector,' Dew admitted.

'Name again?'

'Er . . . Dew.'

'Urdu? That's a bally language, isn't it? Nigger.'

'May I ask the nature of . . .?' Dew ventured.

'No. Private. Go to top. Best man. Always have. Always will. Unfortunately, best man out. Got to make do with Whatsisface.'

'Lestrade.'

'Rank?'

'Chief Inspector,' Dew repeated. Obviously the old man was a little Mutt and Jeff as Hollingsworth would have it.

'Is that all?' Bolsover lowered. 'No bally good. Been sold a pup here. Thought he was bally Assistant Commissioner at least.'

'Oh, I see, sir.' Dew realized the error of his ways. It was not a first for him. 'You mean Mr Lestrade's rank? Oh yes, he's Superintendent.'

'Age?'

'Mr Lestrade? Oh, I don't know. Er . . . fiftyish.'

'I'd killed seventy-six tigers when I was fiftyish. What's he done?'

'Er . . . well, he's solved . . . helped to solve several cases.'

'*Exempli gratia*?'

Dew's tongue protruded in the effort of remembering. 'No, I don't think that was one of his. That was one of Abberline's.'

'Abilene? That's a town in the colonies. In Kansas. This Lestrade. Any good?'

'Very, sir.' Dew was sure. 'As you say, the best.'

'Not what I said.'

An uncanny silence descended. During it, Dew's stomach, cheated of luncheon, gave a gurgling lurch and lay there, mutinous and growling.

'Hot, isn't it, Your Eminence?' he said at last. 'For June, I mean.'

'Flaming,' said Bolsover. And the silence fell again.

It came as the most exquisite relief to the Chief Inspector when the door crashed back and a bowler came whistling through it to ricochet off the green-painted pipes and land squarely on top of the pile of faded paper.

'This had better be good, Dew. I gave up a couple of pints of winkles. Oh.'

'The Marquess of Bolsover, Superintendent Lestrade,' said Dew. 'Superintendent Lestrade. The Marquess o. . .' and realizing his sudden superfluity, crept away.

'My lord.' Lestrade extended a hand. 'I'm sorry, my constable is rather new. I had no idea you'd been kept waiting. I trust that Inspector Dew has been helpful.'

'Doesn't know the meaning of the word.'

'Quite.' Lestrade gestured to a chair and found that Bolsover returned to his, leaving him to perch like a crippled parrot on Dew's, 'Er . . . my Chief Inspector's rather new as well.'

'Come to the point, Lestrade. Busy man. Son. Eldest son. Dead. Shot himself, y'see.'

There was no trace of emotion, no faltering in the Maxim gun delivery of the words.

'I'm sorry,' said Lestrade, reaching for a notepad.

'In the papers. Bally things. Thunderer's not been the same since Buckle. Who is this Harmsworth chappie?'

'Who indeed?' Lestrade stroked his chin ruefully.

'Wanted to do a bally story on me. Cheeky blighter. I sent his man packing.'

'Quite.'

'Wasn't suicide, Lestrade. Not my boy. Not a Fitzgibbon.'

'Quite.' Lestrade was grateful for small mercies at least. Nobody could make a monkey out of him. 'My lord,' he said, 'I shall look into the matter, of course, but I fear, with the Olympic Games so imminent, the entire Yard has its hands full.'

'Damn foreigners!' Bolsover snapped, getting smartly to his feet. 'Bally fool Gladstone. Should've sent a gunboat. Palmerston now, there's the chappie.'

'Yes, indeed. But until the Games are over, I fear I must place your son's demise on file.'

'File be damned.' Bolsover reached the door. 'He'd have beaten all those blighters. He was nimbler than all my boys. Fastest thing on two legs I've seen. Apart from a wallaby on heat, of course.'

'Of course . . . my lord, forgive me.' Lestrade's nostrils began to twitch. 'But do I understand that your son was an athlete?'

'The best,' Bolsover told him.

The words of Mr Edward Henry rang anew in Lestrade's ears – 'The scum of Europe . . .'

'Please, my lord, sit down. Have my chair.' He hopped off Dew's. 'You'd better tell me all about it.'

The two bowler-hatted gentlemen were shown into the bedroom of the late Anstruther Fitzgibbon, eldest son of the Marquess of Bolsover.

'I believe you know Inspector Bland. I am Superintendent Lestrade,' said the shorter of the two, 'You are . . .?'

'Overwrought, sir,' slurred the manservant and he swayed a little as he spoke.

'Yes, of course.' Lestrade wandered the thick pile. 'But what is your name?'

'Botley, sir. Hinksey Botley. I am . . . I was the master's manservant, man and boy.'

'How old was the master?' Lestrade found a silver-framed photograph of a boy in tasselled cap and white knickerbockers showing just a hint of knee.

'He was twenty-seven, sir.' Botley produced a handkerchief and trumpeted into it. 'A mere boy. I had tended him since he was a baby.'

Lestrade mechanically checked the bed.

'You found him?' he asked.

The manservant nodded.

'Tell me, Botley.' The Superintendent placed an avuncular arm around the old man's withered shoulders. 'Would you say the master was the type to take his own life?'

Botley straightened, as cut to the quick by the slur on the family honour as the Marquess had been. 'Never!' he said.

Lestrade smiled and patted the man. 'Well, well. Would you wait outside please? We'll send for you if we need you.'

Botley hesitated, swaying a little, then pivoted on one leg and made a determined bid to reach the door in a straight line. Lestrade followed him, eyeing the moulding intently.

'Again then, John,' he said.

Bland threw his hat on the bed and sprawled on a *chaise-longue*. He consulted the black notepad, bereft of its gold embossing now that economies were in vogue in C Division. 'Anstruther George Hartlepool Fitzgibbon. Third son of the Marquess of Bolsover.'

'Third? I thought he was the eldest?'

'Eldest surviving.'

'What happened to the others?'

'Er . . . eldest died of pneumonia as a child. Second fell prey to a hunting accident. Horse rolled on him.'

'Ah, you don't get that problem with a Lanchester,' Lestrade commented.

'Two other siblings, we think, but somewhat the other side of the blanket. One was a girl born to some American Amazon. She lives over . . . there. Bolsover never married the mother, although he was unencumbered by a wife at the time. The other was a lad, some years older. I got this from old Botley after a lot of haggling. Son of a serving gel. He seems to have been kept on as a boot boy until he was ten or so. Then he ran away.'

'What do we know about Anstruther?' Lestrade asked.

'Educated Harrow. Seemed to be some nonsense involving the games master. Went to Rugby. Some trouble there with the riding instructor. Went up to Cambridge. Some trouble involving a mathematics professor. Gonville and Caius.'

'There were two of them?' Lestrade checked.

'Apparently. Did a short spell with the Durham Light Infantry.'

'No Sandhurst?'

'For three days. There was some trouble with the fortifications lecturer. Don't quite know how he got a commission.'

'And in the Durham Light Infantry?'

'Yes.' Bland flicked over a page. 'Couldn't get much on this. Seems there was some bother with the chaplain and the regimental mascot.'

'Really?'

'Ah, I know what you're thinking,' smirked Bland. 'But it's all right, Sholto. It was a female goat.'

'I'm relieved to hear it. And since the army?'

'Well, he always had this poncho for sport. Quite a good hurdler. Would have got a Blue at Cambridge if he'd been there longer.'

'How long has he lived here?' Lestrade lit a cigar.

'This is the family's second town house. The old man lives in Grosvenor Place. He seems to own half of St James's.'

'No money worries, then.'

'Not judging by the look of this place. Anstruther had been living here on and off since he was eighteen.'

'Tell me about the Night in Question.'

'Last Tuesday. June the ninth. Anstruther had been over to the new stadium at the White City. Before that he'd done some running in the park.'

'Hyde?'

'Regent's.'

'What time did he come home?'

'Ah, now there Botley wasn't sure ' Bland said. 'It must have been after he went to bed. Around ten thirty.'

'So we don't know if he was alone?'

'No. The next thing we know for certain is that Botley knocked on his door as usual at ten o'clock.'

'This door?' Lestrade was drawn to it again.

'Yes. There was no reply.'

'What did Botley do?'

'Nothing. He couldn't get in.'

Lestrade's eyebrows knotted. 'Locked?'

Bland nodded.

'Where's the key?' Lestrade couldn't see one.

'Lost. Years ago.'

'Ah.' Lestrade wandered to the door again. 'The bolt.' It stood an inch or two away from the keyhole. Brass. Highly polished. He touched it with his fingers and it slid back easily. 'Odd,' he said, 'a bolt on a bedroom door.'

'Sholto.' Bland crossed the room to join him. 'I think we must assume that the late Anstruther was not as other men.'

Lestrade narrowed his eyes in the direction of his colleague. 'A Mary Ann, you mean?'

Bland nodded. 'God knows who he was entertaining on that very bed.' The policemen turned collectively to stare at it. 'The bolt was essential.'

'All right,' Lestrade said. 'What happened next?'

'According to my information,' Bland told him, 'Botley got a couple of tradesmen delivering in the street and they took the door off its hinges.'

Lestrade ran his fingers over the jamb. He withdrew them sharply as a couple of splinters got him. 'And not put back with any expertise either.'

'Ah, sorry, Sholto. That's my boys. C Division was never very hot on carpentry.'

'Once they were in, Botley and these tradesmen, what did they find?'

Bland read his book from where he was. 'Anstruther was sitting at his desk.' Lestrade took the same chair. 'He was slumped forward, his head by that paperweight thing.' Lestrade slumped forward.

'Like this?' he asked, in a muffled sort of way.

'Like that,' said Bland, twisting his head. 'Sunny side up. Gunshot wound to the left temple.'

Lestrade sat up. 'You've got the photographs?'

'Ah, well, Sholto.' Bland was realizing this was not his morning. 'I'm afraid my boys in C division aren't really on top of photography. They're a bit blurred.'

Lestrade looked at his man. 'How many came out?'

'Er . . . none.'

Lestrade sighed. 'All right, John. Tell me about the weapon.'

'Ah.' Bland crossed to the far wall and removed a chased box from the sideboard. He lifted the lid to reveal a green velvet lining and a single flintlock pistol. 'The partner to this one,' he said. 'Expensive piece. Made by Egg. We've got the actual one at Vine Street.'

Lestrade took the proffered pistol, letting the silver butt rest in his hand. 'Left temple?' he asked.

Bland nodded.

Lestrade held the gun to his head. 'Awkward bloody thing,' he commented. 'I'm sure your boys in C Division know more about these things than I do, John. How does it work?'

'Buggered if I know, Sholto. I think the bullet thing comes out here.' Bland waved his hand in the general direction of the gun. 'You pull that thing back, don't you?'

'The trigger?' Lestrade was on alien territory.

'Yes, but that curly thing. At the top. No. The other one. Yes, that's it.'

Lestrade clicked back the serpentine. Once. Twice. It would no further go.

'Does it fire bullets?' he asked.

'Well, the doctor dug *something* out of his head,' Bland observed.

Lestrade squeezed the trigger and the serpentine fell with a click. 'Hey presto,' he said.

'I should put it down, Sholto. Bloody thing looks dangerous to me.'

Lestrade glanced to his right. 'John,' he said suddenly, 'was the desk in this exact position?'

'Yes, I think so. Why?'

Lestrade stood up. 'Sit here,' he said, vacating the seat.

Bland did as he was told. 'What?' he asked.

Lestrade squatted beside him, cracking his knee on the desk corner as he did so. 'Agghh!' he screamed.

'A clue?' Bland asked excitedly.

'A minor dislocation,' said Lestrade. 'I'll be all right. Sit upright as though you're smoking. Oh, you are.'

'Like this?'

'Yes.' Lestrade closed one eye, concentrating on the wall beyond Bland's head. He clicked his teeth.

19

'Now lean forward, as if you're writing. That's it.' He frowned. 'Do you always write like that?'

'Well, in C Division, we haven't quite got the hang . . .'

'Yes, I know.' He lined up the wall again, shaking his head. 'All right. Now put your head down on the desk. No, nose down.'

'Sholto,' Bland muttered, 'this isn't very comfortable.'

'Don't move!' Lestrade hobbled across to the far wall. 'Ah ha!' he said.

'What?' mumbled Bland. It wasn't easy to talk through blotting paper.

'What do you make of this?'

Bland joined Lestrade in the corner. 'Wallpaper. Flock. Chinese, I'd say. We're quite good on Oriental wallpapers in C Division.'

'I knew you would be,' nodded Lestrade, 'but I'm talking about this brown stuff.'

Bland pressed his nose against the flock – a slight improvement anyway over blotting paper. 'Camp coffee?' he guessed.

'Blood,' said Lestrade.

'Good God, so it is. I wonder how I missed that?'

'I wonder,' sighed Lestrade. 'What do you make of it?'

Bland looked bland. Clearly he made almost nothing of it.

'Admittedly,' Lestrade helped him, 'I'm not very O'Fay with guns like that, but if I know my gunshot wounds, part of Anstruther's head would have been blown out sideways with the impact. And I think it's a ball, by the way, not a bullet. More or less in a straight line with the angle of the shot.'

'So?'

'So get back to the desk again.'

Bland did.

'Assume the position.'

Bland did.

'Now, pick up the pistol. No. As you were, nose on the desk. Right.'

Bland sat there, his nose back on the blotting paper. 'All right?'

'I don't know. Are you?'

'Well, it's a bit uncomfortable,' admitted Bland.

'Yes, you said. So why do it?'

Bland sat up, a little hurt. 'Because you asked me to, Sholto.'

20

'No, I mean if you were Anstruther, why do it? Why not sit back in the chair? Or sprawl on the *chaise-longue*? Or lie on the bed? Or stand by the window? This thing' – he took up the pistol again – 'must be over eighteen inches long. Why sit with your nose on the desk in order to blow our brains out?'

'What are you saying, Sholto? That Anstruther was murdered?'

Lestrade nodded slowly. 'It had occurred,' he said.

'Impossible,' said Bland. 'You're forgetting one thing.'

'Oh?'

'The locked door.' Bland was triumphant.

'Ah,' said Lestrade. Collapse of stout party.

'Are you seriously saying to me,' Bland was in full flight, 'that the murderer got into the room – yes, he could have been let in by Anstruther without Botley knowing about it. That he killed Anstruther – yes, he could have done, I grant you that, but what then? Did he arrange for Anstruther to get up with half his head missing and neatly lock the door behind him?'

'The window.' Lestrade stumbled to it.

Bland joined him and they peered down. A sheer drop of three storeys, no ledge; and bars six inches apart.

'Joachim the Human Fly?' Bland smirked.

'The walls?' Lestrade began tapping them furiously, listening for a hollow, a concavity that promised a secret passage. All he got was the disappointing pat pat of solid, Georgian brick.

'There's always the chimney, of course.' Bland was in his element. 'Perhaps it was the orang-utan from that bloke's Rue Morgue story. Rather apt, isn't it? Monkey jumps down chimney in Berkeley Square, loads antique gun and kills Fitzgibbon, returning whence he came. The *Daily Mail* will have a field day!'

'You're enjoying this, aren't you?' Lestrade muttered.

'I'm sorry, Sholto,' Bland laughed, 'but you can't pin a murder on this one. It's open and shut. Anstruther took his own life while the balance of his mind was disturbed. And if it wasn't before, it bloody well is now.'

'Where's the body?'

'Vine Street Mortuary. Want to look?'

'I'd better. If this hot weather goes on, he'll be walking to the funeral by himself.'

Lestrade limped painfully to the door. His fingers strayed again to the polished bolt and he shook his head. 'An open and shut case,' he said. And he was gone.

Like what you've read so far?

Then turn the page for a special offer...

Or fill out the form to the right and send it in.

Yes, please send me _____ copies of *Lestrade and the Deadly Game,* Volume V in the Lestrade Mystery Series.

❑ Enclosed is my check for $15.95 per copy

or

❑ Charge my   ❑ **VISA**   ❑ MasterCard   ❑ ⬤   ❑ NOVUS

Credit Card#_____ Exp. Date _____/_____

Signature _____

Phone _____

GSP004   LST4

Please indicate the address to which you would like your copy of *Lestrade and the Deadly Game* sent.

Name _____

Street_____

City_____State _____Zip _____

MAIL THIS FORM TO:

Gateway Mysteries
PO Box 97199 • Washington, DC 20090-7199

OR CALL 1-888-219-4747 TODAY

Take Advantage of a Special Offer!

For <u>only Four Dollars</u> more, you can have a copy of *The Adventures of Inspector Lestrade*, the first book in the Lestrade Mystery Series, sent to a friend or a loved one.

❑ Please send a copy of *The Adventures of Inspector Lestrade* to the address below. I have enclosed an extra $4, along with payment for *Deadly Game.*

Name _____

Street_____

City_____State _____Zip _____

Too good to be true? Take advantage before we change our minds!